CORRECTION SYMBOLS IN ALPHABETICAL ORDER

Boldface numbers and letters refer to chapters and sections of the workbook.

ab	Faulty abbreviation, *28*	,	Comma, *21*
ad	Misuse of adjective or adverb, *9*	;	Semicolon, *22*
agr	Error in agreement, *8*	'	Apostrophe, *23*
appr	Inappropriate diction, *31a*	" "	Quotation marks, *24*
awk	Awkward construction	: — ( ) [ ] . . . /	Colon, dash, parentheses, brackets, ellipsis mark, slash, *25*
ca	Error in case form, *6*		
cap	Use capital letter, *26*	*par*, ¶	Start new paragraph, *3*
coh	Coherence lacking, *1h–3, 3b*	¶ *coh*	Paragraph not coherent, *3b*
con	Be more concise, *31c*	¶ *dev*	Paragraph not developed, *3c*
coord	Coordination needed or faulty, *16a*	¶ *un*	Paragraph not unified, *3a*
		pass	Ineffective passive voice, *7h, 18d*
cs	Comma splice, *11a–b*	*ref*	Error in pronoun reference, *12*
d	Error in diction, *31*	*rep*	Unnecessary repetition, *31c–2*
dev	Inadequate development, *1, 3c*	*rev*	Revise or proofread, *2*
div	Incorrect word division, *30*	*run-on*	Run-on (fused) sentence, *11c*
dm	Dangling modifier, *14g*	*shift*	Inconsistency, *13*
emph	Emphasis lacking or faulty, *18*	*sp*	Misspelled word, *34*
exact	Inexact word, *31b*	*spec*	Be more specific, *3c, 4c*
frag	Sentence fragment, *10*	*sub*	Subordination needed or faulty, *16b*
fs	Fused sentence, *11c*		
gr	Error in grammar, *5–9*	*t*	Error in verb tense, *7e–f*
hyph	Error in use of hyphen, *34d*	*t seq*	Error in tense sequence, *7f*
inc	Incomplete construction, *15c–3*	*trans*	Transition needed, *3b–6, 3e*
ital	Italicize (underline), *27*	*var*	Vary sentence structure, *19*
k	Awkward construction	*vb*	Error in verb form, *7a–d*
lc	Use lowercase letter, *26f*	*w*	Wordy, *31c*
log	Faulty logic, *4*	*ww*	Wrong word, *31b–1*
mixed	Mixed construction, *15a–b*	/ /	Faulty parallelism, *17*
mm	Misplaced modifier, *14a–f*	#	Separate with a space
mng	Meaning unclear	⌒	Close up the space
no cap	Unnecessary capital letter, *26f*		Delete
no ,	Comma not needed, *21j*	∼	Transpose letters or words
no ¶	No new paragraph needed, *3*	*x*	Obvious error
num	Error in use of numbers, *29*	∧	Something missing, *15e*
p	Error in punctuation, *20–25*	??	Manuscript illegible or meaning unclear
. ? !	Period, question mark, exclamation point, *20*		

D0473426

THE LITTLE, BROWN WORKBOOK

THIRD EDITION

Donna Gorrell

UNIVERSITY OF WISCONSIN–MILWAUKEE

With the Editors of Little, Brown

Little, Brown and Company

BOSTON   TORONTO

ISBN 0-316-32138-9

9 8 7 6 5 4 3 2 1

ALP

Published simultaneously in Canada
by Little, Brown & Company (Canada) Limited

Printed in the United States of America

We would like to thank the following authors and publishers for permission to
quote from their works.

Excerpts, pages 51 and 83: Copyright 1984 Time Inc. All rights reserved. Reprinted
   by permission from *Time.*
Excerpt, page 58: From Maya Angelou, *I Know Why the Caged Bird Sings*, copyright
   © 1969 by Maya Angelou. Reprinted by permission of Random House, Inc.
Excerpts, pages 71–72 and 84: From Jerome Nilssen, *Our Church*, copyright © by
   Jerome Nilssen.
Excerpt, page 73: From Ellen Goodman, *Close to Home*, copyright © 1979 by The
   Washington Post Company. Reprinted by permission of Simon & Schuster, Inc.
Excerpt, page 74: From Knut Hamsun, *The Wanderer*, English translation copyright
   © 1975 by Farrar, Straus and Giroux, Inc. Reprinted by permission of Farrar,
Straus and Giroux, Inc., and Souvenir Press (Educational and Academic) Ltd.

Preface

The Little, Brown Workbook, Third Edition, is a composition textbook that can be used by itself as a guide for college writing or as a companion to *The Little, Brown Handbook,* Third Edition. The workbook is patterned after the handbook: they share a common vocabulary and approach to writing, their organizations are parallel, and they use the same rules, correction codes, and correction symbols. But the workbook provides additional exercises on tear-out sheets for removal without destroying textual material. The workbook also differs somewhat from the handbook in its explanations. Though similar to the handbook in approach, the workbook is written more particularly for students requiring additional work in specific areas of composition. It often omits exceptions and fine points of usage, making some explanations briefer than those in the handbook.

Because of the needs of the audience, many of the explanations in this third edition of the workbook are more thorough than those found in the second edition. Some chapters have undergone extensive revision. In particular Chapters 1 through 4 on the whole paper and complete paragraph, Chapter 5 on grammar, and Chapter 31 on diction include new textual material, as well as some new exercises. The revisions are less extensive in chapters where the explanations and exercises seemed serviceable as they were. Many of the new exercises use sentence combination, controlled composition, imitation, and other tasks requiring the writing of sentences, paragraphs, or whole essays. Throughout the book, the tone of both text and exercises is positive, reflecting writing as it is done by careful writers.

This edition still uses self-tests, introduced in the second edition, as lead-ins to the chapters on sentences, punctuation, and mechanics. Because the answers (found at the back of the book) are keyed to sections of the workbook, these tests aim to assist students in identifying their own weaknesses and directing them to helpful material in the text. Answers to all other exercises appear in an answer book that accompanies the workbook (available free to students at the instructor's option).

As a writing teacher, I like the arrangement of the handbook and workbook. It makes sense to me to start with larger issues — discovering and exploring ideas, arranging, composing, and revising them — before getting wrapped up in learning where to put commas and how to get just the right word. Many of our students need help on every facet of writing at once, but focusing first on the word or sentence does not help them to see how these discrete pieces combine and complement one another to make up a coherent essay. I find it is better to start with the whole essay and then deal with the parts as necessary.

Because of its arrangement, this third edition of the workbook (used with or without the handbook) can serve as a main textbook for a writing course. Starting with the paper as a whole, the first section introduces students to composing processes and ways of getting thoughts on paper. Discussions and exercises on prewriting, thesis development, drafting, revising, paragraph composition, and support for arguments encourage students to explore and develop their own ideas. Then the chapter "Understanding Sentence Grammar" explains the system by which sentence parts join and interrelate. Several chapters follow with discussions about individual sentence parts: nouns and pronouns, verbs, agreement of subjects with verbs and of pronouns with their antecedents, and adjectives and adverbs. Once the system of English grammar has been established, the next sections cover common usage problems — sentence fragments, comma splices and fused sentences, unclear pronoun reference, incorrect placement of modifiers, and so on — and the writing of effective sentences. Discussions of punctuation, mechanics, diction, vocabulary, and spelling conclude the text. Although the movement from whole to part is a logical arrangement, it is also flexible in use: each part can be used separately, in class or out, by individuals, groups, or the entire class.

I would like to thank all the people who have helped me in making this revision. In particular, for their helpful comments on an early draft, I owe a debt of gratitude to A. M. Belmont, Jr., of Southern Arkansas University; Donald S. Heines of Cape Cod Community College; Harvey S. Wiener of City University of New York, La Guardia; and Nancy G. Wilds of the National Defense University. I am grateful also for the support given to me by members of the Little, Brown staff: Carolyn Potts for getting this project started; Adrienne Weiss for keeping it in motion; and Lauren Green for seeing it through to completion. Finally, I'd like to thank my husband, Ken, for his patience and my daughter Louisa for allowing me to pick her grammar-sensitive brain.

Donna Gorrell

Contents

xvi

I | The Whole Paper and Paragraphs

1 | *Developing an Essay*

Let's start by saying what an **essay** is *not*. It is not necessarily a response to a teacher's assignment (such as "Write a classification essay on campus architecture"). It's not necessarily 500 words or five paragraphs long. The process of writing an essay is not necessarily something that begins with an outline, continues with a draft, and then ends with revision and correction. Neither does the process necessarily begin with a broad topic and end with a narrow one or begin with an idea, a purpose, or an organizational plan.

There is no right way of writing an essay; there is no right essay. A newspaper reporter may start with an assignment: "Go out and cover the governor's campaign speech this afternoon." She collects details, and when she is ready to start writing she has to make sense of them, discover a unifying idea. A preacher starts with a text: a broad idea, such as the relationship between church and state in the reference to Caesar's image on the Roman denarius. Like the reporter, the preacher must also discover an idea, something he can say about the text that his congregation hasn't already heard many times. The businessman writing a letter to a client may start not so much with an idea as with a purpose: to order 100 cartons of blue widgets, to say that an insurance policy is lapsing, to influence a decision, to share some information. To support his purpose he collects and orders as many details as he needs.

Essay writing does start with an assignment of some kind. The assignment may originate with the teacher, an editor, a sermon text, a boss, or oneself. How a person carries out that writing assignment varies with what the assignment is, who the writer is, who the audience is, and what the audience knows about the subject; it depends also on what the writer's purpose is and on many other factors.

1a | The writing situation and the writing process

We can talk about an essay as a communication of an idea — from someone, to someone, for a purpose. Keep in mind that in any writing situation, ideas may start out broadly but become narrowed as the writer proceeds to write, or they may start out as a loose collection of details that must be held together by a unifying idea.

Also bear in mind that a writer's role changes according to the assignment. The preacher who writes a sermon on Saturday night is the same person every day of the week, but his role changes as his job changes. He may be an administrator on Monday morning and a counselor on Tuesday afternoon. The businessman may be salesman when he tries to convince a client to increase an insurance premium, a boss when he circulates a memo to his staff, and an employee when he writes a report to his supervisor. A student may be a computer expert when describing a program she's written, an investigator when proposing a research project, an interested observer describing a fight that broke out after the soccer game.

Every writing situation takes into account the audience, too: the person or persons who will read the communication — perhaps a teacher, other members of a class, a newspaper's subscribers, a client, a businesswoman, and so on. An audience has a particular relationship to the writer and to the subject based on past experiences and knowledge, and this relationship determines what details the writer must communicate, what vocabulary and types of sentences he decides to use, what attitude he takes in communicating the idea, and so on. As an example, a newsletter to professional ornithologists will be written on a different level from one to members of an amateur bird watcher's society; the language of the professional publication will be more technical and the amount of explanatory information less detailed.

Overriding all considerations is purpose for writing. If the writer has no purpose, then there is little to say. The purpose determines the subject matter and the writer-audience relationship. It influences the tone of the writing as well as its length, organization, details, and style. The purpose must always be more than meeting a deadline. Just as a newspaper columnist meets an imposed deadline, so do student writers. But the newspaper columnist has something else in mind while writing, and so should a student.

This piece of writing you are now reading has a purpose. These paragraphs have been an extended exposition of what an essay is — for the sole purpose of informing you that the writing process is not cut and dried. There is no single writing process; the process varies as its components — writer, subject, audience, and purpose — vary. That means that the way you write differs from the way your classmates write. It means that the way you write depends on whether you are writing a paper for your history teacher or a report for your biology professor.

But the processes of carrying out formal writing tasks do have some things in common: *development* or *planning*, the stage of exploring ideas and gathering information; *drafting*, the stage of writing ideas down in rough, preliminary form; and *revising*, the stage of rethinking and re-working. Although we must separate these stages for the purpose of discussing them, they are not separate and distinct parts of the writing process. Writers revise while they are drafting and even while planning; they continue to plan as they write and sometimes as they revise. Both experienced and inexperienced writers differ in how much of the process appears on paper — some do much of their planning in their heads while others make extensive notes, some do very little revising on paper while others stop revising only when the piece of writing is due — whether to a publisher or to a teacher.

This chapter and the next will assist you in understanding how you write and how you might adjust your process of writing to suit your varying assignments. Experiment with the procedures discussed in the following sections: finding a topic, defining a purpose, developing ideas, shaping ideas, considering an audience, developing a thesis, organizing, drafting, revising, editing. As you try these procedures in a variety of writing tasks, you will find which ones work for you.

1b | Discovering and limiting a subject

You may be assigned a subject for an essay, or you may be required to invent one from your own store of experiences. Discovering your own subject requires you to look within yourself to find out what interests you — something that you know about and can share with others. Maybe you already know what interests you. If you don't, you might try to find answers for these questions:

> What have I read recently (books, newspaper articles, magazines)?
>
> What have I seen recently on television that I had at least a moderate reaction to?
>
> Have I seen any good — or bad — movies lately? If so, what made them good or bad?
>
> Have my attitudes toward local or national issues changed in the last year? What issues? What brought about the change?
>
> What is the most challenging idea I've heard in the last two weeks?
>
> What is the most important goal of my life? What am I willing to do to achieve it? How did I become convinced that this is a worthy goal?
>
> What person do I most admire? Why?

These questions are only starters to convince you that you do have something to say — lots of things.

Ask as many questions as necessary to discover an idea that you care enough about to share with an audience. Once you have a subject, make sure it's narrow enough for you to develop with specific details. Many freshmen, for example, like to compare high school with college, two things they certainly know something about; however, their essays end up being too general because the topic covers too much ground. Better would be a comparison of the high school library with the college library or the high school computer course with the college computer course.

Here are some other examples of narrowing a subject to a manageable topic, that is, to a limited, specific essay subject:

BROAD SUBJECT	SPECIFIC TOPICS
tradition	Christmas dinner
	weddings
	comparison with habit
curiosity	as a learning impetus
	people who pry into the affairs of others
	in cats
cooking	how wok cooking promotes creativity
	the difference exact measuring makes
	teaching a child to bake chocolate chip cookies

| *Discovering a subject*   EXERCISE **1-1**

Use questions 1–12 to discover a subject for an essay when you are not assigned a subject. Answer the questions as completely as you can.

1. What have I read recently?

   a.

   b.

   c.

2. What have I seen recently on television that interested me?

   a.

   b.

   c.

3. What good (or bad) movies have I seen recently?

   a.

   b.

   c.

4. What made those movies good (or bad)?

   a.

   b.

   c.

5. What local or national issues interest me?

   a.

b.

c.

6. Why am I interested in any one of those issues?

7. What is the most challenging idea I've heard in the last two weeks?

8. What is the most important goal in my life?

9. What am I willing to do to achieve that goal?

10. How did I become convinced that this is a worthy goal for me?

11. What person do I most admire? Why?

12. What interesting discussions have I had lately?

|*Limiting a subject* EXERCISE **1-2**

Discovering something to say is only the first step in responding to a writing assignment. The subjects you discovered in Exercise 1-1 are probably too broad for an effectively written short essay. This exercise gives you practice in taking a broad subject and thinking of several ways to limit it to specific topics. Limit each of the following subjects to two or more specific topics that interest you, or limit several of the subjects you discovered in Exercise 1-1.

1. Rituals

    a.

    b.

2. Play

    a.

    b.

3. Libraries

    a.

    b.

4. War

    a.

    b.

5. Computers

    a.

    b.

6.

   a.

   b.

7.

   a.

   b.

1c | Defining a purpose

dev

1

While you're trying to decide what subject interests you enough to write an essay about, probably at the back of your mind is also some kind of purpose for writing. You may not know what it is yet; student writers often don't have a clear sense of purpose when they sit down to write. But there is really no sense writing unless you know what you want to happen in the minds of your readers.

By *purpose* we mean our chief reason for communicating something to a particular audience. We might have one or a combination of four main purposes: (1) to entertain readers, (2) to express our feelings or beliefs, (3) to explain something, or (4) to persuade readers to agree with our opinions. You might want your readers to laugh, to get angry, to know something, or to change something. You may have discovered lately that using the exact amount of water when making Jell-O makes a big difference in how that confection sets, and you would like to save your reader from experiencing the same disaster you did when you used too much water. Or you might want to entertain your reader with the latest escapades of your three cats — little busybodies who seem to be always getting shut up somewhere or knocking something over as a result of their insatiable need to know everything that is going on in the house. In short, you need to explore the recesses of your mind to discover not only why you want to write about this subject but also why any reader would want to read about it.

1d | Developing the topic

When you have a specific topic that interests you and a purpose for writing about that topic, begin thinking of the particular information that will convey your interest convincingly to your readers. Write down the ideas that occur to you. Some writers find that ideas come more easily if they explore the topic while taking a walk, running, riding the bus, or driving on the open road. Somehow the forward movement and the separation from the usual setting seem to encourage new thought and creative solutions to problems. The following are some other strategies that might work if your ideas are slow in coming.

1 | Freewriting

Sometimes just pushing the pencil across the page generates ideas. Perhaps you have decided to write on Christmas dinners. The idea interests you but you can't really think of anything to say about it. You might try freewriting for ten or fifteen minutes. Begin by writing whatever occurs to you. Write fast, without pausing to make corrections or revisions and not worrying about spelling, punctuation, or grammar. Don't stop until you run out of ideas. When you're finished you won't have an essay, but you will have some ideas that you can turn into an essay.

2 | Making a list

Another way to push a pencil across the page is to jot down ideas in list form. If you were writing about Christmas dinners, you would list all the details that occur to you. If you were making a comparison, as between tradition and habit, you would make two columns, one for tradition and the other for habit. Then you would brainstorm, jotting down everything that occurs to you. Here's an example:

TRADITION	HABIT
Family gatherings at Christmas	Brushing teeth before retiring
White wedding dress	Reading bedtime story to a child
Funerals	Dinner at 6:00
Fourth of July parades	Bacon and eggs for Saturday
Has significance	breakfast
Connected with special times	Grocery shopping on Monday
Usually involves family	evenings
Often highly charged with	Mindless repetition
emotion	May involve self alone or others

This is just the start of a list, performed in about ten minutes. Given more time and thought, it could yield the subject matter for an essay. Most subjects will require only one list. "Christmas dinners," for example, would lead you to compose a long list of details about the traditional meal as you know it.

3 | Reading

With most writing assignments, it is not necessary for you to rely solely on your own store of knowledge. You can find out what others think about the subject through reading newspapers, magazine articles, books, and so forth. In fact, something you have read may be what started your ideas on the subject; in that case, try to go back to the same piece of writing and read it more carefully. Whenever you read for increased knowledge of a subject, take notes, jotting down main ideas and facts that you might forget. Note also the author's name and the title and location of a piece of writing you're using so that you can give proper credit in your essay.

4 | Using the journalist's questions

Asking a series of journalist's questions — starting with *who, what, when, where, why,* and *how* — may lead you to useful information for developing ideas.

1. Who is involved? Who cares? Who said it? Who knows?
2. What happened? What are the results? What was said? What is important?
3. When did it happen? When will it happen?

4. Where did it happen? Where are the effects felt?
5. Why did it happen? Why does it matter? Why do I care?
6. How did it happen? How did I react? How did others react?

Keep asking questions until you get enough answers. Just start with the interrogatory word — *who, what,* and so on — and change the subjects and verbs:

> *How* does it happen?
>
> *How* does it work?
>
> *How* do I feel about it?
>
> *How* do others feel about it?
>
> *How* does it look?

5 | Using the patterns of development

Other questions take advantage of how our minds work. When we file information in our heads, we generally relate it to something that is already there. We categorize information, thinking in terms of how it's like or different from something we already know, how things are caused and by what, what the effects of particular events are, and so on. By trying to find out how things relate to one another, we not only are able to explore what we know but may also have a way of developing our ideas. These patterns of development are familiarly known as **illustration** or **support, definition, division** and **classification, comparison** and **contrast, analogy, cause-and-effect analysis,** and **process analysis.**

> Who or what is it? (*definition*)
>
> What are some examples of it? (*illustration*)
>
> What other things are like it? (*comparison, analogy*)
>
> How is it like other things? (*comparison, analogy*)
>
> How does it differ from similar things? (*contrast*)
>
> What are its component parts? (*division*)
>
> How do those parts function? (*process*)
>
> What categories can it be sorted into? (*classification*)
>
> Is it changing? (*process, cause and effect*)
>
> If so, how? (*process, cause and effect*)
>
> How much can it change and still be itself? (*contrast, process*)
>
> What does it mean? (*definition*)

What is its history? (*process, cause and effect*)

What are its causes? (*cause and effect*)

What effects does it have on other things? (*cause and effect*)

Asking these and other questions will help you generate some ideas for writing. Even after you've started writing, you can go back to asking questions any time you get stumped.

1e | Grouping ideas

Once you have some ideas, you can try grouping them in different ways to see how they relate to and complement one another. For instance, if you were writing about tradition versus habit, you might decide that one group would consist of examples of each subject, another their similarities, and another their differences. Such idea groupings might lead you to new insights and understandings about your subject. Try grouping your ideas in other ways, too, moving them around like pattern pieces on fabric until you get a good fit. After a while you may have some sense of the significance, the point, the thing that will make this essay different from all others — your thesis (see 1g).

| *Generating ideas and grouping them* | EXERCISE **1-3** |

Choose one of the specific topics you identified in Exercise 1-2 or a different specific topic. Develop ideas for a brief essay using one of the methods discussed on pages 9–12. Then, on the next page, group the ideas according to their similarities or their differences or in some other ways.

1. Topic: ——————————————————————————

   Ideas: ——————————————————————————

——————————————————————————————————

——————————————————————————————————

——————————————————————————————————

——————————————————————————————————

——————————————————————————————————

——————————————————————————————————

——————————————————————————————————

——————————————————————————————————

——————————————————————————————————

——————————————————————————————————

——————————————————————————————————

——————————————————————————————————

——————————————————————————————————

——————————————————————————————————

2. Groups of ideas: _____

1f | Considering an audience

To communicate effectively with your readers — your **audience** — you must consider their interests and needs as you select a topic, develop an attitude toward it, and decide what specific information to use to express your view.

1 | Using specific information

A student writing about the school library may be addressing an audience of other students, perhaps freshmen who are not yet familiar with the campus. But he might also be an architecture student addressing other architecture students, a librarian addressing other librarians, or a student senator writing to the Board of Regents. The specific information in an essay would differ in each case.

2 | Deciding on an appropriate role and tone

Even though you are the same person wherever you go and whatever you do, your **role** changes with each situation. For example, the way you describe your automobile accident to your insurance representative differs from the way you describe it to your classmates. With the insurance person you are the experienced, competent driver who always observes traffic regulations; with your classmates you are the free-spirited driver who knows when to exceed the speed limit and disregard stop signs, who looked away just for a second. Your role in a given situation depends on your interest in that situation — your purpose, your subject matter, and your audience.

So when you are writing, your role changes according to your purpose, your subject matter, and your audience. Your possible roles are many and varied: reporter, interpreter, storyteller, and so on. As a reporter of a science experiment, your role differs from that of interpreter of a poem. If you want to explain how traffic control devices help move traffic safely, you will write as an informed expert.

As you write, your role will be evident in *what* you say and *how* you say it — your tone.

The **tone** of your writing comes from the use you make of ideas, words, and sentence structures, and it will influence how your readers react to what you say. If you want to be seen as serious and thoughtful, you will use formal sentence structure and words and will develop sensible, well-supported assertions. If you want to adopt a light attitude toward your subject — if you are writing to fellow students, say, about how to choose an easy course — you may want to use an informal sentence structure, a conversational vocabulary, and a humorous approach.

3 | Writing for a general audience

Most writing done for college courses is directed at a general, college-level audience. Even if your only readers are your instructors, you can assume that they are alert and thoughtful, open to what you have to say, but nonetheless insistent that your writing be fresh and clear with strong, well-supported assertions.

1g | Developing the thesis

The **thesis** is the main idea, the controlling idea, the point, the significance of an essay. A **thesis sentence** is a statement of that idea. Not all essays have an explicit statement of the thesis, but in academic expository writing — essays written to inform or explain for an instructor or for other students — readers generally expect to find a clear expression of the main idea. In academic writing, the thesis generally appears near the beginning of an essay, frequently at the end of the introduction, and may be restated in the conclusion. It is the single most important sentence in an essay because it tells the reader what your subject is and how you view that subject. It focuses the essay and thus serves as a unifying device for everything that follows. All your paragraphs will be related in some way to the thesis.

1 | Conceiving the thesis sentence

To arrive at your statement of the thesis, you must first know what your subject is, what point you want to make about it, and how you can support that point. Exercises 1-1, 1-2, and 1-3 for discovering subjects and generating specific ideas will have assisted you in moving toward a thesis for the topic you chose. When you are ready to write your thesis sentence, remember that it must not only *state the subject* but also *assert something about the subject*. A thesis sentence does not begin "The purpose of this essay is" or "This essay is about"; such sentences state only the subject. A thesis sentence must also make an assertion:

> The design of our library invites students to come in and study.
> Successfully repotting a plant is a simple procedure with the appropriate materials and equipment.
> Family rituals assist a child in developing a sense of identity.

Each of these sentences includes not only the subject but also an assertion about the subject.

Another way to describe these two essential parts is as **subject** and **predicate.** In English sentences, subjects present ideas and predicates tell what is important about those ideas — what they do, what they are, what they mean. As illustrated below, the subject of the essay corresponds to the subject of the thesis sentence, and the assertion — the point of the essay — begins with its predicate.

SUBJECT	PREDICATE
The design of our library	invites students to come in and study.
Successfully repotting a plant	is a simple procedure with the appropriate materials and equipment.

SUBJECT	PREDICATE
Family rituals	assist a child in developing a sense of identity.

To describe the thesis sentence in another way, it serves two primary functions and sometimes a third:

1. It narrows the topic to a single dominant idea (subject).
2. It asserts something about the topic, conveying the point the writer is making (predicate).
3. It may provide a preview of ideas and how they will be arranged.

The following thesis sentence fulfills all three functions:

SUBJECT	PREDICATE	ARRANGEMENT
Knitting	is a quiet form of recreation	that relieves the stress of the day and gives a sense of creative satisfaction in the finished product.

2 | Writing and revising the thesis sentence

Developing an effective thesis sentence that conveys your purpose completely and concisely may require several attempts. It is a necessary step in writing an essay because until you know — and can express in writing — specifically what you want to say, your essay is likely to wander. If you see that your writing is wandering, consider the writing you've done so far as preliminary — *prewriting* — something you've done to help you discover what you can say. Then ask yourself, with all your written ideas in front of you, what your perspective on your subject is.

What does this subject have to do with you?

Who are you in relation to the subject?

What purpose might you serve by writing about this subject?

Why do you want to write about it?

What is interesting about it?

Who might be interested in reading about it?

Whom do you want to read about it?

Mull the subject over in your mind until you have a *perspective*, an insight into your subject that is different from what anybody else has said about it — something that will surprise your reader a little. That's your thesis, and now you're ready to put it in a sentence. Make your thesis sentence *specific, limited,* and *unified.* That's the best way to write an essay that is also specific, limited, and unified.

The following thesis sentence provides no insight into the subject and because of its generality would lead to a general, unfocused essay.

Our library is well designed.

This thesis makes an assertion, but the statement is not specific, limited, and unified. If you tried to write an essay with such a general thesis, you would not have any idea where to start and you would not know when you were finished. To write an effective thesis sentence you first would have to ask yourself such questions as the following:

What does the term *well designed* mean when it is applied to a library?

What kind of library is it?

Who uses it?

What in particular makes its design good?

The following thesis statement (used on p. 16) is better:

The design of our library invites students to come in and study.

Here is another sentence. It not only makes a specific assertion but previews the supporting ideas as well.

Because of the wide expanse of windows, the well-lighted stacks, and the easy access to all floors, the design of our campus library invites students to come in and study.

This thesis sentence states that the subject of the essay is the design of the school library; the point is that the design makes the library a desirable place to study; and the specific support for that assertion ranges from the windows to the lighting to the ease of moving around in it. The writer of this essay knows what she wants to say and how she can say it.

| *Developing the thesis sentence*   EXERCISE **1-4**

Select one of the subjects you discovered in Exercise 1-1, perhaps the same one you worked with in Exercises 1-2 and 1-3, or use the subject you were assigned. After answering the following questions about that subject, write a thesis sentence.

1. How am I related to the subject (expert, angry citizen, informed student, mature youth, and so on)?

2. What is my purpose in writing about this subject?

3. Why do I want to write about it?

4. What interests me about it?

5. Who might be interested in reading about it?

6. Who do I want to read about it?

7. What do I want to say?

Thesis sentence:

|*Revising the thesis sentence*   EXERCISE **1-5**

Rewrite the following thesis sentences to make them specific, limited, and unified.

Example: Legislators do not communicate enough with their constituents.

State legislators should improve communication with voters by scheduling local meetings regularly and by mailing newsletters before and after assembly sessions.

1. Many people believe that baseball players have no right to strike.

2. Religious cults serve a valid purpose.

3. Some teachers do not know how to lead a class discussion.

4. The government owes a college education to every citizen who wants one.

5. Sometimes use of slang can be very effective.

6. Hunting wild animals, as long as they are not in danger of extinction, can actually help nature.

7. Travel to foreign countries is educational.

8. Space exploration will change our lives.

9. Silence is often the best response to anger.

10. Coughing can have an important role in communication.

1h | Organizing the essay

By now you know what you're writing about, who you think might read what you write, what point you want to make, and how you intend to support that point. Since you already have all this information in writing or in your head, you may also have some idea of how you're going to organize your ideas. One standard characteristic of essays is **organization,** a logical, coherent arrangement through which readers can follow the progression of the writer's thoughts.

Sometimes it is enough to have just a thesis sentence as a guide for writing, especially for a short essay. The sentence on page 17, for example, might be an adequate guide for some writers:

> Knitting is a quiet form of recreation that relieves the stress of the day and gives a sense of creative satisfaction in the finished product.

It implies that, after the introduction, the essay will show first how knitting relieves stress and then how it gives a sense of creative satisfaction. To help organize their essays some writers would need a few notes in addition to the thesis sentence, a few ideas jotted down and numbered in order of intended use. Still other writers are more comfortable with a formal outline.

1 | Arranging the parts of an essay

There are several common ways to organize an essay that correspond to readers' habitual ways of thinking. One pattern is **spatial,** examining a topic (such as a place or a person) by moving in space from one location to another, as when we survey a scene from the farthest point to the nearest or vice versa. Essays and paragraphs arranged in such a way are largely descriptive. If you were describing your school newspaper spatially, you might start with the first page and move through the paper by sections; if you were describing a painting, you would start with the area of the painting that strikes you first and then move around within the painting, assisting your reader to see it the way you do.

Another common organizing scheme is **chronological,** reporting events as they occur over time, earliest first. Such essays are narrative (telling the history of an event) or process analysis (telling how something is done or how it happens). If you were recounting your drive home over snow-slick highways, you would start with the beginning of your trip, when the roads and weather were deceptively clear, and proceed through worsening conditions, ending with your arrival home and the final frustrating need to shovel out your driveway to get the car in. Or, if you were telling your audience how to make a pot of chili, you'd start again with first things first — getting out the ingredients, browning the meat — and proceed to the end when the chili was completed and ready to be served.

Two other organizing patterns are **general to specific** and **specific to general.** In the first pattern the main ideas come before the details that support them, as in an essay that makes initial strong claims about, say, gun control and then presents the evidence for the claims. In the specific-to-general pattern the details come first and build to the more general ideas, as in an essay that describes the styles of specific big bands before generalizing about the sound they have in common. A similar pattern is **climactic,** which is the arrangement of material in order of importance. You may also arrange items by the principles of **most familiar to least familiar** or **simple to complex.**

The patterns of development discussed in 1d-5 (p. 11) suggest additional patterns. Also see 3c (pp. 71–84) for paragraph-length examples of each pattern.

2 | Outlining

The organizing plan you select will depend on your topic and on what you want to say about it. The amount of detail you include in an outline will be determined by the complexity of your topic and your requirements as a writer. Remember that the only reason for having an outline is to aid *you* the writer. Your readers won't see your outline, but they *will* benefit from the orderly presentation of your ideas. Two useful work plans are informal and formal outlines. They can be used to organize your ideas from whatever form they are in: freewriting, a brainstorming list, even scattered thoughts in your head.

An **informal outline** arranges the general and specific points of the essay in the order in which they will appear in the essay. It may be little more than your preliminary list of ideas with numbers added to indicate the order in which you'll be using them and lines drawn through ideas you've discarded as irrelevant. If you want to get a little more elaborate, you can rewrite the list in the order you prefer, indicating by indentions the ideas that are subordinate to others. Less important ideas will be subordinate to main ideas, specific facts subordinate to general statements. This extra work will make a neater pattern for you to follow so that, when you're writing, each major point together with its subpoints will become a paragraph.

A **formal outline** takes the informal outline one step further. Its more rigid form can help you place elements in careful relation to each other, with levels of subordination (perhaps three or more) clearly indicated. It can also help you fill in gaps, eliminate redundancies, and make wording more precise. For student writers, a formal outline is particularly useful for research papers and other long papers.

The formal outline follows a typical pattern: main points, often corresponding to the topic of an entire paragraph, are preceded by capital Roman numerals (I, II, and so on); chief subpoints, the support for the main points, are preceded by capital letters (A, B, and so on); and specific supporting details, examples, and reasons are preceded by Arabic numerals (1, 2, and so on). (A fourth level of subordination may be indicated by small letters — a, b, and so on.)

You may write the outline in complete sentences or in phrases, but whichever manner of expression you choose, use it consistently throughout the outline. Ideas at the same numbered or lettered level should be parallel in both content and form of expression, and those at sublevels should be logically subordinate to those at the superior level. Be sure that all headings are matched by at least one other heading at the same level, because subheadings in an outline imply that the preceding topic has been divided. An A without a B, in other words, illogically implies that the preceding level is divided into only one part.

The following detailed topic outline, for a paper on the benefits of knitting, illustrates a formal outline.

THESIS SENTENCE

Knitting is a quiet form of recreation that relieves the stress of the day and gives a sense of creative satisfaction in the finished product.

FORMAL OUTLINE

I. Introduction
   A. Need for recreation at the end of the day
   B. Frequent need for recreation that is quiet
   C. Knitting as a fulfillment of this need
   D. Statement of thesis

II. Relief of stress of the day
   A. Physical relief
     1. Activity of fingers
     2. Remainder of body at rest
   B. Mental relief
     1. Little thought required
     2. Other activities possible
       a. Conversation
       b. Television viewing

III. Sense of creative satisfaction
   A. Feeling of accomplishment
   B. Admiration for work well done
   C. Pleasure in using or giving finished product

IV. Conclusion
   A. Summary
   B. Restatement of thesis

3 | Checking for unity and coherence

When your informal or formal outline is completed, examine it for unity and coherence. These are two essential qualities of effective writing that will be dealt with in more detail in Chapter 3. But since you've gone to the trouble of writing an outline, you can anticipate problems by checking your outline for unity and coherence. **Unity** means that the parts of the essay are related to the thesis and to one another. Each paragraph, with its general statements and specific supporting evidence, supports the thesis. Disunity occurs when irrelevant ideas creep in or when the writer moves away from the thesis sentence in mid-essay.

Coherence means that the relations between ideas are clear and that each point leads easily to the one following it. The essay "hangs together," with each part clearly linked to all other parts. The writer leaves clues along the way so that the reader has no trouble following the progression of ideas.

In the formal outline above, notice how all the parts under II support the idea of knitting as a stress reliever and how all parts under III relate to how knitting provides a sense of satisfaction. Paragraphs developed from these parts would be unified, each paragraph dealing with one idea. They would relate to one another and to the thesis. In the outline, they are coherent because of their form: they repeat key ideas expressed in the thesis, and they are in noun form — *relief* and *sense*.

⎸*The formal outline* EXERCISE **1-6**

Rewrite the following informal outline (which has no indications of subordinate ideas) into a formal outline, using as many subdivisions as necessary to put parallel ideas into parallel format. Refer to the outline on page 25 as a guide, remembering that you will have different divisions and subdivisions.

THESIS SENTENCE

Because flying terrifies me, I have developed several techniques to help me cope with that fear both before and during a flight.

INFORMAL OUTLINE

1. Introduction
2. Narrative of last plane trip
3. Recounting fear of flying
4. Statement of thesis
5. Relaxation methods before a flight
6. Trying to sleep the night before
7. Reading an architecture book before sleeping
8. Contemplating pictures before sleeping
9. Riding to the airport
10. Talking to the cab driver
11. Looking out the cab window
12. Reading in the airport lounge
13. Relaxation methods during a flight
14. Taking a seat
15. Choosing a seat location
16. Choosing a travel companion
17. Eating
18. Reading
19. Listening to music
20. Staying in my seat
21. Refraining from looking out the window

22. Conclusion
23. Restatement of thesis

FORMAL OUTLINE

_____

_____

_____

_____

_____

_____

_____

_____

_____

_____

_____

_____

_____

_____

_____

_____

_____

_____

|*Outlining an essay*   EXERCISE   **1-7**

One use for outlines is to check the organization of essays you have already written. Read the following essay and write an outline of it, following the guidelines for formal outlines on pages 24–25. Start by stating the thesis.

INSIDE IS A PERSON

Children are known for their cruelty to others. They'll taunt a girl whose nose is too long, calling her "Eagle Beak" or reciting a line about liars, noses, and telephone wires. They'll tease a kid about his "buck teeth" before he's ever had a chance to go to an orthodontist, and they'll make jokes about the chubby boy whose appetite obviously outstrips his energy needs. When I was growing up in Chicago, we kids used to be cruel too, needlessly hurting others with our words.

I remember one instance in particular. Several of us girls would walk together to school, and on our way each day we passed the house of a particular old woman. I say she was old, but she only seemed that way. As we walked by her house, she was always sitting on her front porch — not doing a thing, just sitting. She was fat. She was so fat that she could hardly walk. She couldn't do her own housework; she couldn't ride in a car or go anywhere; she couldn't even cook her own meals anymore. She just sat. And as we walked by, we taunted her. We called her "Fatso" and "Chubs," and we whispered jokes about her, giggling as we turned around to see if she was still watching us.

When my mother heard about our behavior, she was angry. She scolded me and told me never again to laugh at Mrs. Jackson. "She's a person," she said, "and your name calling hurts her." She also warned me that people who laugh at others might have the same thing happen to them: "What goes around comes around." Well, I certainly never wanted to look anything like "old" Mrs. Jackson, so I never teased her again. When my friends and I walked by on our way to school, I always looked away when they started making jokes. They couldn't understand what had come over me, but they shrugged their shoulders and continued to tease.

Soon I started finding excuses for not walking with my friends.

Instead, I would leave a few minutes early and stop to say "Good morning" to Mrs. Jackson, who was pleased at the unexpected kindness. Sometimes I took her some flowers from my mother's garden and sometimes some fresh-baked cookies. As I came to know Mrs. Jackson as a person, I almost forgot about my mother's warning that had motivated my friendship.

But I remembered it a few days ago when I went back to visit my old neighborhood. Mrs. Jackson is dead and buried, but I had a real shock when I drove down the street and saw, on the porch of the house next door to where Mrs. Jackson had lived, one of my two friends who had been so mean. She was fat — fatter than Mrs. Jackson had ever been. I didn't even recognize her until someone pointed her out to me. And then my mother's words came flooding back: "What goes around comes around." And for my friend it had. I don't know if the old saying is true; I don't really believe that my friend is fat now because she once delighted in teasing Mrs. Jackson. I'm just glad I learned when I was young that cruel words hurt, but kindness makes friends.

OUTLINE

_____

_____

_____

_____

_____

_____

_____

_____

_____

_____

_____

|*Writing an outline for an essay*   EXERCISE   **1-8**

Prepare an outline for an essay, using the ideas you generated and grouped in Exercise 1-3. First, repeat the thesis sentence composed in Exercise 1-4. Then outline the ideas, using the form (informal or formal) specified by your instructor. Be sure the outline is unified (all its parts relate to each other and to the thesis) and coherent (the relations among ideas are logical and clear).

Thesis sentence: _____

_____

_____

Outline: _____

_____

_____

_____

_____

_____

_____

_____

_____

_____

_____

2 | *Drafting and Revising the Essay*

Carefully developing an essay (Chapter 1) often makes writing and revising it easier. But, as this chapter shows, writing is more of a circular, repeating process than a linear progression of prewriting, writing, and revision. If you have carried out the exercises in Chapter 1 in preparation for writing an essay, you have done some prewriting. But you may also have already done some writing and revising. As we begin to discuss writing in this chapter, you should bear in mind that as you write you will probably be doing some additional prewriting and will also be revising as you go along.

2a | Writing the first draft

In developing a thesis and an outline, you settled on a purpose, decided on at least part of what you will need to say to achieve that purpose, and arranged your ideas in a unified and coherent pattern. As a result of this preparation, you are much more likely to write an essay that focuses on a point and supports that point adequately for a given audience than you would be if you had started out without any planning.

But the writing of your essay still requires much thought, for it is often only in the writing that we discover what we really want to say and finally come to know our ideas. Most writers treat their outlines as changeable plans that can vary as they find they need to emphasize one idea, provide greater support for another, and delete yet another. Writers also revise their thesis sentences if it seems reasonable to shift the focus of their essays. Preparation gives a plan, a guide for saying what the writer wants to say.

As a writer you must remember that even with a carefully written thesis sentence and a clearly organized outline before you, *you* are in charge — not your outline, not your prewritten thesis sentence. You can change anything you want as long as you see a reason for doing so. An outline is not a map of fixed territory, like a map of city streets; rather, *you are making up the territory* — it's coming out of your head. So if you see that the original plan — more like a blueprint than a map — is not conforming to what you now want to say, change the outline. If you do change it, though, you'll undoubtedly need to go back and adjust your thesis sentence as well. In most cases it's not necessary to start over from scratch, as if no planning had occurred. But when you do make changes in the plan, do it with thought and for a reason.

As you write, use your outline or thesis sentence as a guide. (As indicated in Chapter 1, some people can organize and hold the plans for a short essay in their heads, while others require at least an informal outline in front of them. If you don't know which kind of person you are, try the written outline.)

In writing your first draft, you are primarily concerned with your ideas, to get them down on paper before you forget what you're thinking. So you write quickly, not stopping to check punctuation or spelling. You might mark words that you want to look up later or leave blank spaces where you can't think of the right word. You may have long paragraphs that need to be divided or unwieldy sentences that require some tinkering later. You may even find strange things happening to your ideas — they change as you write them down, becoming clearer and better focused.

While you're writing (and revising), remember who will be reading what you write and then use vocabulary appropriate to that audience (avoiding technical words, for example, with a general audience or slang for an instructor); include details that your audience requires in order to see your subject as you do. (See Chapters 3 and 4 for further discussions of ways to reach your audience.)

Also keep your purpose in mind as you write. By writing this essay, what do you hope to achieve? Do you want to persuade your audience of something? To entertain? To complain about something that's gone wrong? To explain something? To inform or report? To summarize, criticize, or spiritually uplift? If you were writing about the trip home on snow-slick roads, mentioned in Chapter 1, what details and language would you use to achieve a purpose of entertaining as opposed to, say, a purpose of criticizing the lack of highway repairs? Unless you keep your purpose firmly in mind throughout your writing, your essay will not achieve that purpose. It will become an odd collection of loosely related details — making no point, boring your reader, and, worst of all, boring you.

Once you put down the last period of your rough draft, you'll experience a wonderful feeling of relief, because you finally have all of your ideas out of your head and down on paper. It's like having a child: the "child" exists and is out where you can see it and care for it. Getting your ideas out on paper is a beginning. Before tackling the tough job of shaping and disciplining this child of your mind, it is a good idea to allow your mind to rest for a few hours or even a day or two before you take over the care and feeding of your essay. This rest gives you a chance to clear your mind and take a fresh, new look at what you've written.

2b | Revising the first draft

Though you may end up using substantial portions of your rough draft in the final version, a rough draft is just a start. Except for in-class writing assignments, in which you usually have no time for rewriting, you will probably write several drafts of some sentences, paragraphs, or even the whole essay. Beginning writers often think of revision as proofreading for errors in spelling, grammar, punctuation, and the like. But this is editing, not revision, and it can come fairly late in the writing process. Real revision happens while you are writing and still working with a rough draft. It involves rethinking the arrangement of ideas, their support, and their effectiveness in furthering your purpose. You may decide to add details, statements, or whole paragraphs to sharpen the focus on your purpose; you may decide to strike out details, statements, or entire paragraphs because they detract from your purpose; you may decide to move parts around to achieve greater emphasis or a sense of logical order.

The following checklist may be helpful in guiding your revision. If you need help in any of these areas, read the Workbook or Handbook section given in parentheses.

Checklist for revision

1. Does the body of your essay carry out the purpose and central idea expressed by your thesis sentence (1c, 1g)? Will your reason for writing be apparent to your readers, not only in your thesis sentence but throughout your essay (1f)? If you have drifted away from your thesis sentence in the body, do you need to revise the thesis sentence (to reflect your new direction) or the body (to reflect the thesis sentence)?
2. Have you provided adequate details, examples, or reasons to support each of your ideas (1d)? Will your readers need more information at any point to understand your meaning or appreciate your point of view (1f)?
3. Is your essay unified (1h-3)? Does each paragraph and sentence relate clearly to the thesis sentence?
4. Is your essay coherent (1h-3)? Are the relations within and among its parts apparent? Will readers see the shape of the essay — its overall organization? (Outlining the draft can help you check its structure. See 1h-2 and Exercise 1-7.)
5. Does the tone of your writing accurately convey your attitude toward your topic and the role you are assuming (1g-2)? Is the tone appropriate for your purpose and your audience? Is it consistent throughout the essay?
6. Is each paragraph in the body unified (3a), coherent (3b), and well developed (3c)?
7. Does your introduction engage and focus readers' attention (3c-1)? Does your conclusion provide readers with a sense of completion (3c-2)?

2c | Editing the second draft

By the time you've revised your rough draft according to the guidelines given in 2b, you probably have a pretty messy paper. When it comes to the point where you're having a hard time finding your way through it, copy what you have so far on fresh paper. (If you started out with a handwritten draft, it's best to make a typed draft at this time.) Once you've made this new working draft, use the revision checklist again to see if you want to make more changes. Try to read your fresh draft as some other reader would, remembering that the reader does not know what has been going on in your mind; he or she has only what you put on paper. If you leave out some important details or don't make your points absolutely clear, your reader will miss something.

Now read your paper out loud, listening for rhythms and awkward phrases, for unnecessary repetitions, and for slang and other expressions too casual for written communication. Ask somebody — a classmate, a parent, or a friend — to listen as you read and tell you what is unclear or awkward. You may need to read through your paper many times. If you are inclined to misspell words, read once just for spelling; if you write fragments, read once for nothing but fragments; if verb forms are your problem, read for verbs. Here is another checklist for you to use at this point. As with the list in 2b, the questions are keyed to chapters of the Workbook and Handbook where you can look for help.

Checklist for editing

1. Are your sentences grammatical? Have you avoided errors in case (6), verb form (7), agreement (8), and adjectives and adverbs (9)?
2. Are your sentences clear? Have you avoided sentence fragments (10), comma splices and fused sentences (11), errors in pronoun reference (12), shifts (13), misplaced or dangling modifiers (14), and mixed or incomplete constructions (15)?
3. Are your sentences effective? Have you used subordination and coordination (16) and parallelism (17) appropriately? Are your sentences emphatic (18) and varied (19)?
4. Is your use of commas, semicolons, colons, periods, and other punctuation correct (20–25)?
5. Are your sentences mechanically correct in the use of capitals, italics, abbreviations, numbers, and hyphens (26–30)?
6. Have you relied on standard diction (31a)? Do your words denote and connote what you intend, and have you avoided triteness (31b)? Is your writing concise (31c)?
7. Are your words spelled correctly (34)?

2d | Revising and editing on a word processor

Perhaps instead of composing on paper, either with a pen or on a typewriter, you are writing your paper on a screen in front of you — on a word processor. In that case, it hasn't been necessary for you to type a clean second draft for continued revising and editing, because with word processing you always have a clean script on your screen, and you can print a draft at any time.

Writing on a word processor has several advantages. The one that writers usually discover first is that composing goes faster. A word processor is mechanically faster than a typewriter or a pen, so that the time it takes to write the words corresponds more closely with the time it takes to think of them. Words on the screen or on the disk can be changed much more easily than words on paper, so revision is not such an onerous task. Words, sentences, and paragraphs can be changed, deleted, or added. And once the revision is done the script is ready for printing — no typing of a final draft. Some people using word processors also have programs that are designed for composing and revising text, providing them with the kinds of guidance suggested in this book.

If you do your composing on a word processor or are considering doing so, you might keep a few cautions in mind. First, your machine and program are just mechanical devices; they can't think. The ideas and words must come from you. In plain language, if your paper ends up saying nothing important, that's not the fault of the word-processing program. Everything we have said so far about writing and revising applies just as much to composing on the word processor as it does to composing with pen or typewriter: you must have something to say, a reason for saying it, someone to say it to, and a way to say it. Second, some writers find that, because writing is so easy with the word processor, they write too much, going on and on with whatever comes into their heads. What such writers must learn to do is revise and edit, cutting out irrelevant material using the techniques suggested in this chapter.

The major disadvantage of word processors is that a break in electrical power can destroy all the text you've been working on — a disastrous, irretrievable loss. To be safe, writers must save their text by frequently storing it on a disk.

In short, word processing is a new way to write. It doesn't replace the pen or the typewriter, but it offers special advantages to writers who are adventuresome enough to try it or lucky enough to have it.

2e | Preparing the final draft

After you have edited your essay, following the guidelines suggested in 2c, copy a clean draft. Make sure you don't omit words, parts of words, and punctuation marks. Then proofread for copying errors and other errors you might have missed earlier. When you proofread, read once through for meaning to make sure you haven't skipped lines or omitted words. Then read again particularly for errors. This may be your last chance to make your paper express your idea clearly. Some writers like to read their final drafts backward as well as forward to catch typographical or spelling errors.

2f | Benefiting from criticism

To be an effective writer, you must learn to become a good critic of your own writing. You need to know what is good and what is bad about your compositions and how you can make them better. One way to become a good critic is to observe how other writers write — how they phrase their sentences, what words they choose, how they order their paragraphs, and so forth. Another way is to learn from people who criticize your writing — teachers and, in some classes, classmates. When a teacher or classmate returns a paper with suggestions of ways to improve a paper or your writing as a whole, you can learn something about how to look at your writing. Instead of looking at the markings on your papers as personal criticisms, take advantage of them as suggestions that the instructor — a more experienced writer — or your peers are sharing.

The following typewritten samples show two different methods an instructor may use to correct your essay, followed by a revised paragraph. The first sample uses the correction code on the inside back cover of this book; it directs you to the Handbook or Workbook section where you will find the error discussed. The second sample shows the use of correction symbols, listed on the inside front cover.

(3A)
(8b)
    The trouble with bank credit cards is that they prey on people
where they are most vulnerable. The (banks) take a percentage of
purchases made with the card, but that is not how (it) makes its profit.
Instead, the profit comes from the high interest rate on the balances
people maintain over thirty days. Thus, the higher (your) balance over   (13a)
time, the more money you owe to the bank in interest. Though banks
usually set a low limit at first on the amount (one) can charge, they   (13a)
just as often raise that limit as soon as the balance approaches it.
(10c)
(34a)
Without the customer (even requesting an increase. In this way the
banks encourage (there) customers to incur large debts.   (6h)

Run-
topic
sentence
doesn't
describe
paragraph

    The trouble with bank credit cards is that they prey on people
where they are most vulnerable. The (banks) take a percentage of
purchases made with the card, but that is not how (it) makes its profit.   agr
Instead, the profit comes from the high interest rate on the balances
people maintain over thirty days. Thus, the higher (your) balance over   shift
time, the more money you owe to the bank in interest. Though banks
shift   usually set a low limit at first on the amount (one) can charge, they
just as often raise that limit as soon as the balance approaches it.

38

frag { Without the customer even requesting an increase. In this way the

sp _____ banks encourage (there) customers to incur large debts. ⌣ *case*

A bank credit card can be dangerous for its holder. The bank takes a percentage of purchases made with the card, but that is not how it makes its profit. Instead, the profit comes from the high interest rate on the balance a customer maintains over thirty days. Thus, the higher a person's balance over time, the more money he or she owes the bank in interest. Though a bank usually sets a low limit at first on the amount a customer can charge, the bank just as often raises that limit as soon as the balance approaches it, without the customer's even requesting an increase. In this way the bank encourages the customer to incur a large debt.

❘ Revising the first draft   EXERCISE **2-1**

Read the student essay below and answer the following questions about it:

1. What is the thesis sentence? How could you improve it?
2. What do you see as the writer's purpose for writing this essay?
3. Are the paragraphs unified? Does each one focus on a central idea? Do they contain any unrelated ideas?
4. Is the essay coherent? Do all parts follow one another logically? Are all parts interrelated? Make whatever changes you think necessary to improve the essay.
5. Do you see any errors? If so, correct them.

FEAR OF FLYING

I hate flying. But I am going to school a thousand miles from

home, flying is the fastest way for me to get home and back to school.

Because flying terrifies me, I have developed several techniques to help

me deal with fear both before and during a flight.

My preparations for psychological survival start the night before

I have to get on the plane since I expect my fears to keep me from sleeping,

I read a book on the history of architecture. I have a good book on that subject, and I read it because I need a book that deals with solid structures that are on solid ground, the subject matter gives me comfort. I contemplate the pictures of pyramids which reminds me of stability and permanence. When I get real tired, I study photographs of flying buttresses, which remind me of both air travel and stability. Then I am able to doze off.

Reasonably well-rested the next day, calm will help me get through the next stages of the trip. On my way to the airport, I start out very nervous about the flight.

I encourage the cab driver to tell me about car accidents he has seen, then I think about how much safer flying is. I look out the window at sturdy, solid buildings and divert my eyes when we pass the cemetary. After I check in at the airport, I sit in the flight lounge and read a cheap paperback that has alot of explicit passages about sex — that keeps my mind off flying on the airplane.

The most important thing at first is to find a seat as far away from the windows as possible. If the seats are assigned, I try to choose an aisle seat — far from the windows — near the exit door at the rear of the plane, the safest part in case of a crash. If the seats are not assigned, I still try to get the same location, but I also try to sit next to someone who looks like a calm, experienced traveler, but who does not look too talkative. Because I don't want to be next to anyone as nervous as me but I also don't want to be next to someone who will try to point out sights on the ground and continually remind me how the cars look like ants. During the flight, I try to distract myself from the trip as much as possible by eating constantly, listening to music on the headphones, and by reading my paperback novel. I make sure I don't drink anything for several hours before the flight or during the flight, so that I don't have to go to the restroom. If I had to go to the restroom, then I would have to unbuckle my seat belt. Keeping the seat belt buckled throughout the trip is important to my sense of security. If I keep eating and reading throughout the trip, I am less likely to look out the window inadvertently.

I shall always believe that airplanes violate the law of gravity, but my sense of exhilaration when I get off an airplane would be something I probably would not feel if I did not go through the various stages of suppressed terror before and during a flight.

|*Using the correction symbols*   EXERCISE   **2-2**

The following paragraphs have been marked with some of the correction
symbols inside the front cover of the Workbook. To develop a familiarity
with the symbols, revise these paragraphs according to the markings.

sp

cap —— The worst part of our trip home after chirstmas were the last —— *agr*

fifty miles between the Illinois border and Milwaukee. While the

highway around Chicago was wet and messy; the road as we entered —— *p*

Wisconsin became snow-covered and slick. And the farther we drove into

no cap —— our home State, the worse the roads became. From the 65-mile-per-hour

speed that was common on I-294 and I-94 in Illinois, the traffic slowed

to 60, then to the legal 55. Continuing to drop to about 30 and 35. } *frag*

frag { Even at 30 miles per hour, stoping was impossible, we just drove along *sp*

slowly, hoping there would be no need to stop. All along the way the —— *cs*

shoulders were punctuated by cars and trucks that had tried to do

something different. Then plod along at a regular though agonizingly —— *sp*

frag —— slow rate of speed. The closer we got to Milwaukee, the worse it

became. Only after we got home and turned on the radio did we discover *¶/ref*

why: the storm had dumped eight inches of snow on the city in just a

few hours, whereas areas to the south had received a mere two or three

inches or, farther to the south, rain.

sp —— The absolute worst occured after we entered the city. Choosing to } *frag*

drive through downtown because those streets would most likely be

cleared (and going that way was the most direct route to our house).

We drove into a huge traffic snarl made up of cars, trucks, and buses

stuck in and grinding away at the entire eight inches of damp, slushy, slippery no-longer-white stuff occupying Jackson St. and Wisconsin avenue. The plowing crews were waiting for people to go home so they can clear the streets, but the only way people could go home were to push their cars around the stuck ones and out of the slush.

|*Writing and revising the essay*   EXERCISE   **2-3**

Write the first draft of an essay using the ideas you identified and grouped in Exercise 1-3, the thesis sentence you developed in Exercise 1-4, and the outline you prepared in Exercise 1-8. Use your own paper. Then revise the draft, checking it against the revision checklist on page 35. Work to clarify your purpose in your thesis sentence and consistently throughout the paper. Concentrate on maintaining unity and coherence (see Sections 3a and 3b). Proofread for errors in grammar, spelling, punctuation, mechanics, and word choice, referring to the checklist on page 36. Write the final draft in the form specified by your instructor.

When your instructor returns your corrected paper, revise it further in accordance with his or her comments and suggestions, asking questions about any comments you don't understand. Keep track of the problems and errors pointed out to you, and concentrate on these areas when you prepare your next paper. Also take note of what your instructor says you are doing well, and next time you write try to repeat and improve on those things.

3 | *Composing Paragraphs*

Readers have certain expectations when they read. They expect that there will be a minimum of mechanical and grammatical errors to hinder their understanding of what a writer is saying. They also expect that a piece of writing will make sense, will make a point worth making. And they assume that related ideas will be grouped together and marked with indentions to make what we commonly call paragraphs.

While paragraphs have no specific length and no required number of sentences, they do conventionally have three characteristics: they are unified, coherent, and adequately developed. That is, a paragraph presents a single thought, all its parts are clearly related to one another, and its point is sufficiently supported by details, examples, or explanations.

3a | Maintaining paragraph unity

A paragraph is **unified** when all its parts relate clearly to its central, controlling idea. This idea is often expressed in a **topic sentence.**

1 | Focusing on the central idea

A paragraph is a unit of thought, a central idea supported by relevant details. When writers allow unrelated thoughts to creep in or the paragraph's topic to shift in midstream, the unity of the paragraph is destroyed. As a writer you should examine each paragraph you write to be sure all its parts relate to your topic sentence. To do so, of course, you must know what the topic, or controlling idea, is. In examining your paragraphs, you should be able to point to a given sentence that expresses your controlling idea or be able to summarize the idea of each paragraph in a single sentence.

Read the following paragraph and see how your expectations as a reader are frustrated when it begins to slip off the topic. (The irrelevant sentences are in italics.)

Letter writing seems to be a thing of the past, and with it is gone much of the charm and wit of leisurely composition. When people want to share information today with a friend or relative, they are likely to turn to some form of communication other than the personal letter. You can probably count on one hand the number of personal letters you've received in the past year. But can you count the number of long-distance telephone calls you've received in the past year? Personal letters don't seem to "reach out and touch" in quite the same way a telephone call does. And now that so many people have cassette tape recorders in their homes, another modern communication device is supplanting the letter. Cassette recordings are cheaper than telephone calls, and they can be composed in much the same way a letter can — at leisure and over a long period of time. *Cassettes are like letters in another way too: they need to be mailed, which may be both an advantage and a disadvantage. The cost of postage will be much less than that of a telephone call that transmits a comparable amount of information. The disadvantage is that the sender must trek down to the post office to mail the cassette.*

This paragraph lacks unity because the writer shifts from the topic of "forms of communication other than the personal letter" to a related topic, "how cassette recordings are like letters." The writer clearly expresses the topic of the paragraph in the second sentence but then seems to have lost track of it. The paragraph would have avoided disunity if it ended in the following way:

> Cassette recordings are cheaper than telephone calls, and they can be composed in much the same way a letter can — at leisure and over a long period of time. Perhaps this new form of communication will at least bring back the leisurely composition of the personal letter.

2 | Placing the topic sentence

A paragraph's central idea and supporting details may be arranged in different ways. In the most common paragraph shape, the central idea — expressed in a topic sentence — falls first, sometimes followed by a restricting sentence that narrows the topic and makes it more specific. The paragraph on letter writing in 3a-1 follows this pattern and the following paragraph illustrates it further. The first sentence expresses the topic, and the first part of the second sentence, "On *The CBS Evening News* last night I watched a commercial," restricts the broader topic ("most" of the evening news programs and "most" of the commercials) to a specific news program; the remainder of the examples in the paragraph name specific commercials.

> *Most of the evening news programs consist of commercials, and* 1
> *most of the commercials are for products to treat the infirmities of old*
> *age.* On *The CBS Evening News* last night I watched a commercial 2
> for an iron and vitamin tonic from 6:33 to 6:34. From 6:34 to 6:35 3
> appeared a commercial for arthritis remedies. And that was fol- 4
> lowed by a thirty-second commercial for sleeping pills. At 6:40 ap- 5
> peared three more commercials: One showed an elderly man eating
> bran cereal; a second showed a hemorrhoid salve; a third showed a
> salve for aching muscles. A few minutes later another barrage of 6
> commercials came on, and two more series of them appeared still
> later. These ads dealt with such products as laxatives, life and 7
> health insurance, and pain relievers for head and stomach.
>
> – A student

The central idea may also appear at the end of a paragraph, as in the following example.

> Harvey got two speeding tickets last week. He turned in his [1,2]
> psychology paper two days late. He borrowed ten dollars from me [3]
> and forgot to pay it back. When his girlfriend's parents called to [4]
> invite him to dinner, he got the date mixed up and showed up the
> night after the dinner was held. *Harvey probably would not fit any-* [5]
> *one's definition of "responsible."*
>
> – A student

Or the central idea may appear in the middle of a paragraph.

> Slouched against the weather-beaten doorway of the Burgundy [1]
> Hotel ("Beds $2"), a drunk dozed, shivering in the cold, a wine bottle
> in a paper bag at his feet. Along both sides of the street, several store [2]
> windows were broken. Beer cans, gum wrappers, old newspapers, [3]
> broken glass, and whiskey bottles cluttered the sidewalks and gut-
> ters. *Harley Avenue was a typical street of the North Side.* In a two- [4,5]
> block area there were nine pawn shops, two X-rated movie houses,
> half a dozen bars, and an adult bookstore. Most depressing, though, [6]
> were the drunks, drug freaks, and raggedly dressed people who loi-
> tered near the store entrances.
>
> – A student

The central idea may appear at the beginning of the paragraph and then be restated or added to at the end. The sample paragraph on page 50 about television commercials would have such a shape if it ended with the sentence *I have quit watching television news because it makes me feel old.*

Also, the central idea may appear at the beginning of the para-graph and be amplified in the middle. This shape would characterize the paragraph about the city street if a sentence such as *The signs of decay were obvious* were added at the beginning.

Finally, the central idea may be unstated. Students should use this technique with caution and only if the main idea of the paragraph is obvious from the context. You should be able to sum up in writing the unstated topic sentence even if you leave it out of the paragraph. If you cannot do so, the paragraph needs revision.

In the following description of the revival of Latin in an elemen-tary school class, the central idea, though not explicitly stated, is clearly that the children are enjoying the study of the once-dead language.

> "We're going to play the 'come-up' game," says Leonard, hold- [1]
> ing aloft a picture. "Quid est [What's this]?" he asks. Hands fly up. [2,3]
> "Caseus est [It's cheese]," pipes a nine-year-old named Cheryl. "Op- [4,5]
> time [Super]!" praises Leonard, and calls the proud pupil up front
> to play teacher with a new picture. After a relay of come-ups, Leo- [6]
> nardus leads a Latin sing-along of *Rome Is Burning* to the tune of
> *Are You Sleeping, Brother John?* climaxed by a fire dance with every-
> one shouting *"Flammae, flammae, flammae!"*
>
> – *Time*

Name _____ Date _____

¶
3

| *Identifying irrelevant details* | EXERCISE **3-1** |

The topic sentence is italicized in each of the two paragraphs below. Each paragraph contains sentences that are not directly related to the central idea. Identify these irrelevant sentences by drawing a line through them. Then reread each paragraph to check for improved unity; if all sentences still are not supporting the topic sentence, make further deletions until you are satisfied that all sentences support the central idea.

1.   We tend to view mosquitoes as insects with identical traits and with the primary goal of sucking human juices. *But there is quite a bit of variety among mosquitoes, as their biting behavior illustrates.* The female mosquito tries to lay her eggs where there is water or is certain to be water. It was once thought that only female mosquitoes bite, but in at least one group males also feed and both sexes feed only on flowers, not on animals. In another group, females feed by sticking a tube into an ant's mouth for a secretion the ant has collected from aphids. Mating habits also vary widely among mosquitoes. Feeding on animals, including humans, may occur after mating, when the female needs food for her eggs. But some groups of mosquitoes never do bother humans at all, getting their food instead exclusively from birds or other animals.

2.   *English pubs illustrate English character.* Every neighborhood has a pub that serves as its social center. The local residents congregate in the sedate and homelike atmosphere of soft talk, warm lights, and comfortable furniture, drinking mostly pints of beer or ale. In the United States, in contrast, bars are loud with music, dark and shadowy, and furnished with hard chairs and benches. One can go to an American bar and expect to remain anonymous, hidden from view and free of the annoyances of human interaction. The pubs close their doors promptly at ten on weeknights and eleven on weekends, at which point everyone returns home. Thus the pubs almost dictate English leisure life, whose principle seems to be pleasure under control.

|*Identifying the topic sentence*   EXERCISE **3-2**

The topic sentences in the following paragraphs occur at different points — at the beginning, at the end, or somewhere in between. Underline the topic sentence in each paragraph.

1.   Diamonds are the hardest naturally occurring substance known. They are so hard that they can cut and grind very hard metal. To accomplish such tasks, they are sometimes set in the ends of drills and other tools. At other times they are crushed into dust and baked into industrial tools. Because of their extreme hardness and indestructibility, they are also used as needles in all record players.

2.   Diamonds can be broken with a severe blow. If they are put in acid, they will dissolve. If they are heated in the presence of oxygen, they will burn and form carbon dioxide. If they are heated without oxygen, they turn to graphite, a very soft mineral. So, even though diamonds are the hardest natural substance known, there are ways of destroying them.

3.   Diamonds are made up of many sides, or facets, each of which must be the right size and shape and placed at exactly the right angle. Each must be polished. Because of these facets, diamonds are sparklingly brilliant. Each facet reflects light, bends rays of light, and breaks light up into the colors of the rainbow.

4.   There are only four major sources of diamonds: Africa, India, the Soviet Union, and South America. Africa is by far the largest producer, mining about 80 percent of the world's supply. Most of the remainder come from Siberia in the Soviet Union, which produces about 16 percent. India, while once an important source, mines very few of the gems today, and South America also accounts for a small number.

3b | Achieving paragraph coherence

An effective paragraph is not only unified but also **coherent:** the relation of its sentences is clear and easy to follow.

1 | Organizing the paragraph

The principal way of achieving coherence in an essay is to write a thesis sentence that is specific, limited, and unified and that clearly states your purpose. With such a thesis sentence you will have little trouble achieving the second aspect of a coherent essay: organization that flows naturally and reaches a conclusion logically. In a similar way, clearly stated topic sentences tie related parts of paragraphs together. Patterns of organization for paragraphs are like those for organizing essays. (See also 1h-1.)

One common pattern of paragraph organization, useful in description, is **spatial.** The paragraph begins at one point in space and moves from there to other points, following a logical sequence corresponding to the way we scan a scene or an object: inward to outward, up to down, and side to side. The following paragraph describes a person beginning with the first impression, her dress, and moving to her face:

> The bride was not pretty, nor was she very young. She wore a [1,2] dress of blue cashmere, with small reservations of velvet here and there, and with steel buttons abounding. She continually twisted [3] her head to regard her puff sleeves, very stiff, straight, and high. They embarrassed her. It was quite apparent that she had cooked, [4,5] and that she expected to cook, dutifully. The blushes caused by the [6] careless scrutiny of some passengers as she had entered the car were strange to see upon this plain, underclass countenance, which was drawn in placid, almost emotionless lines.
>
> – Stephen Crane, "The Bride Comes to Yellow Sky"

Another common paragraph pattern is **chronological,** relating events as they occurred over time. The paragraph on page 50 that describes a sequence of television commercials illustrates this pattern.

Paragraphs may also be arranged from specific ideas to increasingly general ones. The **specific-to-general** pattern is well illustrated by the paragraph on page 51 about Harvey, which moves from specific examples of his behavior to a general statement about his irresponsibility. The **general-to-specific** pattern is illustrated below; here the discussion moves from generalities about the highway system to details about a specific stretch.

> Now that much of it is over twenty years old, America's inter- [1] state highway system is growing more dangerous and starting to decay. But the stretches of potholes and weakening bridges are not [2] the only evidence. As suburbs have grown, more and more entrance [3] and exit ramps have been added near metropolitan areas, and the traffic flow in many instances is increasingly heavy. An eight-mile [4] stretch of I-395, near Washington, D.C., is the most heavily traveled

road in Virginia. It is almost constantly jammed, and during rush ₅ hour, cars move at an average speed of thirty miles per hour. One ₆ disabled car can jam up over a hundred thousand commuters for an hour or more and multiply accident hazards a hundredfold. Even a ₇ light rain can add half an hour to a seven-mile commute.

— A student

Finally, a paragraph may be organized in order of **increasing importance or drama,** as in the following paragraph.

The first sign I noticed of the ailing local economy was the ₁ gradual increase in the number of cars parked at the secondhand clothing store near my house. Instead of two or three cars on the ₂ usual Saturday morning, there were now six or eight. Not long after ₃ I noticed that change, our town's only car dealership closed, and the bearing manufacturing plant laid off half its twenty employees, in- cluding my next-door neighbor. A week later, my father, who oper- ₄ ated a hardware store, made his decision to sell out and move the family to the South.

— A student

2 | Using parallel structures

Another way to achieve paragraph coherence is occasionally to use **parallel structures** (see also 17a). By putting related ideas in equiva- lent grammatical form, parallel structures provide a tight link between those ideas. In the following paragraph, the parallel structures are itali- cized. The participles *standing, weighing,* and *wielding,* for example, are parallel forms linking descriptions of the pronoun *she,* referring to Carry Nation. Similarly, the two parallel verbs *terrorized* and *inspired,* linked with the conjunction *but,* provide a smooth, natural flow of action.

After her first husband died of alcoholism, Carry Nation devoted ₁ herself to eliminating consumption of alcohol in the United States. *Standing* nearly six feet tall and *weighing* nearly two hundred ₂ pounds, *she intimidated* any drinker. *Wielding* rocks and hatchets, ₃ *she destroyed* dozens of saloons. In the course of a ten-year rampage, ₄ she *terrorized* thousands of Americans but *inspired* thousands more. Though her campaign ultimately failed, she lives on as a symbol of ₅ powerful conviction and unequaled zeal.

— A student

3 | Repeating or restating words and word groups

Repetition can link sentences in a paragraph. While thoughtless repetition can weaken a piece of writing, intentionally repeating key words and phrases can hold a paragraph together. The key words in a paragraph are generally found in the topic sentence (and those of an essay in the thesis sentence). Notice in the following paragraph how the key word of the topic sentence, *cemetery,* is repeated, as are the words referring to the supporting ideas, the yew tree and the quiet. The concluding sen- tence draws all three ideas together.

The country cemetery today looks, I suspect, much as it did a hundred and fifty years ago, except that there are now more graves. A huge old yew tree dominates the grounds, shading the tombstones of the farmers and merchants. As the sprawling branches of the yew attract the visitor's eye, intense quiet attracts the ear. The intermittent buzzing of insects, whose sounds would go unnoticed in a busier atmosphere, accents the absence of the noises of human activity. Cattle graze silently and placidly beyond the barbed wire that fences the cemetery off from the surrounding grasslands. The scent of newly mown alfalfa from nearby fields permeates the cemetery, but the slightly bitter aroma of the yew dominates, cutting through the quiet and overriding, with the threat of death, the impression of shelter given by the tree's sprawling branches.

– A student

4 | Using pronouns

Pronouns, which refer to and function as nouns (see 5a-2), can link sentences in the same way that nouns do. Instead of continually repeating key words, as in the preceding paragraph, writers can sometimes achieve the same effect by substituting pronouns for those nouns. Such substitutions should be made, however, only when the reference of a pronoun is absolutely clear — that is, when there is no doubt about what the pronoun refers to (see Chapter 12). Reread the paragraph about Carry Nation on page 57 and see how each time the pronoun *she* occurs it relates back to the first, or topic, sentence, where Nation's name, the key word, is mentioned. Then read the following paragraph and see how Maya Angelou uses pronouns to link ideas.

My education and that of my Black associates were quite different from the education of our white schoolmates. In the classroom we all learned past participles, but in the streets and in our homes the Blacks learned to drop *s*'s from plurals and suffixes from past-tense verbs. We were alert to the gap separating the written word from the colloquial. We learned to slide out of one language and into another without being conscious of the effort. At school, in a given situation, we might respond with "That's not unusual." But in the street, meeting the same situation, we easily said, "It be's like that sometimes."

– Maya Angelou, *I Know Why the Caged Bird Sings*

5 | Being consistent

Consistency in the person and number of nouns and pronouns and in the tense of verbs (see Chapter 13) is crucial to paragraph coherence, for a paragraph that shifts unnecessarily from one person, number, or tense to another is hard to follow. In the following paragraph, for example, the meaning is obscured because of inconsistency (the shifting parts are italicized).

SHIFT IN PERSON

If *a person* wants to buy a computer, the first thing *you* do is decide what *your* needs are. When *the person* is primarily interested in word processing, *you* will not be looking at computers that feature graphic capabilities. And if what *one* wants is video games, *you* probably won't want to look at the most expensive machines on the market.

IMPROVED

If *you* want to buy a computer, the first thing *you* do is decide what *your* needs are. When *you* are primarily interested in word processing, *you* will not be looking at computers that feature graphic capabilities. And if what *you* want is video games, *you* probably won't want to look at the most expensive machines on the market.

SHIFT IN NUMBER

Another thing *a computer shopper* has to look for is cost. If *they* have only $2000 to spend, *they* can't be looking at top-of-the-line machines. On the other hand, *a careful shopper* can get some very good equipment for that amount of money; *they* just need to look around a bit.

IMPROVED

Another thing *computer shoppers* have to look for is cost. If *they* have only $2000 to spend, *they* can't be looking at top-of-the-line machines. On the other hand, *careful shoppers* can get some very good equipment for that amount of money; *they* just need to look around a bit.

VERB SHIFTS (TENSE AND MOOD)

One of the best ways to start looking around at what *is* available in the computer market *would be* to go to the local library and read the latest computer magazines. These publications *will contain* reviews of some of the most recent equipment and software. They also *have provided* price ranges and recommendations about how to use both the machines and the programs to run them.

IMPROVED

One of the best ways to start looking around at what *is* available in the computer market *is* to go to the local library and read the latest computer magazines. These publications *contain* reviews of some of the most recent equipment and software. They also *provide* price ranges and recommendations about how to use both the machines and the programs to run them.

6 | Using transitional expressions

Transitional expressions are words or word groups that connect ideas, both within sentences and between them. Some common transitional expressions are listed below by the connecting function they perform.

TO ADD OR SHOW SEQUENCE

again, also, and, and then, besides, equally important, finally, first, further, furthermore, in addition, in the first place, last, moreover, next, second, still, too

TO COMPARE

in the same way, likewise, similarly

TO CONTRAST

although, and yet, but, but at the same time, despite, even so, even though, for all that, however, in contrast, in spite of, nevertheless, notwithstanding, on the contrary, on the other hand, regardless, still, though, yet

TO GIVE EXAMPLES OR INTENSIFY

after all, an illustration of, even, for example, for instance, indeed, in fact, it is true, of course, specifically, that is, to illustrate, truly

TO INDICATE PLACE

above, adjacent to, below, elsewhere, farther on, here, near, nearby, on the other side, opposite to, there, to the east, to the left

TO INDICATE TIME

after a while, afterward, as long as, as soon as, at last, at length, at that time, before, earlier, formerly, immediately, in the meantime, in the past, lately, later, meanwhile, now, presently, shortly, simultaneously, since, so far, soon, subsequently, then, thereafter, until, until now, when

TO REPEAT, SUMMARIZE, OR CONCLUDE

all in all, altogether, as has been said, in brief, in conclusion, in other words, in particular, in short, in simpler terms, in summary, on the whole, that is, therefore, to put it differently, to summarize

TO SHOW CAUSE OR EFFECT

accordingly, as a result, because, consequently, for this purpose, hence, otherwise, since, then, therefore, thereupon, thus, to this end, with this object

You can see these transitional expressions at work in many of the examples of paragraphs in this chapter. You might want to look at the paragraph about letter writing on pages 49–50, where you'll find these words: *when, today, but, and now, another.* Another one you might observe describes the ailing economy on page 57: *the first sign, not long after, a week later.*

Organizing paragraphs: spatial and chronological

EXERCISE **3-3**

The following paragraph topics are suitable for spatial and chronological organization. Select one topic for each pattern, or make up similar topics of your own. For each topic you choose, write a topic sentence, list at least three details related to the topic sentence, and write one paragraph. Use parallel structures, repetition, pronouns with clear reference, and transitional expressions to achieve paragraph coherence.

1. Topics for spatial paragraph: a stadium during a game, a variety store shortly before Christmas, a school playground, a local gym, a person.

Topic sentence: _____

_____

Details: 1. _____

_____

2. _____

_____

3. _____

_____

Paragraph: _____

_____

_____

_____

_____

_____

2. Topics for chronological paragraph: a parade, a wedding, cleaning your room, a particular basketball game or other sports event.

Topic sentence: _____

_____

Details: 1. _____

_____

2. _____

_____

3. _____

_____

Paragraph: _____

_____

_____

_____

_____

_____

_____

_____

_____

_____

_____

_____

_____

Organizing paragraphs: specific, general, dramatic

EXERCISE **3-4**

The following topics are suitable for paragraphs organized from (1) specific to general and general to specific or (2) less dramatic to more dramatic. Select two topics, or make up topics of your own, that are suitable for two of these paragraph patterns. For each topic you choose, write a topic sentence, list at least three details related to the topic sentence, and write one paragraph. Use parallel structures, repetition, pronouns, and transitional expressions to achieve paragraph coherence.

1. Topics for specific to general or general to specific: the benefits of exercise, the results of having made a particular decision, the appeal of music videos.

   Topic sentence: ————————————————————————————

   ——————————————————————————————————————

   Details: 1. ——————————————————————————————

   ——————————————————————————————————————

   2. ————————————————————————————————————

   ——————————————————————————————————————

   3. ————————————————————————————————————

   ——————————————————————————————————————

   Paragraph: ——————————————————————————————

   ——————————————————————————————————————

   ——————————————————————————————————————

   ——————————————————————————————————————

   ——————————————————————————————————————

_____

_____

_____

2. Topics for less dramatic to more dramatic: why I hate (or like) family reunions; an embarrassing incident; a serious accident

Topic sentence: _____

_____

Details: 1. _____

_____

2. _____

_____

3. _____

_____

Paragraph: _____

_____

_____

_____

_____

_____

_____

_____

_____

_____

|*Being consistent*   EXERCISE   **3-5**

The following paragraphs are consistent in person, number, and tense. To help you avoid writing that has unneeded shifts, rewrite each paragraph on separate paper according to the instructions, concentrating on being consistent.

1.   Counting bald eagles on the Mississippi River is an experience to remember. It's different from most bird watching because you do it in the middle of winter (in January, to be specific). Furthermore, you don't need to get up before dawn to do it. However, you do need warm clothing and a car for moving from one place to another. Since eagles migrate down the river toward open water, you need to position yourself wherever ice and water meet. Sometimes you find the eagles feeding at the edge of the ice; sometimes you see them perched in a tree overhanging the river; and sometimes you have the magnificent experience of seeing these large white and black birds in flight over the water.

Rewrite the paragraph, copying the first sentence as it is and changing the second to read:

> It's different from most bird watching because *bird watchers* do it in the middle of winter (in January, to be specific).

Make all other sentences consistent with this change. Use pronouns and repeat *bird watchers* where necessary.

2.   One year I went to Dubuque, Iowa, from my home in Milwaukee, Wisconsin, to count the bald eagles in their migration down the Mississippi. As I traveled between Madison and the river in early January, I saw several huge flocks of geese flying south. I saw five or six thousand at one time. They probably spent the early winter at Horicon

Marsh, being unwilling to move on until their food supply there was exhausted.

Rewrite the paragraph, changing the first sentence as follows:

> Each year I *have gone* to Dubuque, Iowa, from my home in Milwaukee, Wisconsin, to count the bald eagles in their migration down the Mississippi.

Make all other sentences consistent with this change. Your verbs will be altered to use *have* plus the past participle (*gone* is the past participle of *go* and *went*).

Name _____ Date _____

*Identifying parallelism,
repetition, pronouns,
transitional expressions*   EXERCISE **3-6**

Read the following paragraph, looking for the ways in which parallelism, repetition, pronouns, and transitional expressions link sentences. Then answer the questions after the paragraph.

> The most notable house in Plainville has always been a large ₁ and distinguished Victorian on Grant Avenue. The house was built in ₂ the 1890s by a wealthy industrialist who claimed to see great promise in the backwater town. The promise was never fulfilled, however, and ₃ the town settled instead into permanent shabbiness and obscurity. Despite his disappointments, the industrialist and three succeeding ₄ generations of his family stayed on in the mansion, preserving it for themselves and thus for their neighbors. Standing a full story above ₅ anything else in Plainville, the house remained a source of pleasure and pride for the community. Painted royal blue with red trim, it ₆ provided a bright island in an otherwise colorless setting. Even when ₇ the house was finally abandoned in the 1970s, it still recalled Plainville's optimistic past. Last week that past was demolished along with ₈ the old house. Now all that remains in Plainville is the drab present. ₉

1. List at least five transitional expressions in the paragraph.

   a. _____ c. _____ e. _____

   b. _____ d. _____

2. Two key words in the first sentence are repeated or restated throughout the paragraph. Identify the two key words and then list five repetitions or restatements of each one in the order in which they appear in the paragraph.

   a. Key word: _____

      Repetitions or restatements: _____; _____;

      _____; _____; _____

67

b. Key word: _____

    Repetitions or restatements: _____; _____;

    _____; _____; _____

3. The paragraph also contains three other words that are repeated in at least two sentences each. List them.

    a. _____ b. _____ c. _____

4. Pronouns substitute for three different nouns in the paragraph. Identify each noun and list the pronoun or pronouns substituting for each one.

    a. Noun: _____ Pronoun(s): _____

    b. Noun: _____ Pronoun(s): _____

    c. Noun: _____ Pronoun(s): _____

5. Two sentences in the paragraph are closely linked by parallelism. Identify the sentences by number.

    a. _____ b. _____

|*Arranging and linking sentences* EXERCISE **3-7**

The following list provides all the details for a unified and coherent paragraph about a volcanic eruption on the island of Krakatoa. Through combining sentences, rearranging details, and using some of the coherence devices discussed in this chapter, you can write a paragraph that describes the explosion and its effects. Begin with the topic sentence and combine it with the restrictive sentence, reducing unnecessary words by using only the *when* clause of the topic restriction. Select details in chronological order, and finish with the concluding sentence. Use parallel structures, repetition of key words, pronouns with clear references, and transitional expressions.

TOPIC SENTENCE

The greatest volcanic eruption of modern times occurred on August 27, 1883.

TOPIC RESTRICTION

The great eruption occurred when the island of Krakatoa, in what is now Indonesia, blew up.

CONCLUDING SENTENCE

In the aftermath nearly forty thousand people were discovered to have died.

1. The mountains exploded.
2. The island sank into the ocean.
3. At first the island's mountains spewed rocks and ash into the air for a day, blackening the sky.
4. The earth calmed down again.
5. The explosion roared.
6. The collapse of the island caused gigantic tidal waves.
7. Almost nothing remained of the island when things were calm again.
8. The sound could be heard three thousand miles away.
9. The tidal waves swallowed up coastal cities and inland towns.
10. The explosion created winds that circled the earth several times.
11. The waves appeared finally as unusually large waves on the English coast, half a world away.

¶ 3

Paragraph: _____

_____

_____

_____

_____

_____

_____

_____

_____

_____

_____

_____

_____

_____

_____

_____

_____

_____

_____

_____

_____

_____

_____

_____

_____

3c | Developing the paragraph

An effective paragraph is **developed;** that is, the central idea of the paragraph (usually expressed in a topic sentence) is well supported with enough details, examples, or reasons to convince the reader of the point being made.

1 | Using specific information

A paragraph may be developed by details. Compare the following undeveloped paragraph with the one on page 58 by Maya Angelou:

> The education of black children differs from that of white children in that the black children learn language in two places: in the classroom and on the street.

The details of the original provide interest and clarity.

2 | Using a pattern of development

As a writer, you sometimes know exactly what you want to say and how you want to say it. You sit down and start writing, and it comes out right. At other times, however, you may be at a loss as to how to begin; you know what you want to say, but you don't know the best way to say it. At other times your paragraphs need some tinkering; they're not convincing, and they're not clear. At such times you can draw on established methods of paragraph development to generate specific supporting information or to give shape to the information you have. (These methods correspond to the exploratory questions on pages 11–12.) Useful methods of development include illustration and support, definition, division and classification, comparison and contrast, analogy, cause-and-effect analysis, and process analysis.

How can it be illustrated or supported?

As we have seen, some paragraphs may be developed simply by **illustration** or **support** — that is, by well-detailed examples or reasons that explain and clarify the paragraph's central idea.

For instance, the paragraph on page 51 about the city street uses examples for development, and the paragraph on pages 56–57 about the highway system gives reasons and a specific example to develop its main point. In the following paragraph the main idea (expressed in the second sentence) is supported by a specific example.

> Since I'm on the subject, I might as well mention another thing about cats. They seem to enjoy killing: random, senseless killing. The other day the dark-colored cat landed on a robin, toyed with it for half an hour, and then, when I scolded the animal, walked away from the scene of the crime without so much as a backward glance. Meanwhile, what was I supposed to do? The robin had a broken wing, a punctured eye, no doubt several assorted internal injuries. I wasn't going to take it to a veterinarian, so I put it out of its misery. Meanwhile the cat was back on our doorstep, crying to go inside and eat. What did the cat care?

For her the robin was only idle recreation. And that's a deplorable attitude. But just try to change it; a cat takes to self-improvement about as readily as a turtle takes to flight.

– Jerome Nilssen

What is it? What does it encompass, and what does it exclude?

In **definition** you name the category of things to which something belongs and then distinguish it from other members of its category.

> Every class has certain kinds of students, and one kind who is [1] always present is the hand raiser. I mean the too-eager student who [2] does all the required *and* suggested reading two weeks in advance and who needs to show off all that work. Not long after class starts, [3] the hand goes up — not merely raised, with a slightly bent arm, fingers relaxed, but *waved*, arm and fingers straight as sticks, hand turning 180 degrees as fast as the muscles will allow. The face is [4] bright-eyed and smiling. And the desire to say "Call on me!" is [5] barely repressed. When the hoped-for moment comes, the answering [6] voice is full of pride. But is the answer worth hearing? Almost never. [7,8] In the end, real thought about the reading and the question seems [9] to get lost in the compulsion to answer.

> – A student

What are its parts or characteristics? Or what groups can it be sorted into?

In **division** or **analysis,** you investigate a subject by asking, "What are its parts?" You might analyze the syllabus for a course, for example, by looking at the individual units of material to be covered. In a related method, **classification,** you ask, "What groups can it be sorted into?" In looking at a syllabus you might group the work of all the individual days in the semester into several related units. The following paragraph employs classification to discuss psychic phenomena.

> Psychic phenomena — occurrences unexplained by modern [1] laws of physics and psychology — are usually classified as one of three types. The first and probably best-known is extrasensory per- [2] ception, or ESP. A person who is supposed to have ESP receives [3] messages from his or her environment, whether from people or from objects, without reasoning or using the senses of sight, hearing, smell, taste, or touch. The second category, psychokinesis, or PK, is [4] said to allow its possessor to influence the behavior of objects or people in the environment without touching them. And the third [5] category, often called spiritualism, supposedly enables its possessors to communicate with people who have died and who reside in a "spirit world."

> – A student

How is it like, or different from, other things?

Comparison and contrast are methods of development for which you ask, "How is it like or different from other things?" Comparison usually shows similarities between things we perceive as different; contrast usually shows differences between things we perceive as similar. These methods of development can be used separately or together. Contrast is used in this paragraph about two attitudes toward taking pictures.

> Several years ago, *Time* photographer Steve Northup, who had covered Vietnam and Watergate, took a group of students around Cambridge shooting pictures. He quietly insisted that they ask every pizza-maker, truck driver and beautician for permission. His attitude toward private citizens was one of careful respect for the power of "exposure." In contrast to this, the average camera bug — like the average tourist — too often goes about snapping "quaint" people, along with "quaint" scenes: See the natives smile, see the natives carrying baskets of fruit, see the native children begging, see the drunk in the doorway. As Milgram wrote, "I find it hard to understand wherein the photographer has derived the right to keep for his own purposes the image of the peasant's face."
>
> — Ellen Goodman, *Close to Home*

Is it comparable to something that is in a different class but more familiar?

Analogy is useful for explaining something complex or abstract by comparing it loosely with something simple, concrete, and familiar. You might describe an answering machine as a butler that receives and screens one's calls, or the act of writing in terms of designing a building. The writer of the following paragraph uses the analogy of washing a car to explain the lack of reward from taking a certain course.

> Philosophy class reminds me of the summer I spent washing cars at a service station. A wealthy lady brought her Cadillac to be washed every Saturday, whether or not the car had gotten the least bit dirty the previous week. Doing a good job of washing the car seemed absolutely pointless, because I knew I would have to go through the same motions and exert the same effort the next Saturday regardless of how clean I got the car. In philosophy class I have to master one thinker's viewpoint each week. And each subsequent week I master another thinker's argument that logically rejects the views of the previous philosopher. The mental effort each week seems to me as pointless as washing that Cadillac. Regardless of how I work to embrace "truth," the next week my efforts are undone and I start anew.
>
> — A student

What are its causes or its effects?

To develop a paragraph by **cause-and-effect analysis,** you analyze why something happened or might happen. You look at the events (causes) that brought something about or the results (effects) of a sequence of events. In the following paragraph the writer first notes the effect — the absence of birds — and then guesses about a cause.

73

Strange, this absence of birds. On quiet evenings, at sundown, [1,2]
the great enclosed log pond lay there, deep, its surface immobile;
midges and butterflies swarmed over it; the trees on the bank were
mirrored in it; but no birds perched in the trees. Perhaps the deafen- [3]
ing roar of the torrent was to blame: no birds could thrive where
they could not hear each other sing. And that was why the only [4]
winged creatures here were midges and flies — though God alone
knows why even the crows and the magpies shunned our town.

– Knut Hamsun, *The Wanderer*

How does it work?

When you develop a paragraph by telling how something works
or how something is done, you are using **process analysis.** The organization of such development is usually chronological, describing a thing as it
occurs or has occurred. Process analysis is often used to tell a reader how
to do something. In the following paragraph the author examines how to
deal effectively with an emotionally disturbed person.

If a friend or relative loses emotional control in your presence, [1]
what should you do? The important thing is to help the person pass [2]
through the difficult moment and restore the balance between emotion and reason. First, listen carefully. Try to understand the per- [3,4]
son's view of the problem. Second, stay calm and attentive. Do not [5,6]
panic, and do not allow yourself to become impatient or bored or
angry. Third, if you feel that the person or the problems are too [7]
much for you to cope with, by all means seek help. But, fourth, be [8]
honest. Do not mislead the person about your intentions or conspire [9]
behind his or her back, for you will lose the trust that is essential
for helping.

– A student

Combining patterns of development

Even when you develop a whole essay by one of the methods
above, you will probably use other methods to develop individual paragraphs, and you may even *combine* methods (say, definition and comparison and contrast) in a single paragraph.

3 | Checking length

The length of a paragraph depends on the paragraph's topic and
your purpose. Long paragraphs are not necessarily well developed, nor
are short paragraphs necessarily underdeveloped. But very long paragraphs (more than 150 words, or about eight sentences) may contain irrelevant information. And very short paragraphs (less than 100 words, or
about four sentences) may lack the specific details, examples, or reasons
needed to convey your point adequately. It's a good practice to check all
paragraphs that seem extra long or extra short. The long ones may need
to be divided or have irrelevant information removed, and the short ones
may need to have specific details added.

¶

3

Developing paragraphs with illustration or support

Drawing on the topics suggested below or on topics of your own, develop (1) one paragraph supported by examples and (2) one paragraph supported by reasons. Write a topic sentence for each paragraph, and list at least three of the items to be used in its development; then write your paragraph. An alternative to the three examples for developing the first paragraph is one narrative example, as in the paragraph about cats on pages 71–72. Refer to that paragraph about cats and to the one about black children and language on page 58 as examples of how these paragraphs can be written.

1. Topics for examples: how television commercials mislead; the ideal shopping center; what stage fright is like.

    Topic sentence: _____

    _____

    Examples: 1. _____

    _____

    2. _____

    _____

    3. _____

    _____

    Paragraph: _____

    _____

    _____

    _____

    _____

¶

3

2. Topics for reasons: why not to buy sweetened cereals; why read news-papers; why a particular person makes you feel important.

Topic sentence: _____

_____

Reasons: 1. _____

_____

2. _____

_____

3. _____

_____

Paragraph: _____

_____

_____

_____

_____

_____

_____

_____

_____

_____

_____

¶

3

Developing paragraphs with definition; with division and classification   EXERCISE   **3-9**

Drawing on the topics suggested below or on topics of your own, develop (1) one paragraph using definition and (2) one paragraph using division, classification, or both. Write a topic sentence for each paragraph, and list at least three pieces of supporting information (details, examples, or reasons) to be used in its development. Then write the paragraph. Refer to the paragraphs on page 72 as examples of how these paragraphs can be written.

1. Topics for definition: loyalty; authority; education.

   Topic sentence: _____

   _____

   Supporting information: 1. _____

   _____

   2. _____

   _____

   3. _____

   _____

   Paragraph: _____

   _____

   _____

   _____

   _____

   _____

_____

_____

_____

_____

2. Topics for division: (parts of) a football team; a concert; a newspaper. Topics for classification: (types of) diets; students; comic strips.

Topic sentence: _____

_____

Supporting information: 1. _____

_____

2. _____

_____

3. _____

_____

Paragraph: _____

_____

_____

_____

_____

_____

_____

_____

_____

Developing paragraphs with comparison and contrast; with analogy

EXERCISE **3-10**

¶

3

Drawing on the topics suggested below or on topics of your own, develop (1) one paragraph using comparison, contrast, or both and (2) one paragraph using analogy. Write a topic sentence for each paragraph, and list at least three pieces of supporting information (details, examples, or reasons) to be used in its development. Then write the paragraph. Refer to the paragraphs on page 73 as examples of these ways of looking at ideas.

1. Topics for comparison, contrast, or both: two persons' ways of laughing; news reports on radio and on television; two diet plans.

   Topic sentence: _____

   _____

   Supporting information: 1. _____

   _____

   2. _____

   _____

   3. _____

   _____

   Paragraph: _____

   _____

   _____

   _____

   _____

   _____

_____

_____

_____

_____

2. Topics for analogy: a classroom is like a church or a synagogue; a telephone answering service like an electronic butler; jealousy like hunger.

Topic sentence: _____

_____

Supporting information: 1. _____

_____

2. _____

_____

3. _____

_____

Paragraph: _____

_____

_____

_____

_____

_____

_____

_____

_____

| Developing paragraphs
with cause-and-effect analysis;
with process analysis   EXERCISE   **3-11**

Drawing on topics suggested below or on topics of your own, develop (1)
one paragraph using cause-and-effect analysis and (2) one paragraph
using process analysis. Write a topic sentence for each paragraph, and list
at least three pieces of supporting information (details, examples, or reasons) to use in its development. Then write the paragraph. Refer to the
paragraphs on page 74 as examples of these ways of looking at ideas.

1. Topics for cause-and-effect analysis: the physical effects of anger; the
   effects of a snowstorm (or some other natural event); why you're taking
   a particular class; why you never (or always) travel by bus or train.

   Topic sentence: _____

   _____

   Supporting information: 1. _____

   _____

   2. _____

   _____

   3. _____

   _____

   Paragraph: _____

   _____

   _____

   _____

   _____

   _____

_____

_____

_____

_____

_____

2. Topics for process analysis: how to argue with a traffic officer; how dogs (or cats or some other pet) let you know it's time for them to eat; how to clean a room.

Topic sentence: _____

_____

Supporting information: 1. _____

_____

2. _____

_____

3. _____

_____

Paragraph: _____

_____

_____

_____

_____

_____

_____

_____

3d | Writing special kinds of paragraphs

The opening and closing paragraphs of an essay, transitional paragraphs, and paragraphs in dialogue serve special purposes and may not conform to the guidelines for unity, coherence, and development discussed in preceding sections.

1 | Opening an essay

The introductory paragraph of an essay has some special jobs:

1. To present the subject
2. To arouse the interest of the reader
3. To express the writer's viewpoint on the subject
4. To convey the writer's attitude toward the subject (serious, cynical, humorous, angry, straightforward)

You can open an introductory paragraph with a statement of the essay's subject, some background information, a brief anecdote (relating something you have seen or heard that applies to the subject), a startling opinion, a historical fact or event, or an intriguing or apt quotation. You will generally end an introductory paragraph with a statement of your thesis. Here are two examples of introductory paragraphs:

> After nearly 30 years of warnings from health officials, most Americans are well aware of the perils of too much cholesterol. The problem is, how much is too much? What level of cholesterol in the blood should be considered acceptable, and at what point does treatment become necessary to reduce the risk of heart disease? For three days last week the National Institutes of Health in Bethesda, Md., convened a panel of 14 experts to try to answer these questions. The group reviewed the extensive scientific evidence linking high levels of cholesterol and fatty diet to heart disease, the leading cause of death in the U.S. They heard testimony from dozens of people and then retired to draft a report, working into the early hours of the morning. The result is the most far-reaching recommendation yet made on the subject of cholesterol and heart disease.
>
> — *Time*

> Contrary to what my parents and teachers always told me, I have found daydreaming a very useful pastime. Daydreaming not only has helped me through some boring classes but also has helped me discover my career goals.
>
> — A student

The first paragraph gives extensive background in preparation for an essay that discusses the recommendation named in the thesis sentence. The second paragraph, though much briefer, is equally effective in leading the reader into the subject of the essay.

An effective opening paragraph is concise, direct, sincere, and interesting. Be sure to state your own viewpoint on the subject, perhaps in your thesis sentence (see 1d). In the thesis sentence of the first paragraph above, the viewpoint is expressed in the word *far-reaching*. In the second, the verb *helped* states the perspective the writer is taking toward daydreaming. Make your writing easier for you and its reading easier for your reader by avoiding a simple announcement of your intentions; and don't wander vaguely over subjects broader than or unrelated to your own.

If you have trouble writing an introduction, you might start with your thesis sentence, write your essay, and then come back to write your introduction. Likewise, if you discover after you've written your essay that your introduction is not doing what you want it to, scratch it and start it over. Sometimes, even though you know what you want to say in an essay, you may have trouble getting started effectively; in that case, you're better off plunging into the middle and coming back to work on the introduction after your writing has warmed up.

2 | Closing an essay

A proper close to an essay indicates that you have not just stopped writing but have completed what you wanted to say. Whether in a single sentence or in several sentences, a conclusion may, among other things, summarize, ask a question, introduce a startling or weighty fact or quotation, or suggest a course of action. The first paragraph below ends with questions (and a partial answer), the second with a quotation.

> Well, what do you think? Should I send the cats packing, back to the Humane Society for a quick and painless trip to cat-heaven? Or despite everything shall I keep caring for them? I guess there's precedent for that.
>
> – Jerome Nilssen

> The art of putting daydreams to practical use should be studied and encouraged by every high school counselor. Other college students can profit just as I have. "We are such stuff / As dreams are made on," Shakespeare wrote.
>
> – A student

In writing a conclusion, avoid several common pitfalls: restating the introduction, starting in an entirely new direction, concluding more than your evidence allows, and apologizing for your essay.

3 | Using short transitional or emphatic paragraphs

You may use a brief, one- or two-sentence paragraph to make a transition from one part of an essay to another.

> The causes of child abuse are familiar to all of us, but what can we do about them? The experts have several suggestions.

Avoid using transitional paragraphs simply to mark time while you think of what to say next.

Short emphatic paragraphs are sometimes used to draw attention to a particular idea:

The significance of the governor's actions may not be fully known until long after he has left office.

4 | Writing dialogue

In recording a conversation between two or more people, begin a new paragraph for the speech of each person so the reader can tell when one person stops talking and another begins.

"Why should I be the one to tell him you wrecked his car?" she asked. "I wasn't even there."

"That's why we want you to do it. The rest of us are too frightened."

3e | Linking paragraphs in the essay

Very seldom do paragraphs stand by themselves; more often they are part of a larger work, which in academic writing is likely to be an essay. Each paragraph in a well-written essay supports the thesis statement; each is directly linked to the thesis and is clearly related to other paragraphs in the essay. The introductory paragraph presents the main point, and the concluding paragraph reinforces it. Paragraphs in the body develop the idea in such a way as to make the essay interesting and convincing. Carefully linked paragraphs provide **coherence** to an essay, and if each paragraph in the body supports and develops the single main idea of the entire paper, the essay has **unity.**

Note that the paragraphs in a coherent and unified essay may be and often are developed by different patterns. Thus an essay on advertising ploys to sell skin cream might use *definition* of appeals to snobbery and sexuality in one paragraph and provide *details and examples* in the next. An essay on corruption in college sports might use an *analogy* with air pollution in one paragraph to suggest the seriousness of the problem and *cause-and-effect analysis* in subsequent paragraphs. The combination of patterns makes it possible to look at a subject in several different ways, giving a complete view. At other times an essay will be developed by mainly one pattern. Thus you might have an essay on acid rain that is largely a *cause-and-effect analysis* or one on the mating behavior of bull sea elephants that is largely *process analysis*. You should learn to be proficient in using both a combination of patterns of development and a single pattern, knowing what patterns to use depending on your subject and assignment.

¶

3

|*Opening and closing an essay*   EXERCISE **3-12**

Write opening and closing paragraphs for essays with two of the following thesis sentences (or with thesis sentences of your own), using devices appropriate for the topic. For the introductions, choose from quotation, anecdote, opinion, and historical incident, ending your opening paragraph with your thesis sentence. For the conclusions, choose from question, fact, quotation, and suggested action.

THESIS SENTENCES

1. In some ways raising a dog is like raising a baby.
2. In the last few days I've seen several incidents that convince me that college students need to improve their manners.
3. Getting a charge card entails more responsibilities than privileges.
4. One of the most embarrassing moments of my life occurred (last week) when I was (waiting in line to pay my fees). (Fill in the specifics that apply to you.)
5. Having grown up in a small town (big city), I have several reasons for wanting to settle in a city (small town). (Choose any combination that suits you.)

1. Thesis sentence: _____

Opening paragraph: _____

_____

_____

_____

_____

_____

_____

_____

Closing paragraph: _____

_____

_____

_____

_____

_____

_____

2. Thesis sentence: _____

Opening paragraph: _____

_____

_____

_____

_____

_____

_____

Closing paragraph: _____

_____

_____

_____

_____

4 | *Convincing Your Readers*

In a way, whenever you write you are trying to persuade your readers to accept your point of view. But particularly in argument it is essential that you as a writer aim to convince your readers of your ideas. In this chapter we examine some of the basics of putting together an argument and some problems to avoid in writing such essays.

4a | Constructing an argument

Most important for making your readers take your ideas seriously is to follow the conventions of essay writing discussed in the first three chapters. An effective argument meets certain criteria of structure and content:

1. It presents a thesis, which may be contained in a thesis sentence (see 1g).
2. It backs up that thesis with specific assertions, which may be expressed in topic sentences (see 3a).
3. It supports each assertion with specific evidence.

The framework for a convincing argument is constructed out of a balance between the general and the specific required by these conventions, combined with a balance between reason and emotion and a consideration of the likely attitudes of your reader.

1 | Combining the general and the specific

General statements, or assertions, are important to writing. In them we state our ideas, the significance of what we're saying. Thesis sentences are general statements. So are topic sentences. When we say, "The United States should stop meddling in Central American affairs," we are making a general statement. This statement might also be a thesis sentence. If we make such a statement, we must be prepared to back it up with specifics. An argumentative essay developing such a thesis must contain specific details as to how the United States is meddling in Central American affairs, what countries it is involved in, and so on — in other words, answers to the journalist's questions discussed in Chapter 1: *who, what, when, where, why,* and *how*. Good argumentative writing calls for a balance between the general and the specific.

89

2 | Appealing to reason and emotion

The most convincing argument is one that appeals to both reason and emotion. It avoids absolute words like *all* and *never*, and it shows that the writer has recognized and weighed all the alternatives before reaching his or her conclusions. Uncontrolled anger or dislike makes readers skeptical about the writer's opinions. For this reason you should avoid "shouting" with exclamation marks and loaded words. In the following example the loaded words of the first, emotional sentence overshadow the reason of the point the writer is making.

EMOTIONAL APPEAL — It is ridiculous for elderly people, who usually do not have school-age children, to have to pay high property taxes, since most of that outrageous, legal rip-off goes to pay for schools to educate others' children.

BALANCED APPEAL — Since most of the elderly have paid taxes all their lives, are now living on reduced incomes, and do not have school-age children, they should pay lower public education taxes.

The second sentence appeals to readers' sense of fair play by stating rationally why the elderly should pay lower school taxes; at the same time it relies on compassion for older citizens in their economic plight. It avoids loaded words such as *ridiculous*, *high*, *outrageous*, and *rip-off* that contribute no clear meaning to the sentence (for example, how much does *high* mean?). The angry tone of the first sentence is moderated in the second, which expresses the same opinion though in a way more acceptable to a skeptical reader.

3 | Anticipating objections

Writers of arguments must assume that *all* readers are skeptical and must be convinced. After all, if there were no contrary views, there would be no need for arguments. Writers who disregard differing opinions give the impression of not having full knowledge of the subject, and they risk losing credibility with their audience.

Writers of effective arguments acknowledge their opposition, grant whatever truth they see in opposing views, and then show how their own positions are better. For example, a writer using the thesis that the United States should discontinue involvement in Central American affairs must face directly the warning that Communism is knocking at our back door. Without considering the problem of Soviet influence in Cuba, the writer would seem to be poorly informed about the situation.

You can acknowledge your opposition briefly in the introduction of your essay, or you can give it a full paragraph somewhere in the body. If you think the opposition is strong, you should probably deal with it early in your essay, shortly after the introduction, and be done with it. If, however, you think the opposing view is weak, you may want to present your argument first, showing up the weakness of the opposition by contrast.

4b | Making assertions

If you strike a balanced tone in presenting your argument, you give the appearance of being reasonable; however, convincing your reader of your view also requires some substance to your argument. A believable assertion distinguishes among fact, opinion, belief, and prejudice; defines terms clearly; and confronts the issue directly.

1 | Distinguishing among fact, opinion, belief, and prejudice

A **fact** is a verifiable statement: *Shakespeare was born in 1564.* A reader can check a fact and determine if it is true.

An **opinion** is a judgment based on fact: *Shakespeare was a great writer.* Opinions are essential to an argument but must be based firmly on facts to reduce disagreement about them. Because opinions can be contested, writers don't convince readers by simply stating their opinions and implying, "I know I'm right." Writers must present the facts and show how those facts led to their opinions.

An opinion is not the same as a **belief.** An expression like "non-striking employees ought to respect picket lines" cannot be called an opinion because it cannot be contested on the basis of fact. It therefore cannot serve as a thesis statement. But you can at times use statements of belief to support arguments, especially if the audience is likely to agree with you. The preceding statement of belief, for example, might be used in support of a thesis advocating striking to improve working conditions.

A **prejudice** is like an opinion in that it expresses a viewpoint, but a prejudice is based on little or no examination of the evidence. It is a biased view, one that results from prejudging people or issues. A statement like "Women don't know anything about sports" oversimplifies; *some* women don't know anything about sports, but neither do some men, and some women know a great deal about sports. Responsible writers will examine the evidence before expressing their views; if the evidence doesn't support their views, they will refrain from stating them and will perhaps change their views to suit the facts.

An effective argument is based on facts or on opinions backed up with facts, not on prejudice.

2 | Defining terms

For your assertions to be believable, you must define your terms clearly and use them consistently. When you fail to define your terms, you make it difficult for the reader to understand and accept your argument. The first sentence in the following example leaves the term *arts* undefined, making the statement vague and unconvincing; the revision, by being more specific, clarifies what the writer means.

VAGUE   The city arts council is supposed to be supporting the arts, but the arts in our town have not improved since the council was set up.

91

CLEARER   The city arts council was created to give financial support to local performing groups, but the number of theater, music, and dance programs in our town has declined since the council was set up.

3 | Facing the question

Arguments center on questions: "Is the city arts council doing the job it was created to do?" "Should the government have the right to tell a woman whether she can have an abortion?" An argument attempts to answer the question by stating opinions and relevant facts. In answering the question, your essay must not oversimplify complex issues or make an emotional rather than a rational appeal. **Begging the question** and **ignoring the question** are two faults of argumentative writing that come from failure to look at all the evidence.

Begging the question treats an unproved assumption as if it were a fact. The statement below — that eighteen-year-olds are old enough to drink alcohol — is based on the unsupported assumption that they are old enough to vote and serve in the military.

> If eighteen-year-olds are old enough to vote and do military service, they are old enough to drink alcohol.

The argument speaks against government legislation concerning a social right based on age, assuming that two other instances of government legislation regulating civil obligations on the basis of age are correct. The writer must prove that legislation regarding civil matters can be equated with legislation regarding social matters.

Ignoring the question substitutes appeals to the readers' emotions for facts or other evidence.

> Louise Smith understands our children's educational needs because she is a devoted mother.

This statement relies on a reader's emotional response to Louise Smith's motherhood. Furthermore, calling her "devoted" is begging the question, as is the assumption that mothers understand children's educational needs; while they may be true, neither assertion has been supported.

Another way to ignore the question is through flattery or snob appeal:

> All intelligent people recognize the need for gun control.
> An advertisement: "If you can read this, you need a videotape as sensitive to color as you are."

These statements appeal to people's desire to be considered intelligent and sensitive. Questions are also ignored in **ad hominem** arguments, which criticize not an opposing view but instead the defenders of that view:

> How can you accept the commission's conclusion that marijuana should be legalized when one of the members has admitted she once smoked pot?

Careful writers will avoid these faulty appeals based on lack of reason because skeptical readers will not be swayed by them.

4c | Supporting assertions with evidence

Although taking a moderate tone and avoiding faulty appeals are necessary parts of convincing readers, you have no argument at all unless you support your position with evidence. Specific information as discussed in 3c gives weight to general or abstract assertions. In addition you should consider the following kinds of evidence.

1 | Distinguishing among the kinds of evidence

One common form of support is **facts,** statements that can be verified by checking the right sources:

> Richard Caswell was the first governor of North Carolina.
> Nuclear reactors used in the United States consist of three main parts: the reactor, the core, and the control rods.

Facts that use numbers are **statistics:**

> About half the people of Norway live in villages of fewer than 200 persons, and only six Norwegian cities have populations over 50,000.

Another kind of evidence is **examples.** The paragraph on pages 56–57, in which the writer states that the interstate highway system is dangerous, uses a specific example of a stretch of I-395 near Washington, D.C., to back up the assertion.

Expert opinion is still another way to support assertions. Experts are recognized authorities in a given field who can speak knowledgeably on the subject.

2 | Providing reliable evidence

To work effectively, evidence must meet four criteria. It must be **accurate, relevant, representative,** and **adequate.**

1. *Accurate* — correctly reported, drawn from a reliable source, quoted exactly, and undistorted in meaning.
2. *Relevant* — relating directly to the point and drawn from a source with authority on the topic.
3. *Representative* — accurately reflecting the sample from which it is said to be drawn.
4. *Adequate* — sufficient and specific enough to justify your conclusions.

In the paragraph on the highway system, the evidence is accurate if true; a skeptical reader would want to check its truth. The evidence is relevant; it describes a specific stretch of the interstate system, showing how the heavy traffic can be hazardous. Is it representative? If the reader thinks that this example does not reflect the interstate highway system as a whole, the argument is weakened. The same result occurs if the reader decides that there is not enough evidence to support the assertion.

4d | Reasoning effectively

Writing, like thinking, typically employs two types of reasoning: inductive and deductive.

1 | Reasoning inductively

Inductive reasoning involves beginning with one piece of information and adding others until enough evidence has been accumulated to justify making a general conclusion, or **generalization.** Each piece of evidence implies the conclusion, but no one piece is sufficient for it. When a detective gathers clues and infers from them who may have committed a crime, he or she is reasoning inductively. In writing, you use induction when you present a succession of relevant facts that together lead to a logical conclusion. Here is an example.

> In April, Representative Smith told a religious coalition that he favored a total cutoff of government funds for abortions. In May, the representative told a medical convention that he favored liberal government funding for abortions. In July, a newsletter from Smith's office stated that "abortions should be legal, but not one cent of government money should go toward paying for one." I refuse to vote for Smith because he appears unwilling to take a consistent stand on this important issue.
>
> – A student

2 | Reasoning deductively

Deductive reasoning involves beginning with two or more related generalizations and drawing a conclusion from them. No one generalization alone implies the conclusion; information from each one is needed. If a detective knows a crime was committed in the drawing room, and the drawing room was locked until 9 P.M., the detective can deduce that the crime must have been committed after 9 P.M. or by someone with a key. In writing, you use deduction when you combine two or more generalizations to reach a conclusion.

> Because heavy traffic is hazardous and because the traffic on I-394 is heavy, I-394 is a hazardous highway.

Often one of the generalizations, or **premises,** is unstated. Therefore you might write either of the following.

> Because heavy traffic is hazardous, I-394 is a hazardous highway.
> Because of its heavy traffic, I-394 is a hazardous highway.

Premises, whether stated or not, must be backed up with evidence. To support the assertion that I-394 is a hazardous highway, the writer of any of the preceding statements must show (1) that heavy traffic is hazardous and (2) that the traffic on I-394 is heavy. Sometimes writers are unaware that their statements have unstated premises and consequently do not support them; the result is that they beg the question. Here is the example used in 4b:

> If eighteen-year-olds are old enough to vote and do military service, they are old enough to drink alcohol.

The unstated premise is that if you are old enough to perform certain civil acts, you are old enough to enjoy certain social rights, a generalization that must be supported in order to make the conclusion believable — that eighteen-year-olds are old enough to drink alcohol.

3 | Avoiding faulty reasoning

Fallacies are flaws in inductive or deductive reasoning that can weaken an argument.

A **hasty generalization** is a fallacious assertion based on too little evidence.

> Vegetarian diets are unhealthful.

A variation of the hasty generalization is the use of words like *all* or *never* when the evidence supports only words like *some* or *sometimes*. The example sentence above implies *all* vegetarian diets even though *all* is not explicitly stated; a more supportable statement is "Some vegetarian diets are unhealthful." Another variation of the hasty generalization is the *stereotype*, which is an oversimplified characterization of a group of people.

> Vegetarians are pale and sickly looking.

Oversimplification of causes and effects is an interpretation of two events that are coincidental or are related in a complex way as if one were the direct cause of the other.

> Giving up smoking causes people to gain weight.

The **post hoc fallacy** is the assumption that because one event followed another, the first was the cause of the second.

> I went out in the cold without a hat this morning, and now I have a cold.

The **either/or fallacy** is the assumption that a complicated question has only two answers.

> Either we maintain a strong presence in Central America or all the countries there will become Communist.

A **non sequitur** is a connection of two unrelated ideas that implies a logical relation between them. One does not follow the other logically.

> It is said that Indians never invented the wheel, but in fact much of their art includes circles.

A **false analogy** is a comparison between things that cannot be compared.

> If Rockwell Springs, Minnesota, can keep a balanced budget, why can't New York City?

While analogy can be useful for illustration by showing how two things are alike (see 3c-2), it cannot prove a point. And even for purposes of illustration, the similarity between the two things must be valid.

Convincing your readers EXERCISE 4-1

A. Identify each of the following sentences as (1) fact, (2) opinion, (3) belief, or (4) prejudice.

Example: ___1___ Michael Conrad, sergeant on TV's *Hill Street Blues*, died November 22, 1983.

_____ 1. George Washington was the most honorable chief executive the United States has ever had.

_____ 2. George Washington was inaugurated on April 30, 1789.

_____ 3. The Babylon built by Nebuchadnezzar II was a magnificent city.

_____ 4. Captain William Kidd was hanged in 1701 for piracy.

_____ 5. Indira Gandhi, the prime minister of India, was assassinated on October 31, 1984, in New Delhi.

_____ 6. Truth comes out of heated discussion.

_____ 7. Every college student should take at least one history course in order to have a better understanding of world events.

_____ 8. Pro-abortionists have little regard for human life.

_____ 9. These economic policies are designed to encourage local entrepreneurial activity.

_____ 10. Working mothers neglect their children.

B. Identify each of the following sentences as representing one or more of the following: (1) begging the question, (2) inappropriate emotional appeal, (3) snob appeal or flattery, or (4) *ad hominem* argument.

Example: __1, 4__ Do not vote for Wayne Russo as mayor; his parents were not born in this country.

_____ 1. Seat belts are unnecessary; I do not need the U.S. government's conscience in my car to make me a safe driver.

_____ 2. How can anyone believe that a car made by dedicated American workers in an American factory is unsafe?

_____ 3. People who really know automobiles usually prefer British cars.

_____ 4. Cars wouldn't be so outrageously expensive if it weren't for all the unnecessary extras like pollution control devices, ignition locks, and padded dashboards.

_____ 5. If you want four more years of graft-free city government, re-elect Charles Smythe as mayor.

_____ 6. How can I vote for Charles Smythe for mayor when he just divorced his wife last year?

_____ 7. Most of the people I know on the fashionable East Side will be voting for him.

_____ 8. The Mothers for a Decent Government will be voting for him as well.

_____ 9. If young people just set their goals high and work hard, they'll have successful careers.

_____ 10. You'll find that the smartest young people do set their goals high.

C. Each sentence below illustrates one or more of the following fallacies: (1) hasty generalization, (2) stereotype, (3) oversimplification, (4) *post hoc* fallacy, (5) either/or fallacy, (6) non sequitur, or (7) false analogy. Identify the fallacy or fallacies of each sentence by writing the appropriate number(s) in the blank to the left.

Example: __1, 2__ The problem with Russian novelists is that they're all so serious.

_____ 1. He must have been drinking, because he is always happy when he has been drinking, and he is happy now.

_____ 2. If El Salvador's government is overthrown, Costa Rica's will be next.

_____ 3. Jane is a lovely, gracious woman, but she has a very sharp business sense.

_____ 4. If anything can go wrong, it will.

_____ 5. People's right to adequate medical care will be guaranteed only if Congress passes Senator Schmidt's health insurance bill.

_____ 6. Be careful of your grammar when you talk to an English teacher, or you will be criticized.

_____ 7. If scientists can send a spaceship to Mars, they should be able to cure the common cold.

_____ 8. If we don't build nuclear power plants, we will be forever dependent on imported oil.

_____ 9. It always snows as soon as I put my down jacket in storage.

_____ 10. The game will be exciting because it is for the championship.

_____ 11. Parachute jumping is just like roller skating — as long as you are careful, you will not get hurt.

_____ 12. So many workers belong to unions that high-quality work is rare.

_____ 13. If you light a cigarette, the bus will come right away.

_____ 14. Bureaucrats are concerned only with putting in their time, not with serving the public.

_____ 15. The reason our country is still respected by the Soviet Union is that we stood firm during the Cuban missile crisis.

II | Grammatical Sentences

5 | *Understanding Sentence Grammar*

Grammar is a way of describing how words work in relation to one another. Learning grammar is not the same as learning to write, any more than learning how all the parts under an automobile hood work is the same as learning to drive. As long as the car is running right, you don't need to know what's happening under the hood in order to drive your car around town. But knowing how the automobile parts are supposed to work can be a big help if something goes wrong. The same is true with grammar: when your sentences are coming out right, you don't need to think consciously about how all the parts interrelate; in fact, if you do you may forget how to write. But when your sentences need some tinkering, it's much more convenient to know how to do it yourself than to take them to a mechanic — to a grammarian, that is.

Let's extend this analogy a bit further. Many people consider it a personal challenge to understand the mechanics of their automobile; in fact, they don't even think of going out for a drive unless they know that everything is in good working order. These people derive great pleasure in tinkering with the carburetor, spark plugs, and other functioning parts under the hood. Some people feel the same way about their language: they consider their education incomplete if they don't understand how their language works. And some of these people really enjoy tinkering with sentences — adjusting their phrases, cleaning up their verb tenses, balancing their parallel structures, checking out their pronoun references. This chapter and those that follow can help you become a better sentence mechanic, and in the process you may come to enjoy working with your sentences.

5a | Understanding the basic sentence
1 | Identifying subjects and predicates

The sentence is the basic unit of writing. It makes a statement — an assertion — about something. The part that names the something is the **subject,** and the part that makes the assertion is the **predicate.**

SUBJECT	PREDICATE
Alfred	lives in New York.
My uncle who works in São Paulo	calls Brazil a country of mystery.
The chemical	leaked from the truck.
The doctors at the convention	were women.

101

Observe that these sentences have simple subjects (*Alfred, uncle, chemical, doctors*), but that the complete subjects include all the words that modify each simple subject.

2 | Identifying the basic words: nouns and verbs

Within the subject and the predicate are two basic words: a noun and a verb. In the sentences above, nouns serve as the subjects (*Alfred, uncle, chemical, doctors*), and verbs make the assertions (*lives, calls, leaked, were*). Nouns and verbs are the basic **parts of speech,** or classes of words.

NOUNS

Nouns name. They may name people, places, things, and qualities or ideas.

PEOPLE	PLACES	THINGS	QUALITIES
Alfred	New York	chemical	mystery
uncle	country	truck	justice
doctors	Mount Rainier	Carroll College	beginning
women	home	lettuce	permission

Nouns take different forms. Most nouns name things that can be counted and have a plural form usually denoted by an *-s* ending: *book, books; coat, coats; pencil, pencils.* Some **count nouns,** rather than taking an *-s* ending to indicate the plural, take an irregular plural form: *man, men; child, children; sheep, sheep.* Other nouns name things that cannot be counted; they are called **mass nouns,** and they ordinarily do not take an *-s* ending: *music, sugar, literature, anger.* **Collective nouns** such as *committee* or *team* name groups of people or things.

Another way of classifying nouns is as **common nouns,** such as *doctor* and *chemical,* which name general classes of people, places, or things, and as **proper nouns,** such as *Alfred* and *Brazil,* which name specific people, places, or things. Proper nouns are capitalized.

Nouns are often preceded by the **articles** *a, an,* and *the* — sometimes called noun markers because they indicate that a noun will soon follow.

VERBS

Verbs describe action or occurrence (*live, call, leak*) or a state of being (*be, seem*). One characteristic of verbs is that, through changes in their form, they tell time, called **tense.** *Opens* indicates action in present time, while *opened* means action in past time, *have opened* means action begun in the past and continuing into the present, and *will open* indicates future action. In present time, all verbs add *-s* or *-es* when their subjects are singular nouns, indefinite pronouns, or the singular pronouns *he, she,* and *it.*

Carla writes.   He whistles.
The dog stretches.   She is here.
Everyone wants to go.

Verbs used with subjects that are plural nouns or the pronouns *I, you, we,* and *they* in present time do not take an ending.

Carla and Jim write.   They whistle.
Dogs stretch.   I am here.

Most English verbs indicate tense by a regular change. To show past time they add *-d* or *-ed* to the plain, or dictionary, form: *open, opened; call, called; require, required; type, typed; wash, washed.* Some of the most common verbs have irregular ways of showing past tense: *make, made; see, saw; is, was; read, read; begin, began.*

Verbs often combine with **helping,** or **auxiliary, verbs** to form verb phrases that express complex time relations and other attributes: *is living, has lived, will go, should call, may survive, can run.* (See pages 129–130 and Chapter 7 for further discussion of verbs and verb forms.)

A note on form and function

A word may serve different functions in different sentences. *Support*, for instance, is a noun in *I need your support* but a verb in *I support the representative. Work* is a noun in *She looked for work* but a verb in *I work on Sundays.* Thus, determining a word's part of speech often requires examining its function in its sentence.

PRONOUNS

Pronouns function in sentences as nouns do. They can take the place of nouns when their meaning is clear. That is, we can say *She looked for work* when we have already established that the pronoun *She* refers to Carla (or any other person specified by name). **Personal pronouns** refer to specific individuals (*I, you, he, she, it, we, they*). **Demonstrative pronouns** (*this, that, such,* for example) identify or point to nouns (*This is the right place*). **Relative pronouns** (*who, which, that*) refer to other words or a group of words and introduce subordinate clauses (*This is the person who saw it happen*). **Indefinite pronouns** such as *everyone, somebody, each,* and *other* function as nouns but do not substitute for any specific nouns (*Everybody should be here by now*). **Intensive pronouns** (*himself, themselves*) emphasize a noun or pronoun (*We did it ourselves*). **Reflexive pronouns** (the same forms as intensive pronouns — *myself,* for example) indicate that the subject not only performs the action but receives it as well (*She pictured herself as an actress*). **Interrogative pronouns** (*who, what*) introduce questions. For a discussion of form changes in pronouns, see Chapter 6.

Identifying subjects and predicates

EXERCISE **5-1**

In the following sentences, draw a vertical line between the complete subjects and predicates. After identifying subjects and predicates, on separate paper write a sentence of your own that follows the pattern of each sentence.

Example: Bill, a friend of mine in California, | drinks fruit juice every day.

Steamboat, a young golden labrador puppy, sits on the freshly planted flowers.

1. The dead leaves blew into the swimming pool.

2. I talked to the professor after class.

3. The judge sent him back to prison.

4. She put too much faith in her ability to ski.

5. Raw garlic keeps rude people away.

6. The foul shots won the game for us.

7. I would rather read biographies than anything else.

8. We trained the parakeets to sing duets.

9. Elmo City has a crime problem.

10. Tom's souvenir album of Waco, Texas, rested on the top of the bureau.

11. The refrigerator contained nothing.

12. He forgot to prepare the speech.

13. A broken ashtray indicated the presence of my cat in the room.

14. Two reams of paper were missing from the storage cabinet.

15. The coffee table in the living room was imported from Holland.

16. The electrical contractor is three weeks behind schedule.

17. Long sideburns have been popular in the South at least since the Civil War.

18. The aromatic herb coriander may be the most popular spice in Jordan.

19. Three perfect robin's eggs were in the box.

20. Tourists from all over the country flock to the Clair County Sheep Festival each year.

Identifying nouns, verbs, and pronouns

EXERCISE **5-2**

In the following passages, identify all words functioning as nouns by writing *N* above them, all words functioning as verbs or verb phrases with *V*, and all pronouns with *P*. Sentences will often have more than one of each.

<pre>
           N   V   P V V   N
</pre>
Example: Herb decided he had seen enough violence.

1.   A cat makes a fine pet for a family. Two cats are even better because each entertains the other. But three or four cats are definitely too many cats. Independent creatures that they are, when you have more than two they get the idea that they own the house. They think they are kings and queens in their own castle. They are lords and ladies with obedient servants who care for all their needs. Their slaves prepare meals at the appropriate times, brush their coats so they stay gleaming, and keep their sanitary facilities clean. Meanwhile, you, the person who pays the taxes and buys the groceries, wonder sometimes about whether you are really the one in charge.

2.   Another problem that arises when you have four cats in the household occurs at the grocery store. As you browse the shelves for new delicacies that might tempt the appetites of your finicky live-in guests, you come to the conclusion that everyone in the country must own a cat. On the other side of the aisle, where the dog food is kept, are

107

bags upon bags and cans upon cans of food for man's best friend. But here on the cat food side the shelves are nearly bare. Man's second-best friend surely exists in greater numbers than his best friend. So you pick what you can from what remains on the shelves. For four cats that means a cart full of cans plus boxes of dry stuff; the twenty-five pounds of litter you stow on the rack below. As you proceed to the checkout lane, you hope no one will notice how much of your grocery purchase consists of supplies for your cats.

| Using nouns and verbs

The words shown below can be used as both nouns and verbs. For each word, first write a sentence using it as a noun and then write a sentence using it as a verb.

Example: whistle (noun) *Ruth carried a dog whistle on a chain around her neck.*

(verb) *Ruth whistled for her dog.*

1. bomb (noun)

   (verb)

2. condition (noun)

   (verb)

3. stamp (noun)

   (verb)

4. swing (noun)

   (verb)

5. store (noun)

   (verb)

6. dump (noun) _____

   (verb) _____

7. load (noun) _____

   (verb) _____

8. run (noun) _____

   (verb) _____

9. wash (noun) _____

   (verb) _____

10. flag (noun) _____

    (verb) _____

gr

5

3 | Forming sentence patterns with nouns and verbs

The English language is capable of an infinite number of sentences, each different from all the others. However, most sentences are built on just five basic patterns. In the following example sentences notice how the subjects remain similar — a noun with perhaps an article — but how the predicates differ.

        N   **V**
1. A storm approached.

       N   **V**   **N**
2. Timothy hid the key.

    N   **V**   **N**
3. Jill was the chairperson.

       N   **V**   **N**   **N**
4. The observer told his supervisor the story.

      N   **V**   **N**   **N**
5. The tornado left the city a disaster area.

Because their predicates differ, each of these sentences represents a different sentence pattern. The difference is in the nature of the verbs and in the relations between the verbs and the nouns that follow them. Let's look at each pattern more closely.

Pattern 1: A storm approached.

The simplest form of this pattern consists of just the subject and verb. With the addition of modifiers, the pattern has many variations, as illustrated in the following sentences:

SUBJECT	PREDICATE
A storm	approached.
Your friend who lives in California	called.
Your friend	was here but just left again.
Your friend and ally	called about the movie tonight.

The verbs in these sentences are called **intransitive,** and none of them when used in sentences of this type takes an object, as verbs in pattern 2 do. All these sentences fit pattern 1, even though the third sentence has two verbs (*was* and *left*) and the fourth has two subjects (*friend* and *ally*).

Pattern 2: Timothy hid the key.

In this pattern a noun always follows the verb. This noun is called a **direct object;** it receives the action of the verb.

SUBJECT	PREDICATE	
	Verb	*Direct object*
Timothy	hid	the key.
My mother	typed	the letter.

Detroit, Michigan,	has	thirteen universities and colleges.
Forests	cover	a third of the nation's land.

The verbs in pattern 2 sentences are called **transitive** because they transfer the action from the subject to the object. The third sentence above has two direct objects (*universities* and *colleges*).

Pattern 3: Jill was the chairperson.

In this pattern the noun following the verb does not receive the action of the verb as a direct object does, but instead it refers back to the subject. The noun following the verb is called a **subject complement** because it renames, or completes, the subject. A subject complement may also be an adjective, as in *I was angry*. The adjective *angry* describes the subject. In the following sentences, the first two subject complements are nouns and the second two are adjectives.

SUBJECT	PREDICATE	
	Verb	*Subject complement*
Jill	was	the chairperson.
Roosevelt	became	the first college graduate in his family.
The pediatrician	seemed	well qualified.
My brother	has been	late every day this week.

These verbs are called **linking** because they connect the subject complement with the subject.

Pattern 4: The observer told his supervisor the story.

Like the verbs in pattern 2 sentences, the verbs in sentences that fit pattern 4 are transitive and have direct objects that receive the action. In addition, they have **indirect objects,** which come before the direct objects and indicate to or for whom or what the action of the verb is directed.

SUBJECT	PREDICATE		
	Verb	*Indirect object*	*Direct object*
The observer	told	his supervisor	the story.
The tour guide	showed	me	the place.
Charles	gave	himself	a haircut.

Pattern 5: The tornado left the city a disaster area.

This is another pattern that takes a transitive verb and a direct object. Following the direct object is a noun or an adjective that renames or describes the direct object. It is called an **object complement** because it completes the direct object. In the following sentences, the first two object complements are nouns and the second two are adjectives.

SUBJECT	PREDICATE		
	Verb	*Direct object*	*Object complement*
The tornado	left	the city	a disaster area.
The members	elected	Jill	chairperson.
She	made	me	angry.
Charles	considered	his haircut	masterful.

gr

5

Most English sentences fit into some variation or combination of these five basic patterns.

| *Identifying parts of the sentence*   EXERCISE   **5-4**

The following sentences are grouped by pattern. Within each group identify subjects, verbs, objects, and complements by writing the appropriate abbreviation above the word. Disregard modifiers.

Pattern 1:   *S* (subject), *V* (verb)

1. Bats live a long time.

2. Bamboo plants grow for many years without flowering.

3. Some fishes cluck, croak, or grunt.

4. Sound waves must travel through a medium.

5. Some unanswered questions about quark matter still remain.

Pattern 2:   *S, V, DO* (direct object)

6. Some foods may increase chances of getting cancer.

7. However, other foods may provide an effective means of preventing the disease.

8. Pandas eat almost nothing except bamboo.

9. Computer camps offer computer training in a camplike setting.

10. Scientists group butterflies into families according to their physical features.

Pattern 3:   *S, V, SC* (subject complement)

11. Bats are intriguing creatures because of their unusual characteristics.

12. Freon is a common cooling agent.

13. The Doppler effect is an apparent change in pitch.

14. Infrasound means sound with frequencies below the range of human hearing.

15. The sun's rays are strongest between 10 a.m. and 2 p.m.

Pattern 4: *S, V, IO* (indirect object), *DO*

16. A male frog sends a female frog a hoarse mating call.

17. Zoo officials sometimes must feed baby animals milk from a bottle.

18. Medical technologists very seldom give people high doses of ionizing radiation.

19. Trilobites have given paleontologists evidence of continent formation.

20. According to some botanists, trees sometimes send other trees chemical messages when under attack by insects.

Pattern 5: *S, V, DO, OC* (object complement)

21. Scientists call butterflies and moths Lepidoptera.

22. They sometimes call computers "artificial intelligence."

23. Some botanists consider the Cretaceous period the time of the first flowers.

24. Environmentalists have declared the spread of airborne pollutants a major environmental concern.

25. Physicians have named some birth defects "fetal alcohol syndrome."

| *Using sentence patterns*   EXERCISE **5-5**

Choosing from the verbs suggested for each pattern, write two sentences of your own that imitate the pattern of the model sentences below. In your own sentences, identify the sentence parts.

Pattern 1:   *S, V*   study, talk, go, sit, wait

1. Our neighbor's dog barked in the alley.

Example: $\overset{\text{S}}{\text{My little brother}}$ $\overset{\text{V}}{\text{talked}}$ on the telephone.

2.

3.

Pattern 2:   *S, V, DO*   buy, see, intimidate, want, collect

1. Traffic jams always upset me.

2.

3.

Pattern 3:   *S, V, SC*   be (am, is, are, was, were), seem, become, feel, taste

1. Flying is a costly way to travel.

2.

3.

Pattern 4:   *S, V, IO, DO*   give, buy, send, offer, make

1. Our English teacher gave us a long assignment.

2.

3.

Pattern 5:   *S, V, DO, OC*   consider, make, declare, elect, call

1. The plant employees named my father boss of the year.

2.

3.

5b | Expanding the basic sentence with single words

Most sentences we use are longer and more complex than the simple subject-predicate pattern made up of nouns, pronouns, and verbs. We regularly expand this basic pattern with single words and groups of words.

1 | Using adjectives and adverbs

The simplest way to expand sentences is to add details with single modifying words. Adjectives and adverbs describe or limit the words they modify.

ADJECTIVES	ADVERBS
quick trip	walked *slowly*
strawberry yogurt	spoke *very carefully*
this person	*never* swore
her coat	*not* known

Adjectives modify only nouns and pronouns; **adverbs** primarily modify verbs but may also describe or limit other modifiers. An adverb indicates intensity (*very*) or explains how, why, where, or when.

Although adverbs often end in *-ly* (*slowly, carefully*), the ending does not always signal an adverb because some adjectives also end in *-ly* (*friendly*) and some adverbs do not (*never, very*). To determine whether a word is an adjective or an adverb, you must look at how it functions in its sentence.

Adjectives usually precede the words they modify, although sometimes they follow: in *the equipment necessary for the trip*, the adjective *necessary* follows the noun it modifies, *equipment*. As we have seen, adjectives may also serve as subject complements after linking verbs and as object complements:

       S   V   SC
The house was *huge.*

       S   V   DO   OC
The critic declared the movie *pornographic.*

When they modify verbs, adverbs are usually movable: *walked slowly* or *slowly walked, spoke very carefully* or *very carefully spoke.* They generally precede adjectives or adverbs that they modify: *very carefully.*

Adjectives and adverbs have three different forms, or degrees. The **positive** form is the one listed in the dictionary: *red, bad, serious; well, stupidly.* The **comparative** form indicates a greater degree of the quality named by the word: *redder, worse, more serious; better, more stupidly.* The **superlative** form indicates the greatest degree of the quality named by the word: *reddest, worst, most serious; best, most stupidly.* (See also 9e.)

2 | Using other words as modifiers

We have already seen how some words can function as either nouns or verbs depending on their function in the sentence. Words that normally function as nouns, and some verb forms as well, are sometimes classified as adjectives because of their function: in *ticket booth, government intervention,* and *taste test,* the first word functions as an adjective modifying the noun that follows it, even though the first word is usually considered a noun. (See also 9f.)

Words that sometimes function as pronouns (*this, that, which*) can also serve as adjectives (*this person, that book, which address*). Special forms of verbs also function as modifiers: *the banging door, curled hair.* (See 5c-2 and Chapter 7.)

Name _____ Date _____ Score _____

Identifying adjectives and adverbs   EXERCISE   **5-6**

5

In the following sentences underline each word functioning as an adjective (modifying a noun) once and each word functioning as an adverb (modifying a verb, an adjective, or an adverb) twice. Then draw an arrow from the modifier to the word it modifies.

Example: She entered the store quickly and bought a paperback dictionary.

1. Layla usually wore a corduroy jacket.

2. Most aids for hearing can only amplify sound.

3. The law insists on lower speed in densely populated areas.

4. Whales are an endangered species.

5. The movie about orchards was tiring.

6. The first national highway in the United States was constructed in the 1800s.

7. This problem is easier than the previous one.

8. Ed always travels first class.

9. The newest member of the committee represents a large group of lawyers.

10. The meat, tender and juicy, sizzled temptingly.

11. Zimmer often offends people.

12. An enormous iceberg ripped a hole in the keel of the ship.

13. A pattern of gold and green trumpets decorated the dress.

14. After receiving the battered box, Homer put in a claim for damages.

15. The military prosecutor demanded the death sentence.

16. The radical leaders managed to execute a thousand people.

17. A hippopotamus actually can move rapidly.

18. She asked the question impatiently.

19. The buzzing mosquito woke me from a deep sleep.

20. Cars that move slowly can be a hazard on the highway.

21. We moved the cabinet upstairs.

22. Wheat farmers in Kansas expect a record crop.

23. Pointed or rounded arches characterize the different styles of architecture.

24. A brick house, like a wooden house, can catch fire quickly.

25. I would not say the aircraft landed smoothly.

|Rewriting modifiers

In each of the following sentences rewrite the italicized words as a single-word adverb modifying the verb. As you rewrite, put the adverb in the sentence position where it sounds best.

Example: Robert approached the growling dog *in a reluctant manner.*

> *Robert approached the growling dog reluctantly.*
> *Robert reluctantly approached the growling dog.*

1. Harry read the chapter *in a slow way.*

2. Rebecca is considering *with seriousness* a degree in medicine.

3. Uncle Howard drove his van around the icy corner *in a very careful way.*

4. Everybody completed the test in forty-five minutes *with ease.*

5. The temperatures have dropped *with steadiness* since Tuesday morning.

6. It has also been snowing *in a heavy way* since Monday.

7. One thing I can say about this teacher is that she grades *with fairness.*

8. She seems to apply her grading standards *in a consistent way.*

9. Elaine translated the passage *with perfection.*

10. That perfection is surprising because she also translated it *with quickness.*

5c | Expanding the basic sentence with word groups

We have so far looked at single words as building blocks of sentences. We have seen nouns and pronouns function as subjects and objects, verbs as predicates, and adjectives and adverbs as modifiers of nouns, pronouns, and verbs. In this section we examine how groups of words fulfill the functions of single words. A **phrase** is a group of related words that functions as a single part of speech and lacks a subject or a predicate or both. A **clause** is a group of related words that contains both a subject and a predicate.

1 | Using prepositional phrases

A **preposition** is a part of speech that links one word or word group to another. Unlike nouns and verbs, prepositions never change form. Here are the most common ones:

about	beneath	inside	since
above	beside	in spite of	through
according to	between	instead of	throughout
across	beyond	into	till
after	by	like	to
against	concerning	near	toward
along	despite	of	under
along with	down	off	underneath
among	during	on	unlike
around	except	onto	until
as	except for	out	up
at	excepting	outside	upon
because of	for	over	up to
before	from	past	with
behind	in	regarding	within
below	in addition to	round	without

A preposition always takes an object, called the **object of the preposition.** Together the preposition, its object, and any modifiers make up a **prepositional phrase.** The preposition serves to connect its object to another word in the sentence, usually the one immediately preceding the preposition. Prepositional phrases function as adjectives, adverbs, and sometimes nouns. In the following sentences the prepositional phrases are italicized.

> The doll is a souvenir *of Cyprus.* [Adjective phrase modifying *souvenir.*]
> A woman *in a brown shirt* stole my car. [Adjective phrase modifying *woman.*]
> The neighbor's dog ran *into my garden.* [Adverb phrase modifying *ran.*]
> *Out of sight* is *out of mind.* [Noun phrases serving as sentence subject and subject complement.]
> The bus will leave *in an hour.* [Adverb phrase modifying *leave.* Because adverbs are often movable, the sentence could also read *In an hour the bus will leave.*]

Punctuating prepositional phrases

Prepositional phrases are ordinarily not set off from the rest of the sentence with commas or other punctuation:

> Northfield, Minnesota, is located *in the center of Minnesota's dairy country.*

However, sometimes introductory prepositional phrases are set off with commas:

> *As a thematic link in many operas,* the orchestra repeats a melody from an earlier scene.

Do not punctuate prepositional phrases like sentences; if you do, you'll have a sentence fragment:

> In front of the house.

The preceding fragment is only part of a sentence, perhaps this one:

> There were two tall evergreens *in front of the house.*

Identifying prepositional phrases EXERCISE **5-8**

In the following sentences underline each prepositional phrase and draw an arrow from the preposition to the word the phrase modifies.

Example: The fence post was embedded in cement.

1. Economists seem inconsistent in their use of terms.

2. She prefers going against the tide in everything.

3. The dog can perform all kinds of tricks with its tail.

4. The pup came into the kitchen and looked eagerly into the dish.

5. The officials from the zoo bought six alligators from a dealer.

6. The doors in this building close after six o'clock.

7. The food in the dish had spoiled in only a few hours.

8. She enrolled yesterday for the course in Shakespeare.

9. Only five points separated the winner from the loser.

10. A trophy was awarded to the player with the best record.

11. The difficulty of negotiation is often underestimated by many people.

12. In the winter the courts in the park are closed.

13. We are planning a tour of the cathedrals in France.

14. After dinner we skated for an hour on the Lake Park ice.

15. Bruce was disqualified for his fight with the referee.

16. We did not attend the debate between Mailer and Vidal.

17. He could not understand the instructions for the clock.

18. Through the mountains runs a tunnel for the railroad.

19. Typing can at times be a welcome relief from studying.

gr

5

20. Included among the guests were two students from Africa.

2 | Using verbals and verbal phrases

Verbals are forms of verbs, such as *falling, written,* and *to go,* that can function as nouns, adjectives, or adverbs. As grammatical structures, verbals are a useful stylistic option to writers. Compare these sentence pairs:

WORDY   In the 1870s, the federal government signed several treaties with Indians who lived in the Dakota Territory. The treaties gave the Indians land on reservations.

REVISED   In the 1870s, the federal government signed several treaties with Indians *living in the Dakota Territory, giving them land on reservations.*

Verbals cannot stand alone as verbs in sentences. The word groups *The rocks falling* and *The paper written* do not have complete verbs, and they are therefore not sentences. If we add a helping verb (*are, has been*), we have sentences: *The rocks* are *falling, The paper* has been *written.* There are three kinds of verbals: participles, gerunds, and infinitives.

PARTICIPLES

Participles function as adjectives modifying nouns and pronouns. The present participle is the *-ing* form of the verb (*smoking, ringing*). The past participle is usually the dictionary form of the verb plus *-d* or *-ed* (*smoked*), but many irregular verbs form their participles in other ways (*rung, understood*). (See 7a.)

> The *whirling* kite broke from the string. [Present participle modifies *kite.*]
>
> *Stunned,* he stared at the open door. [Past participle modifies *he.*]

GERUNDS

Gerunds function as nouns. Like present participles, gerunds are the *-ing* form of the verb. They are distinguished from participles only by their function in a sentence. If the *-ing* form functions as a noun, it is a gerund. If the *-ing* form functions as an adjective, it is a present participle.

> *Flying* terrifies me. [Gerund as sentence subject.]
>
> *Flying* gravel struck the headlight. [Participle as adjective.]

INFINITIVES

Infinitives function as nouns, adjectives, and adverbs. They consist of the plain form of the verb — the form listed in the dictionary — and they are usually preceded by *to* (*to smoke, to ring*). They never take an *-s* or *-ing* ending.

> I do not plan *to work.* [Infinitive as noun, direct object of the verb *plan.*]
>
> That is the most economical car *to buy.* [Infinitive as adjective modifying *car.*]
>
> That lesson was hard *to learn.* [Infinitive as adverb modifying the adjective *hard.*]

gr

5

Infinitives, participles, and gerunds may take subjects, objects, complements, and modifiers to make up **verbal phrases. Participial phrases** function as adjectives:

> *Sailing against the wind,* we made little headway. [Participial phrase as adjective modifying *we.* The participle *sailing* is modified by the prepositional phrase *against the wind.*]

Gerund phrases function as nouns:

> *Watching skydivers* makes me anxious. [Gerund phrase as sentence subject. *Skydivers* is object of the gerund.]
> After *getting on the bus,* I discovered that I had left my English textbook at home. [Gerund phrase as object of preposition *after.*]

Infinitive phrases function as nouns, adjectives, and adverbs.

> I wanted *to win the prize.* [Infinitive phrase as noun, direct object of the verb *wanted.* The infinitive *to win* has an object of its own, *prize.*]
> The team lost its will *to finish the season.* [Infinitive phrase as adjective modifying *will.* The infinitive *to finish* has an object, *season.*]
> Andy worked *to overcome his handicap.* [Infinitive phrase as adverb modifying *worked.* The infinitive *to overcome* has an object, *handicap.*]
> We urged *him to run for office.* [Infinitive phrase as noun object of *urged.* The infinitive *to run* has a subject, *him,* which is in the objective case (see 6f), and the phrase is modified by the prepositional phrase *for office.*]

(To avoid faulty use of verbal phrases, see 14g.)

Punctuating verbals and verbal phrases

Verbal phrases that appear at the beginning of sentences are usually set off with commas.

> *Circulating about 350,000 copies a day, De Telegraaf* is Amsterdam's largest newspaper.

Verbals and verbal phrases elsewhere in sentences are set off if they do not restrict, or limit, the meaning of the words they modify (see 21c).

> Optometrists prescribe about two-thirds of the glasses and contact lenses *worn by people in the United States and Canada.* [A restrictive participial phrase, essential to the meaning of the sentence.]
> Optometrists, *prescribing about two-thirds of the glasses and contact lenses in the United States and Canada,* are skilled professionals *devoted to the care of vision.* [Two participial phrases; the first is nonrestrictive, the second is essential to the meaning of the sentence.]

Do not punctuate verbals and verbal phrases as sentences; doing so will make sentence fragments.

> Prescribing about two-thirds of the glasses and contact lenses worn by people in the United States and Canada.

Even though this participial phrase is long, it is still a sentence fragment because it has no subject and verb. It must be part of a main clause, as in the second sentence above, or written as a clause like the first sentence above.

3 | Using absolute phrases

An **absolute phrase** usually consists of a noun or pronoun and a participle. Unlike participial phrases, absolute phrases contain a subject and do not relate grammatically to any word in the rest of the sentence.

gr

5

ABSOLUTE PHRASE	The warning forgotten, we plunged into the woods. [The participle *forgotten* has its own subject, *warning*, but the phrase does not relate to any other word in the sentence.]
PARTICIPIAL PHRASE	Forgetting the warning, we plunged into the woods. [The participle *forgetting* modifies the subject of the sentence, *we*.]

The participle is often omitted from an absolute phrase when it is some form of *be:*

> My hands (*being*) black with ink, I finally gave up trying to change the typewriter ribbon.

Punctuating absolute phrases

Absolute phrases are always set off from the rest of the sentence with a comma or commas (see 21d).

> I used fifteen references in my paper, *five of them being interviews.*

Identifying verbals and verbal phrases

In the following sentences underline each verbal or verbal phrase. Note that some sentences contain more than one verbal. Then fill the blank to the left with the part of speech each verbal or verbal phrase functions as — adjective (*adj.*), adverb (*adv.*), or noun (*n.*).

Example: *n. n.* A lack of <u>understanding</u> caused <u>her to fail</u>.

_____ 1. To go to his class is to suffer an hour of tedium.

_____ 2. Closed for the season, the camp seemed strangely empty.

_____ 3. I never go to flea markets because bargaining for the best price makes me uncomfortable.

_____ 4. After selling his last picture, the painter closed his stand.

_____ 5. Before finishing dinner, we got into an argument.

_____ 6. To adjust the voltage, turn the dial clockwise.

_____ 7. The runner collapsed on the track, exhausted from the heat and humidity.

_____ 8. Listening carefully, I could just hear the voice inside tell me to open the door.

_____ 9. Fishing came naturally to the cub.

_____ 10. She taught me that dancing adds spirit to life.

_____ 11. Swimming is a useful skill as well as good exercise.

_____ 12. At the gate the car halted, flashing its lights.

_____ 13. A refreshing voyage changed her desire to find a new job.

_____ 14. We hoped to win the game but knew our chances were slim.

_____ 15. Experiencing Albanian cuisine is disappointing.

_____ 16. Crying, the child backed away from the clown.

_____ 17. Karen thought that raking leaves was a job for Ben.

_____ 18. Robert Burns's poems, written in dialect, are the continuing pride of Scotland.

_____ 19. Bandaged beyond recognition and mumbling incoherently, the patient was a pathetic sight.

_____ 20. Though she objected constantly to my dating, my mother never ordered me to stay home.

| Using verbal phrases   EXERCISE **5-10**

Rewrite the following sentences by reducing the underlined words to verbal phrases using the verbals in parentheses. Be careful not to alter the meaning when you make your changes.

Example: Grandfather planted seeds indoors in February *so that he could have* an early start on his garden in May. (*to have*)

Grandfather planted seeds indoors in February to have an early start on his garden in May.

1. Ever since *he attended high school* James has been going to Iron Mountain in the winter to ski. (*attending*)

2. Do you want to know how far you can go before *you make me angry?* (*making*)

3. You can paint the fence with the white paint *that is stored in the garage.* (*stored*)

4. You very seldom find a meat market anymore *that displays freshly cut, unwrapped meat in a glass case.* (*displaying*)

5. My brother came home on the train because he had forgotten *that he had taken the car to work.* (*having taken*)

6. *Because I had just seen the movie a few months earlier,* I didn't want to watch it on television. (*Having seen*)

gr

5

7. After school Leonard stopped at the drugstore *so he could buy a pint of ice cream.* (*to buy*)

8. *Before I go to school,* I have to dress and feed my little brother and sister. (*going*)

9. Wouldn't it be nice *if we could take a vacation this summer?* (*to take*)

10. The person *who told you class was canceled* must have been playing a joke on you. (*telling*)

4 | Using subordinate clauses

A **clause** is a group of related words that contains both a subject and a predicate. A **main,** or **independent, clause** forms a sentence and makes a complete statement by itself. A **subordinate,** or **dependent, clause,** like a phrase, functions as a single part of speech and cannot stand alone as a sentence.

TWO MAIN CLAUSES	*The waves washed over their houses.* The people fled.
FIRST CLAUSE SUBORDINATED	*When the waves washed over their houses,* the people fled.

Subordinate clauses are connected to main clauses by subordinating conjunctions or relative pronouns. **Subordinating conjunctions** appear at the beginning of their clauses and never change form. Some common ones are the following:

after	even if	since	until
although	even though	so that	when
as	if	than	whenever
as if	in order that	that	where
as though	once	though	wherever
because	rather than	unless	while
before			

Subordinating conjunctions have no function in their clauses other than to connect subordinate clauses to main clauses. **Relative pronouns,** however, not only link the two clauses but also serve as pronouns and sometimes adverbs within their own clauses. Here's a list of relative pronoun connectors:

which	whatever	who (whose, whom)
whichever	when	whoever (whomever)
that	where	why
what		

(See 6g for how to use the alternative forms of *who* and *whoever.*) The following sentences illustrate how relative pronouns function within their clauses:

Jeff is rooming with Chuck Janssen, with *whom* he went to high school. [*Whom* functions as a pronoun, object of the preposition *with.*]
They are both staying in Kirkland Hall, *which* is the tallest building on campus. [*Which* serves as a pronoun, subject of the verb *is.*]
Can you show me a place *where* I can leave my coat? [*Where* functions as an adverb modifying the verb *can leave.*]
This is Tony Pagliaro, *whose* party we attended last week. [*Whose* serves as an adjective, modifying *party.*]

Subordinate clauses themselves function as parts of speech — as adjectives, adverbs, or nouns.

ADJECTIVE CLAUSES

She longed to return to the house *that she had grown up in.* [Adjective clause modifying *house.*]

People *who can remain calm in emergencies* are well suited for medical careers. [Adjective clause modifying *people.*]

ADVERB CLAUSES

Children should start reading *whenever they are ready.* [Adverb clause modifying *start.*]

As he was bowing to the audience, the conductor fell forward. [Adverb clause modifying *fell.* Since adverbs are often movable, the sentence could also read *The conductor fell forward as he was bowing to the audience.*]

NOUN CLAUSES

We all guessed *how the movie would end.* [Noun clause, object of *guessed.* Compare *We all guessed the outcome.*]

Whoever destroyed the car will be punished. [Noun clause as subject of sentence. Compare *Jack will be punished.*]

ELLIPTICAL CLAUSES

Some very common subordinate clauses, called **elliptical clauses,** omit the relative pronoun or the second half of a comparison, but their meaning is still clear from the context.

I knew *(that) she meant me.*

Monkeys are not as intelligent *as apes (are).*

Some elliptical clauses omit other elements:

When (I am) in Paris, I will visit Andrew.

Punctuating subordinate clauses

Subordinate clauses punctuated as complete sentences are sentence fragments. They must be connected to a main clause. An alternative that works with adverb clauses is to make them main clauses by omitting the subordinating word.

FRAGMENT Because the house was left unlocked.

REVISED The thieves were able to enter easily because the house was left unlocked.

REVISED The house was left unlocked. [Omission of the subordinating word *because* makes the clause complete in itself.]

See Chapter 10 on sentence fragments.

Like phrases, subordinate clauses are set off from the rest of the sentence by commas if they do not restrict the meaning of the word they modify. Adverb clauses are usually set off when they come at the beginning of the sentence and are usually not set off when they follow a main clause. (See 21b and 21c.)

ADJECTIVE CLAUSES

Greenland, *which lies along North America's coast*, is actually a province of Denmark. [Adjective clause does not restrict the meaning of *Greenland*.]

Cuba and the West Indies are other islands *that lie off the North American coast*. [The adjective clause restricts the meaning of *islands*; the meaning would be altered if the clause were omitted.]

ADVERB CLAUSES

Because newspapers in the United States earn most of their income from the sale of advertising space, they have a large staff of personnel to prepare these ads. [Adverb clause begins the sentence.]

The United States had its first major news service *when the Associated Press established an office in New York in 1848*. [Adverb clause follows the main clause.]

5 | Using appositives

An **appositive** is a word or word group that renames the word or word group it follows. Appositives are usually nouns.

The Edsel, *Ford's biggest commercial failure*, is now a classic car.
Bob Hope and Milton Berle, *two veterans of vaudeville*, have been active performers for years.

Appositives can be seen as reduced forms of *who* or *which* clauses that have linking verbs and subject complements.

The Edsel, which is Ford's biggest commercial failure, is now a classic car.
Bob Hope and Milton Berle, who are two veterans of vaudeville, have been active performers for years.

Appositives are therefore economical alternatives to such clauses.

Punctuating appositives

An appositive punctuated as a sentence is a sentence fragment. (See Chapter 10 on fragments.) A non-restrictive appositive should be separated from the word it refers to by a comma, a dash, or a colon. When the appositive restricts the meaning of the word it refers to, it follows or precedes that word with no punctuation.

The largest lake in South America, *Lake Maracaibo*, covers 5000 square miles. [non-restrictive appositive]
Lake Titicaca — *the highest body of water in the world on which steamships operate* — is 12,507 feet above sea level. [non-restrictive appositive, set off with dashes because of its length]
South America's animal population includes many unusual creatures: *armadillos, giant anteaters, capybaras, and sloths*. [non-restrictive ap-

positive, set off with a colon because it is a list coming at the end of the sentence]

The island group *Tierra del Fuego* is separated from the South American mainland by the Strait of Magellan. [restrictive appositive, essential to the meaning of *The island group*, not set off with punctuation]

gr

5

Identifying phrases and clauses

Identify each word group below as a phrase (*phr.*) or a clause (*cl.*) by writing the appropriate abbreviation in the blank to the left. In each clause, underline the subject once and the predicate twice.

Example: ___*cl.*___ because <u>he</u> <u><u>was sick</u></u>

_____ 1. banned for a week from the restaurant

_____ 2. the Spanish arriving first

_____ 3. from soup to nuts

_____ 4. because of a flat tire

_____ 5. under the tree was a book

_____ 6. during the last quarter

_____ 7. men in the professional ranks

_____ 8. lack of understanding

_____ 9. asked a question

_____ 10. when the crystal broke

_____ 11. who she was

_____ 12. that long bench

_____ 13. above the ridge

_____ 14. if you save your money

_____ 15. the game was lost

_____ 16. why the game was poorly played

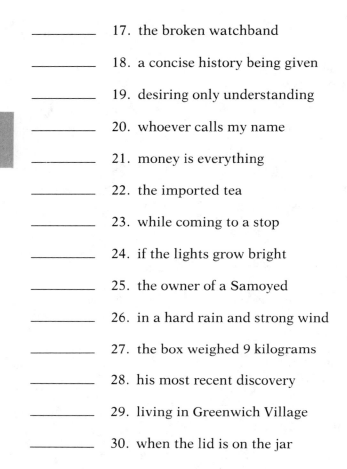

_____ 17. the broken watchband

_____ 18. a concise history being given

_____ 19. desiring only understanding

gr
5   _____ 20. whoever calls my name

_____ 21. money is everything

_____ 22. the imported tea

_____ 23. while coming to a stop

_____ 24. if the lights grow bright

_____ 25. the owner of a Samoyed

_____ 26. in a hard rain and strong wind

_____ 27. the box weighed 9 kilograms

_____ 28. his most recent discovery

_____ 29. living in Greenwich Village

_____ 30. when the lid is on the jar

Identifying subordinate clauses   EXERCISE **5-12**

Each sentence below has one subordinate clause. Underline it and in the blank on the left tell what part of speech the clause functions as — adjective (*adj.*), adverb (*adv.*), or noun (*n.*).

Example: ___*n.*___ I understand <u>why I made an error</u>.

_____ 1. The woman whom the police arrested was charged with arson.

_____ 2. The cat's favorite hiding place, under the bed, is a quiet spot that is also cool and dark.

_____ 3. Although our television was broken, we still heard the game on the radio.

_____ 4. The mayor said that the rat-infested slum should receive a municipal subsidy.

_____ 5. Whoever offers Oliver a job will get a trustworthy employee.

_____ 6. This version of "Stardust," which is fast and slick, would be good to dance to.

_____ 7. After the robber grabbed the cash, the manager rang the alarm.

_____ 8. The waiter sneaked out while the after-dinner lull continued.

_____ 9. The family lived in an apartment that had no fire alarm and no extinguisher.

_____ 10. The building was erected to house an insurance company; however, when it burned down, it was uninsured.

_____ 11. Apples, which are inexpensive, are good for your gums.

_____ 12. He sent her money so that she could come home, but she spent it on a lavish dinner for herself and her roommate.

_____ 13. She got the lawyer who had represented her husband.

_____ 14. Frustration arose near the end of the summer program when funds were cut.

_____ 15. We left on the fishing trip when the sun came up; the fish, however, were already too alert to be caught.

_____ 16. This open letter is for whoever will read it.

_____ 17. To be eligible for student rates, you must show an identification card, which you do not have.

_____ 18. Bill thinks that the owner of the College Restaurant puts Johnson grass seed in the hamburger.

_____ 19. After reading about problems with the mail, I was surprised when the parcel arrived with its contents intact.

_____ 20. Lack of organization was a characteristic of all the lectures Mr. Donaldson gave.

| *Using subordinate clauses*   EXERCISE **5-13**

gr

5

In the following sentences underline each subordinate clause and circle each subordinating word (subordinating conjunction or relative pronoun). Then compose a complete sentence of your own that uses the same subordinating word.

Example: Elephants never forget (how) a trainer treats them.

  Charlene doesn't remember (how) she made the cookies.

1. She did not stop crying until the ceremony ended.

2. Adam jogged through the park while his cat loped behind.

3. Pedestrians are increasingly menaced by bicyclists who ride on sidewalks.

4. If the dog is not confined, it will chew on the saplings.

5. I would have passed if I had understood the question.

6. Whatever money remains goes to the children's home.

7. We will put off our trip to West Virginia until the huckleberries are ripe.

8. I knew that I should not have eaten so much.

9. The tenants, who complained regularly, found no remedy.

10. The council decided against establishing a dress code because so many students protested.

11. People who complain all the time never have time to smile.

12. The surprise is that the governor was not convicted sooner.

5d | Compounding words, phrases, and clauses

Single words and groups of words may be linked to show that they refer to related ideas; such linking — called **compounding** — also has the effect of reducing repetition. We can compound any element of the sentence — clauses, phrases, and any part of speech — but the elements must be equivalent in both grammar and meaning. In a **compound subject,** two or more nouns or word groups join in a single subject. In a **compound object,** two or more nouns or word groups join in a single object.

> *John* and *the boy* from Nebraska played *tennis* and *darts.*

In a **compound complement,** two or more nouns, adjectives, or word groups join in a single subject or object complement.

> After exercising, I feel *healthy, strong,* and *confident.*
> The critic called the movie *thoughtless* and *dull.*

In a **compound predicate,** two or more sentence predicates or verbs join in a single predicate.

> The firecracker *sizzled* and then *exploded.*

In a **compound sentence,** two or more main clauses join in a single sentence.

> *I hoped for a good grade,* and *I got what I wanted.*

1 | Using coordinating conjunctions and correlative conjunctions

The word *and,* which links the parts of the compound constructions above, is a **coordinating conjunction.** The other coordinating conjunctions are *but, or, nor,* and sometimes *for, so,* and *yet.* As in the sentences above, these conjunctions connect words or word groups of the same kind: nouns, verbs, adjectives, adverbs, phrases, clauses, or whole sentences.

Some conjunctions, called **correlative conjunctions,** come in pairs: *both . . . and, not only . . . but also, not . . . but, either . . . or, neither . . . nor.*

> *Both* John *and* the boy from Nebraska were defeated.
> After exercising, I feel *not only* healthy and strong *but also* confident.
> *Either* you *or* I will have to go.
> *Neither* sizzling *nor* exploding, the firecracker seemed to be a dud.

Punctuating compounded words, phrases, and clauses

Two main clauses in a single sentence are separated in one of two ways: with a comma and a coordinating conjunction (21a) or with a semicolon (22a).

> Space has neither air nor the sensation of gravity, *and* it is subject to extremes of temperature. [Two main clauses separated with a coordinating conjunction and a comma.]

Overcoming gravity is the biggest problem for getting into space; gravity pulls everything back to earth. [Two main clauses separated with a semicolon.]

Separating two main clauses with only a comma results in a comma splice. (See Chapter 11.)

Compounded words, phrases, and clauses in a series of three or more are separated by commas.

A space launch vehicle is used to launch satellites, space probes, *and* other spacecraft. [Three nouns plus their modifiers; note the comma before the coordinating conjunction.]

A comma is used before the coordinating conjunction in only two cases: with a series of three or more sentence elements and between two main clauses. (See 21j-2.)

2 | Using conjunctive adverbs

Here are some of the most common **conjunctive adverbs.**

accordingly	furthermore	moreover	similarly
also	hence	namely	still
anyway	however	nevertheless	then
besides	incidentally	next	thereafter
certainly	indeed	nonetheless	therefore
consequently	instead	now	thus
finally	likewise	otherwise	undoubtedly
further	meanwhile		

There are two main things to remember about **conjunctive adverbs:** (1) they are *not* conjunctions, and (2) they *are* adverbs. As we have seen, conjunctions have the function of joining sentence elements — either equal elements (coordinating conjunctions) or unequal elements (subordinating conjunctions). They have no function in their sentences other than to join parts. Adverbs, on the other hand, serve a modifying function; they describe or limit verbs, other modifiers, or groups of words. Conjunctive adverbs modify groups of words, showing how their clauses relate to preceding clauses.

Like other adverbs that modify verbs or clauses, these connectors are usually movable; conjunctions, in contrast, are not. Compare the following sentences, the first using a conjunctive adverb, the second a coordinating conjunction.

Mr. Androni talks of nothing except himself; *however,* he is one of the most interesting people I know. [The conjunctive adverb *however* could appear at the end of the clause.]

Mr. Androni talks of nothing except himself, *but* he is one of the most interesting people I know. [The coordinating conjunction *but* can be used only at the beginning of its clause.]

Punctuating sentences containing conjunctive adverbs

Conjunctive adverbs connect equal clauses; they relate the idea of one main clause to that of a preceding main clause. Between the two clauses the punctuation mark must be either a semicolon or a period.

> Mr. Androni talks of nothing but himself; *however,* he is one of the most interesting people I know.
>
> The season's last game was canceled. *Nonetheless,* we won the championship.

Separating two main clauses with only a comma — even though the second one has a conjunctive adverb — results in a comma splice (Chapter 11).

Writers usually, but not always, follow the conjunctive adverb with a comma. Note the two examples above and the one following.

> Read the directions for the test carefully; *then* follow them exactly.

gr

5

Writing compound constructions: clauses

EXERCISE **5-14**

Make two kinds of compound sentences by joining the following pairs of sentences *twice*, first with coordinating conjunctions and then with conjunctive adverbs. Try to use the most appropriate connectors. Remember that coordinating conjunctions should be preceded by commas, conjunctive adverbs by semicolons.

Example: He failed the final exam. He passed the course anyway.

He failed the final exam, but he passed the course anyway.

He failed the final exam; however, he passed the course anyway.

1. Madison is the capital of Wisconsin. Milwaukee is the largest city.

2. In summer Wisconsin's lakes attract swimmers and boaters. In winter they attract iceboaters and snowmobilers.

3. Wisconsin is the nation's leading milk producer. It is called "America's Dairyland."

4. Wisconsin's cities are mainly Democratic. Its rural areas are largely Republican.

5. Milwaukee was once a fur-trading center. Now it is known for its manufacturing.

6. Milwaukee is known also for its variety of ethnic cultures. Most of its residents were born in the United States.

7. The Wisconsin climate is characterized by warm summers and severely cold winters. Along the lake shorelines the temperatures are somewhat modified.

8. The Lake Michigan shoreline is a flypath for migrating birds. Bird watchers flock to eastern Wisconsin every spring and fall.

9. Jean Nicolet, a French explorer, landed on the shore of Green Bay in 1634. He is said to be the first white person to set foot in Wisconsin.

10. The Ringling Brothers started their first circus in Baraboo, Wisconsin, in 1884. The Circus World Museum there commemorates this event with circus memorabilia.

Writing compound constructions:
words and phrases   exercise **5-15**

The following pairs of sentences are wordy and repetitious. Rewrite each of them into a single main clause by compounding words and phrases. Since the coordinating conjunction will not be joining main clauses, it should *not* be preceded by a comma.

Example: Social insurance is a basic type of welfare program. Public assistance is a basic type of welfare program.

Social insurance and public assistance are basic types of welfare programs.

1. The sun's rays strike the earth at a ninety-degree angle at the equator. They strike the earth at acute angles at the poles.

2. Hurricane Hannah uprooted trees. Hurricane Hannah uprooted telephone poles.

3. Forecasters analyze reports from hurricane hunters. They learn where the hurricane's center is located.

4. Hurricane hunters are U.S. Air Force pilots. Hurricane hunters are U.S. Navy pilots.

5. Methods of weather forecasting differ in the kinds of maps used. They differ in the details given.

6. To forecast weather, meteorologists must know present conditions. They must know past conditions.

7. High-pressure winds blow clockwise in the Northern Hemisphere. They blow counterclockwise in the Southern Hemisphere.

8. Precipitation is water droplets that fall to earth. Precipitation is ice crystals that fall to earth.

9. Clouds precede the arrival of a warm front. Steady rain or snow precedes the arrival of a warm front.

10. Much of the sun's energy is absorbed by the earth. This energy is changed into heat.

5e | Changing the usual order of the sentence

Most English sentences follow the basic word order of subject, verb, and object or complement. This basic order also has some very common variations.

1 | Forming questions

We form questions mainly in two ways: by inverting normal subject-verb order and by using a question word such as *who, what, when, where, which.*

    V   **S**   **SC**
Was the movie interesting? [Normal order: *The movie was interesting.*]

    S   **V**
Who plays in it?

2 | Forming commands

To form commands, we simply omit the sentence subject *you.*

Turn to the diagram on the next page.
Don't expect much from that course.

3 | Writing passive sentences

The normal **voice** of a verb is **active.** That means that when a verb is transitive, the subject performs the action of the verb and the direct object receives the action.

The cat killed the rat.

In this sentence the subject, *the cat*, performs the action, *killed*, and the direct object, *the rat*, receives the action. In the **passive voice,** however, this order is reversed.

The rat was killed by the cat.

In this passive sentence, the subject receives the action, and the performer of the action is the object of the preposition *by.*

The passive verb consists of some form of *be* plus the past participle of the verb. Here are a few examples.

ACTIVE VERB	PASSIVE VERB
gives	is given
gave	was given
is giving	is being given
has given	has been given

Sometimes the performer of an action is left out of the passive sentence:

The rat was killed.

Perhaps the writer of the sentence doesn't know who killed the rat; maybe it's not important who did it; or maybe the writer just doesn't want to say. Passive voice can be particularly sneaky for ducking responsibility (who did kill the rat, anyway?), and so it is often mistrusted by careful readers and avoided by careful writers. (See 7g, 7h, and 18d for additional discussions of passive sentences.)

4 | Writing sentences with postponed subjects

In some sentences the normal subject-predicate order is inverted for emphasis:

High in the tree sat an eagle.

Other sentences, called **expletive constructions,** begin with *it* or *there* followed by the verb, a form of *be.* In such sentences the subject follows the verb.

There are fifty-seven varieties. [*Varieties* is the subject of *are.*]
It is unclear how they got there. [*How they got there,* a noun clause, is the subject of *is.*]

Expletive constructions can provide variety in sentences but should be used sparingly. (See 18e.)

|*Changing the order of sentences*   EXERCISE   **5-16**

Rewrite the passive sentences below in active voice and the sentences with postponed subjects in normal order. Be careful to keep meaning and verb time the same.

Examples: French could never be spoken by me.

     I could never speak French.

     There are twenty people in the class.

     Twenty people are in the class.

CHANGE FROM PASSIVE TO ACTIVE

1. The porcelain vase was broken by my little brother.

2. Unfortunately, the parking ticket was blown away by the wind.

3. Last week my car was towed by our friendly neighborhood towing service.

4. The table had not been cleared by the waitress.

5. The credit-card payment has been made by me.

CHANGE FROM INVERTED TO NORMAL ORDER

gr

5

6. There are ten people coming to the party.

7. It is not known what time the party will start.

8. It is clear that you need to practice parallel parking.

9. There is an extra chair in the kitchen.

10. There were only a few members present.

5f | Classifying sentences

We have already seen how sentences can be described by their subject-predicate patterns (5a). Another way to classify sentences is according to their clause patterns: by how many main clauses they contain and whether they have any subordinate clauses. There are four basic structures: simple, compound, complex, and compound-complex.

1 | Writing simple sentences

A **simple sentence** consists of one main clause. The clause may contain many modifying phrases and compound subjects, verbs, or objects, but as long as it is just one clause it is a simple sentence.

> He cleaned the typewriter.
> Last June Mr. Snapp cleaned Mr. Rollo's typewriter for a small fee.

2 | Writing compound sentences

A **compound sentence** contains two or more main clauses separated by a comma and a coordinating conjunction or by a semicolon. It may have many modifiers, but it has no subordinate clauses.

> Mr. Snapp cleaned Mr. Rollo's typewriter, but some of the keys continued to stick.
> Mr. Snapp cleaned Mr. Rollo's typewriter; however, some of the keys continued to stick.

3 | Writing complex sentences

A **complex sentence** contains one main clause and one or more subordinate clauses.

> After Mr. Snapp cleaned Mr. Rollo's typewriter, some of the keys continued to stick. [The first half of the sentence is the subordinate clause; the second half is the main clause.]

4 | Writing compound-complex sentences

A **compound-complex sentence** contains two or more main clauses and one or more subordinate clauses.

> Mr. Snapp cleaned Mr. Rollo's typewriter, but some of the keys continued to stick after he had finished. [Main clause, main clause, subordinate clause.]

Writing compound, complex, and compound-complex sentences

The following sentences have compound, complex, or compound-complex structure. Observe the structure of each one; then write a sentence of your own that imitates the clause pattern. Use appropriate conjunctions and punctuation.

Example: (*Complex*) Even though the lake was cold and wide, we could swim across it.

> *After I finish this macramé hanger,*
> *I'll make a wall hanging for you.*

1. (*Complex*) I learned to read before I started school.

2. (*Complex*) Teachers who grade on the curve are fairer than those who do not.

3. (*Complex*) All the union members who went on strike to protest a lack of safety regulations were fired.

4. (*Compound*) Falling and freezing are dangers for mountain climbers, but heat exhaustion and dehydration are greater perils.

5. (*Compound-complex*) Before 1967 the city seemed to have no profile, but a skyscraper that was built in that year now dominates the city's horizon.

6. (*Compound*) The movie script was generally well written; however, the direction was often weak.

7. (*Compound*) The snowplows cleared the streets overnight, but now the driveways are blocked with banks of snow.

8. (*Compound-complex*) You've changed your hairstyle since I last saw you, and I hardly recognized you.

9. (*Complex*) Whenever I go to a concert, I like to read the newspaper reviews of it the next day.

10. (*Complex*) The road commissioner was fired for conflict of interest because a building supply company that he owned sold materials to the government.

6 | Case of Nouns and Pronouns

Self-test

Circle the correct pronouns in the following sentences.

Example: (*Us,* (We)) Americans often neglect our right to vote.

1. My roommate and (*I, me*) became close friends.
2. The meal was prepared especially for (*they, them*) and (*we, us*).
3. For (*we, us*) students, attendance is required.
4. There is a problem between you and (*I, me*).
5. The river rose after the Browns and (*us, we*) had safely crossed.
6. The audience did not know (*who, whom*) to applaud.
7. Either (*he, him*) or (*I, me*) will wait for the shuttle.
8. The music drew Sylvia and (*I, me*) closer.
9. The substitutes were (*her, she*) and (*I, me*).
10. Both (*he, him*) and (*her, she*) were admitted to the hospital.

Case is the form of a noun or a pronoun that shows how it functions in a sentence: as a subject, an object, or something else. The pronouns *I, we, he, she, they,* and *who* have different forms for three cases: the **subjective,** used when the pronoun is a subject or a subject complement; the **objective,** used when the pronoun is an object or the subject of an infinitive; and the **possessive,** used to show ownership. The following list shows the case forms of the personal and relative pronouns that have changing forms.

SUBJECTIVE				
I	we	he, she	they	who

POSSESSIVE				
my	our	his, her	their	whose
mine	ours	his, hers	theirs	

OBJECTIVE				
me	us	him, her	them	whom

All other pronouns and all nouns have only two cases: a possessive case (*woman's, everybody's, your, its*) and a plain case (the dictionary form), which serves all other functions (*woman, everybody, you, it*).

6a | Use the subjective case for all parts of compound subjects and for subject complements.

The subjective form is used when a pronoun is a subject or a subject complement. (See 5a and 5c.) It is therefore used for all compounds of these functions.

SUBJECT

I came late.
Carlos and *I* came late.

SUBJECT COMPLEMENT

The guilty persons were *he* and *Jacob*.
The guiltiest one was *he*.

In speech and other informal usage, it is common to say *It's me* or *It's him*, but these forms are not generally acceptable in formal, written English. If as a writer you're uncomfortable using the correct forms, such as *The guiltiest one was he* (and you're right — that sentence does sound awkward), you have the option of revising your sentence to some other grammatically correct phrasing, such as *He was the guiltiest one*.

6b | Use the objective case for all parts of compound objects.

The objective form is used when the pronoun is the direct or indirect object of a verb or verbal or the object of a preposition. (See 5a and 5c.) It is therefore used for all compounds of these functions.

OBJECT OF VERB

We provided *him* with dry clothes.
We provided *Jodie* and *him* with dry clothes.

INDIRECT OBJECT

We gave *him* dry clothes.
We gave *him* and *Jodie* dry clothes.

OBJECT OF PREPOSITION

The party was for *me*.
The party was for *Stavros* and *me*.

OBJECT OF A VERBAL

After taking *him* home, she went shopping. [Object of gerund.]
Having nominated *Lin Wong* and *me*, the committee adjourned. [Object of participle.]
We tried to find *him* in the crowd. [Object of infinitive.]

Another use of pronouns in the objective case is as subjects of infinitives.

Nunzio's mother wanted *him* to register for classes by mail.

6c | Use the appropriate case form when the plural pronouns *we* and *us* occur with a noun.

In the following sentences, the pronoun — *we* or *us* — is in apposition to the noun that follows it, and the case of the pronoun is determined by the function that it and its appositive noun fulfill. They both have the same case. If you are not sure about which pronoun to use, try the sentence without the appositive; your acquired sense of grammar will tell you which pronoun is correct. (See also 5c-5.)

> The coach threw a party for *us* players. [*Us* is the object of the preposition *for*, and *players* is its appositive.]
> *We* players also held a party of our own. [*We* is the subject of the sentence, and *players* is its appositive.]

6d | In appositives the case of a pronoun depends on the function of the word it describes or identifies.

In the following sentences (in contrast to the sentences above), the pronoun is the **appositive,** renaming the preceding noun. The case of the pronoun is determined by the function of the noun it renames. They both have the same case. If you are not sure about which pronoun to use, try reading the sentence without the word the appositive identifies; your acquired sense of grammar will tell you which pronoun is correct. (See also 5c-5.)

> Two victims, Homer and *I*, sued the company. [The appositive *I* renames *victims*, the subject of the sentence.]
> The company was sued by two victims, Homer and *me*. [The appositive *me* renames *victims*, the object of a preposition.]

6e | The case of a pronoun after *than* or *as* in a comparison depends on the meaning.

The case of a pronoun after *than* or *as* in comparisons is what it would be if the clause were completed.

> Axel likes pizza more than *I* (like pizza).
> Axel likes pizza more than (he likes) *me*.
> Axel likes pizza as much as *I* (like pizza).
> Axel likes pizza as much as (he likes) *me*.

If you don't like the sound of sentences like *Axel likes pizza more than I*, add the verb form at the end: *Axel likes pizza more than I do.*

6f | Use the objective case for pronouns that are subjects or objects of infinitives.

Infinitives, being verbals, can take subjects and objects even though they cannot function as verbs.

We want *him* to learn. [*Him* is subject of the infinitive *to learn*.]
To win *her* over requires patience. [*Her* is object of the infinitive *To win*.]

6g | **The form of the pronoun *who* depends on its function in its clause.**

1 | **At the beginning of questions use *who* if the question is about a subject, *whom* if it is about an object.**

Who ate the macaroni? [Question about a subject. Compare *He ate the macaroni*.]
Whom are you kidding? [Question about an object. Compare *You are kidding them*.]

In speech, *who* is commonly used whenever it begins a question. Writing, however, requires *whom*.

SPOKEN

Who did you appoint to the position?
Who did you write the letter to?

WRITTEN

Whom did you appoint to the position?
To *whom* did you write the letter?

2 | **In subordinate clauses use *who* and *whoever* for all subjects, *whom* and *whomever* for all objects.**

The case of the relative pronoun is determined by its function *in its own clause*, not by the function of the clause in the sentence.

I do not know *who* can help me. [*Who* is the subject of the subordinate clause *who can help me;* the entire subordinate clause is the direct object of the verb *know*. Compare *She can help me*.]
Whoever wants the dog can have it. [*Whoever* is the subject of the subordinate clause *Whoever wants the dog*. Compare *He wants the dog*.]
I know *whom* he was writing about. [*Whom* is the object of the preposition *about*. Compare *He was writing about him*.]
I do not know *whom* to criticize. [*Whom* is the object of the infinitive *to criticize*. Compare *to criticize him*.]
She will hire *whomever* she chooses. [*Whomever* is the object of the verb *chooses*. Compare *She chooses him*.]

6h | **Ordinarily, use the possessive form of a pronoun or noun immediately before a gerund.**

A *gerund* is the -*ing* form of a verb used as a noun (see 5c-2).

We couldn't listen to *his* singing.
Oxnard College's running ruined our game plan.

While these sentences are grammatically correct, the use of the possessive might at times sound awkward to the ears of both writers and readers. If you are in doubt about the sound of your sentences, revise them. The second sentence above would be better recast as follows:

The running *of Oxnard College* ruined our game plan.

See 23b on the avoidance of apostrophes in possessive personal pronouns.

Using the appropriate pronoun case I

Circle the correct pronoun in each pair below.

Example: (Who, (Whom)) did the dean reprimand?

1. (*His, Him*) feeding the animals was illegal.
2. The sale was less than profitable for you and (*we, us*).
3. The drop in circulation left (*we, us*) and (*they, them*) confused.
4. (*We, us*) Americans should use all the imported fuel we can get.
5. We appreciate (*you, your*) taking the job.
6. Why were Carl and (*he, him*) given the blame?
7. The traffic congestion delayed (*she, her*) and (*I, me*).
8. Ben and Bruce sold more tickets than Karen and (*I, me*).
9. The winners were really (*we, us*) and (*they, them*).
10. (*Who, Whom*) will be responsible for bringing the food?
11. The cameras were damaged by Linda and (*her, she*).
12. We wondered (*who, whom*) to give the assignment to.
13. To (*who, whom*) should I give the book?
14. Jamie and (*he, him*) caught the last flight.
15. The tickets are for (*whoever, whomever*) I give them to.
16. The award will go to (*whoever, whomever*) prepares the best essay.
17. (*His, Him*) installing deadbolt locks deterred the burglar.
18. You and (*I, me*) should get tickets for the play.
19. One representative, either Kathy or (*I, me*), will go to the meeting.
20. We asked (*he, him*) to represent the club.
21. (*Whoever, Whomever*) paid for the item forgot to claim it.
22. The tuition was more than (*we, us*) students could afford.
23. We fight harder than (*they, them*).

24. What are (*he, him*) and Jones doing here at this hour?

25. (*Who, Whom*) expected so much rain?

26. The referee had to break up a fight between (*he, him*) and (*I, me*).

27. The Lamberts and Merediths gave (*he, him*) and (*I, me*) a farewell party.

28. (*Who, Whom*) is the ecology course designed for?

29. I expected (*she, her*) to open the gifts earlier.

30. My brother is taller than (*I, me*).

Using the appropriate pronoun case II

EXERCISE **6-2**

ca

6

Cross out any incorrect case form in the following sentences and write the correct form or forms on the blank to the left. If a sentence is correct as given, write *OK* on the blank.

Example: **whomever**   Wendy will date ~~whoever~~ she likes.

_____   1. The handmade ornament is one donated by her and I.

_____   2. I explained to the policeman, "I'd appreciate you giving me just a warning."

_____   3. I am not as smart as him, but my grades are just as good.

_____   4. We hoped that you could tell us who this car belongs to.

_____   5. Whom will the new dean be?

_____   6. Elizabeth and her were born the same day.

_____   7. It must have been them who left the books.

_____   8. When my mother sees we children watching television, she tries to start a conversation.

_____   9. The dispute was between he and the clerk.

_____   10. Show the map to whomever plans to drive.

_____   11. Me and my brother bought a tape deck.

_____   12. Whom can we count on to work at the hospital?

_____   13. Ed is much more willing to drive a truck than me.

_____   14. Us students all get discounts.

_____   15. Hardly any love remains between she and I.

_____ 16. John lifts weights every day, so he is stronger than either Larry or me.

_____ 17. Chris tells old jokes to whoever will listen.

_____ 18. After practice, the batboy brought Carl and I cold drinks.

_____ 19. Dave wanted to know whom to ask about organic gardening.

_____ 20. The two latecomers, Judith and I, agreed on who would do the work.

_____ 21. She and the teacher disagreed over her grade.

_____ 22. The police should protect you and I from peeping Marys as well as from peeping Toms.

_____ 23. Us freshmen no longer are subject to hazing from sophomores.

_____ 24. Between you and me, the play was a flop.

_____ 25. We expected him to win, not Delgado.

|Pronoun case: Review

Rewrite this short narrative, changing the beginning sentence to read as follows:

> This morning Neal decided that the rabbit needed some attention.

Then, as you write, change all first-person *I* references to third-person pronouns referring to Neal: *he, his,* and *him.* Where necessary, repeat *Neal.* When you finish, the narrative will describe something Neal did rather than something the writer did.

This morning I decided that my rabbit needed some attention. So far this winter, Milwaukee has accumulated nineteen inches of snow on the ground, with drifts and piles of shoveled snow much higher. Because of the high winds overnight, all my previous tracks through the yard were filled in. But the bunny, for whom I was feeling particularly sorry today, had no food, no hay, and only ice in place of water. So I plunged out into the drifts, plodding through snow several inches above my knees.

First I had to get some hay from under the porch. My pulling and tearing at the hay from the bale might have sent me flat into the snow if the drifts hadn't been packed around my legs so tight that they held me up. Next was the matter of getting myself and the hay across the yard to the rabbit hutch. The hay survived better than I. Except for a few bits trailing across the yard, it arrived intact. I, however, had snow packed on my jeans and into my boots.

The next task was for me to lift the cover of the rabbit hutch, snow and all. As I struggled with it, I was thinking about the eight-year-old bunny and half expected to find her in a corner, stiff and feet up. But as I raised the lid, sliding the snow off onto the ground and tossing the hay inside, out from her enclosed, insulated house hopped old Checker, ready to begin another day. I removed the icy food and water dishes and trekked back over the yard and into the basement to fill them. My going back to the hutch wasn't any easier than it was the first time out, for this time I was carrying a sloshing water dish in one snow-encrusted glove and the pellet-filled food dish in the other. But Checker and I were both glad when I managed to get most of the water and food out there — she definitely more than I. I myself was a lot gladder when I had my cold, wet jeans off and had put something warm and dry on my legs and feet. For Checker and me, that was enough snow adventuring for one day.

ca

6

7 | *Verb Forms, Tense, Mood, and Voice*

Self-test

Circle the correct verb form in each of the following sentences.

Example: The doctor had not (*took,* (*taken*)) too long.

1. We (*swam, swum*) the length of the pool.
2. A (*broke, broken*) chair leaned in the corner.
3. I would buy tickets if I (*was, were*) you.
4. They were surprised when the new guest (*shows, showed*) up.
5. The milk had (*set, sat*) on the table all night.
6. He would be unhappy if the test score (*was, were*) low.
7. She was (*lying, laying*) in the sun by the pool.
8. The phone had (*rang, rung*) ten times that morning.
9. The race had (*last, lasted*) all afternoon.
10. We were (*mistook, mistaken*) for intruders.

VERB FORMS

All verbs except *be* have five forms.

INFINITIVE	talk, write
PAST TENSE	talked, wrote
PAST PARTICIPLE	talked, written
PRESENT PARTICIPLE	talking, writing
-S FORM	talks, writes

The first three forms are the verb's **principal parts:** the infinitive, the past tense, and the past participle. The **infinitive** — the dictionary, or plain, form of the verb — has no endings. We use this plain form for present-time verbs when the subject is *I, we, you, they,* or any plural noun:

I *go.*   You *swim.*   Dogs *scratch.*   Cars *pass.*

The **past tense** form indicates action that occurred in the past. Each verb has only one past form, and that form is used with all subjects:

I *went* (you *went*, they *went*, the car *went*, cars *went*).
You *swam.*   Dogs *scratched.*   Cars *passed.*

The past tense is usually formed by adding *-d* or *-ed* to the plain form, although some of the most common verbs (for example, *be, do, have*) are formed irregularly (see 7a).

The **past participle,** which for regular verbs has the same form as the past tense, combines with *have, has,* or *had:*

I *have gone.*   You *have*   Dogs *have*   Cars *have*
                   swum.   *scratched.*   *passed.*

It also combines with a form of *be* in the passive voice:

The windows *have been washed.*   The floors *are being scrubbed.*

The past participle may be used to modify nouns and pronouns:

The *scrubbed* floors look shiny.
The *closed* door is *unlocked.*

Here is a chart of the principal parts of a few verbs, comparing the three forms for both regular and irregular verbs.

	INFINITIVE	PAST TENSE	PAST PARTICIPLE
REGULAR VERBS	open	opened	(have) opened
	close	closed	(have) closed
	talk	talked	(have) talked
	scratch	scratched	(have) scratched
	pass	passed	(have) passed
IRREGULAR VERBS	bring	brought	(have) brought
	take	took	(have) taken
	write	wrote	(have) written
	swim	swam	(have) swum

In addition to the three principal parts, all verbs have two other forms: the present participle and the *-s* form. All verbs form their **present participle** by adding *-ing* to their infinitive form: *going, swimming, scratching, being, having.* This form may combine with a helping verb to form a verb phrase called the *progressive form* or *progressive tense.* (See 7d, p. 180.)

I *am going.*   The dog *has been*   Joshua *is swimming.*
                       scratching.

The *-ing* form may also serve as a modifier or as a noun:

Scratching dogs don't bite. [Adjective modifying *dogs.*]
Joshua cools off after work by *swimming.* [Noun functioning as object of the preposition *by.*]

The *-ing* form can never stand alone as the verb in a sentence. (See 10c.)

The *-s* form of all verbs except *be* and *have* is made by adding *-s* to the infinitive, or plain, form of the verb: *opens, closes, brings, takes.* The *be* and *have* forms also end in *-s: be* changes to *is,* and *have* to *has.* The *-s* form of all verbs is used to show present-time or habitual action when the subject is *he, she, it,* or any singular noun or pronoun:

He *goes.*	Joshua *swims.*	The dog *scratches.*	Everybody *passes.*

In addition to the *-s* form, *be* has other irregular forms:

	I	*he, she, it,* and singular nouns	*we, you, they,* and plural nouns
PRESENT	am	is	are
PAST	was	was	were

Helping, or **auxiliary, verbs** combine with other verbs in verb phrases to indicate time and other meanings. The common helping verbs are the forms of *have, do,* and *be,* plus *shall, will, can, could, may, might, must, ought, should,* and *would.*

We *did expect* to go.
They *were flying.*
The mayor *will come.*
The prize *should have been awarded.* [Not *should of been.*]

7a | Use the correct form of regular and irregular verbs.

Most verbs are **regular,** meaning that they form their past tense and past participle by adding *-d* or *-ed* to the infinitive, or plain, form: *expect, expected, (have) expected; wash, washed, (have) washed.* Regular forms do not often cause problems in writing.

Some verbs, however, do not form their past tense and past participles predictably, by adding *-d* or *-ed* to the infinitive, so writers must either memorize the principal parts of these **irregular verbs** or look them up in a dictionary. (Dictionaries list principal parts for irregular verbs in this order: infinitive, past tense, and past participle; sometimes the present participle — the *-ing* form — is also included.) The following list contains sixty-nine of the nearly two hundred irregular verbs in English. Read the list and check the forms that sound strange to you; those are the ones that may give you trouble in your writing.

INFINITIVE	PAST TENSE	PAST PARTICIPLE
arise	arose	(have) arisen
become	became	(have) become
begin	began	(have) begun
bid	bid	(have) bid
bite	bit	(have) bitten, bit
blow	blew	(have) blown
break	broke	(have) broken
bring	brought	(have) brought

INFINITIVE	PAST TENSE	PAST PARTICIPLE
burst	burst	(have) burst
buy	bought	(have) bought
catch	caught	(have) caught
choose	chose	(have) chosen
come	came	(have) come
cut	cut	(have) cut
dive	dived, dove	(have) dived
do	did	(have) done
draw	drew	(have) drawn
dream	dreamed, dreamt	(have) dreamed, dreamt
drink	drank	(have) drunk
drive	drove	(have) driven
eat	ate	(have) eaten
fall	fell	(have) fallen
find	found	(have) found
flee	fled	(have) fled
fly	flew	(have) flown
forget	forgot	(have) forgotten, forgot
freeze	froze	(have) frozen
get	got	(have) got, gotten
give	gave	(have) given
go	went	(have) gone
grow	grew	(have) grown
hang	hung	(have) hung
hang	hanged (executed)	(have) hanged
hear	heard	(have) heard
hide	hid	(have) hidden
hold	held	(have) held
keep	kept	(have) kept
know	knew	(have) known
lay	laid	(have) laid
lead	led	(have) led
leave	left	(have) left
let	let	(have) let
lie	lay	(have) lain
light	lighted, lit	(have) lighted, lit
lose	lost	(have) lost
pay	paid	(have) paid
prove	proved	(have) proved, proven
ride	rode	(have) ridden
ring	rang	(have) rung
rise	rose	(have) risen
run	ran	(have) run
say	said	(have) said
see	saw	(have) seen
set	set	(have) set
shake	shook	(have) shaken

INFINITIVE	PAST TENSE	PAST PARTICIPLE
sing	sang, sung	(have) sung
sink	sank, sunk	(have) sunk
sit	sat	(have) sat
slide	slid	(have) slid
speak	spoke	(have) spoken
spring	sprang, sprung	(have) sprung
stand	stood	(have) stood
steal	stole	(have) stolen
swim	swam	(have) swum
take	took	(have) taken
tear	tore	(have) torn
throw	threw	(have) thrown
wear	wore	(have) worn
wind	wound	(have) wound
write	wrote	(have) written

7b | Distinguish between *sit* and *set* and between *lie* and *lay*.

The principal parts of *sit* and *set* and *lie* and *lay*, shown in the preceding list, are often confused. *Sit* and *lie* are **intransitive verbs**, meaning they do not take objects. *Sit* means "be seated"; *lie* means "recline." *Set* and *lay* are **transitive verbs**, meaning they usually take objects. Both *set* and *lay* mean "put" or "place" something. All four words can be used with both animate and inanimate subjects, persons or creatures, as well as things, qualities, and so on.

> They *sit* (*sat, have sat*) in class like zombies. [No object.]
> The books *are sitting* on the table. [No object.]
> We *set* (*have set*) the pole against the wall. [Object: *pole.*]
> She *set* the baby in the chair. [Object: *baby.*]
> I often *lie* awake at night. [Present of *lie;* no object.]
> Last night I *lay* awake half the night. [Past of *lie;* no object.]
> I *have lain* awake every night this week. [Present perfect of *lie;* no object.]
> *Lay* the books on the table. [Present of *lay;* object: *books.*]
> I *laid* the books on the desk this morning. [Past of *lay;* object: *books.*]
> I *haven't laid* the books down yet. [Present perfect of *lay;* object: *books.*]

7c | Use the *-s* and *-ed* forms of the verb when they are required.

The present-tense verb form *-s* (*asks*) and the past-tense and past-participle form *-ed* (*asked*) often are not pronounced in speech and might therefore mistakenly be omitted in writing. Be especially careful not to omit the ending when the verb's infinitive ends in sounds like *s*, *sk*, or *g* and when the ending does not add another syllable. In such sentences as the following, use the verb forms in parentheses.

> When Bobbie *ask* (*asks, asked*) to leave the table, his mother *excuse* (*excuses, excused*) him.

Ramon was *suppose* (*supposed*) to be here at five o'clock.
I *use* (*used*) to read more than I do now.

In some familiar dialects, the *-s* form of some verbs is replaced by other forms.

He *don't* (*doesn't*) want to go home.
Elaine *ain't* (*isn't*) ready to take the test yet.
Don't nobody *have* books. (*Nobody has books.*)

While such forms are appropriate in everyday speech in some communities, they should be avoided in writing, in favor of the forms in parentheses.

7d | Use helping verbs when they are required.

Helping verbs are used with infinitives, present participles, and past participles to indicate time and other kinds of meaning. Some familiar dialects omit them in everyday speech.

Felicia (has) *been* at school all day.
You told your mother you (would) *be* home early tonight.

In written English the helping verbs, shown here in parentheses, are required for completeness.

Identifying the principal parts of irregular verbs

Circle the correct form of the verb from each pair in parentheses. On the blanks to the right, fill in the principal parts (infinitive, past tense, past participle) of the correct verb. If necessary, consult a dictionary or the list of irregular verbs on pages 177–79.

Example: I had to (*lie,* *lay*) down.   *lie*   *lay*   *lain*

1. The cold wind (*blowed, blew*) up the alley. _____ _____ _____

2. Jerry had (*wrote, written*) down the directions. _____ _____ _____

3. The professor (*began, begun*) the class with a joke. _____ _____ _____

4. He had (*ran, run*) the mile in record time. _____ _____ _____

5. That is an album you have not (*heard, heared*). _____ _____ _____

6. She (*drunk, drank*) Gatorade during the game. _____ _____ _____

7. He (*drove, drived*) the golf ball 250 yards. _____ _____ _____

8. She had not (*gave, given*) a minute of her time. _____ _____ _____

9. The problem of boarding the dog had not (*come, came*) up before. _____ _____ _____

10. The book had (*laid, lain*) on the shelf for many years. _____ _____ _____

11. She (*finded, found*) the gift on her pillow. _____ _____ _____

12. The team had (*swum, swam*) an hour that morning. _____ _____ _____

13. They (*knew, knowed*) that the class was easy. _____ _____ _____

14. The cat (*bitten, bit*) him on the wrist. _____ _____ _____

15. They had (*ate, eaten*) before going out.   _____   _____   _____

16. He is (*suppose, supposed*) to arrive Monday.   _____   _____   _____

17. Wilson (*brung, brought*) a guest along.   _____   _____   _____

18. The platter (*broke, breaked*) when it hit the floor.   _____   _____   _____

19. They (*flew, flied*) in from Pittsburgh.   _____   _____   _____

20. The patient had (*went, gone*) to the examination room.   _____ · _____   _____

21. The balloon had (*burst, bursted*) against the power lines.   _____   _____   _____

22. The skunk has (*become, became*) Denny's favorite pet.   _____   _____   _____

23. The attorney (*proved, proven*) his case.   _____   _____   _____

24. No problem with cheating has (*arose, arisen*).   _____   _____   _____

25. Someone has (*sat, set*) on Martha's broken chair.   _____   _____   _____

26. May and Raymond have (*took, taken*) the train.   _____   _____   _____

27. The driver (*swore, sweared*) at the pedestrian.   _____   _____   _____

28. He managed to (*shake, shook*) loose from the dog's grip.   _____   _____   _____

29. We (*seen, saw*) the accident on our way home.   _____   _____   _____

30. The shortstop (*throwed, threw*) him out.   _____   _____   _____

Using the -s forms of verbs	EXERCISE **7-2**

Rewrite the following paragraphs with Beverly in the present. Begin by changing the first sentence to read:

> Beverly learns something about writing today.

Then, as you rewrite, change verbs as necessary to describe the action as if it is happening right now. Be sure to use the *-s* forms, not the *-ing* forms.

Beverly learned something about writing last week. She learned

that writing is a way of thinking, a way of learning. Her teacher told her

that somebody said, "How can I know what I think until I see what I say?"

Beverly discovered that by writing something down she could learn. First

she asked herself how this could be. Then she tried it.

Her teacher asked the class to write about the question of

whether the government should pay for all education, including college.

Beverly had never thought about that subject before, and she wondered

what she would say about it. But she started writing, and pretty soon she

had written several paragraphs in which she stated that students should take the responsibility for their own education and that this would not

happen if somebody else paid for that education.

Suddenly Beverly understood how people could learn through

writing. When she was required to put some thoughts down on paper, she

began thinking about things she had never thought about before. And by

writing down those thoughts, she remembered them longer.

|*Using the* -ed *forms of verbs*

Rewrite the following short essay to read as if the writer is recounting experiences in the past. Your first sentence will read:

> When I was learning to write, my dictionary was always a close companion.

As you rewrite the essay, you will need to change all verbs to the past tense, in many cases using *-ed* forms. Avoid using *would* or *used to* with the verbs.

When I write, my dictionary is a close companion. I refer to it

throughout the writing process for several purposes. Before I start writing,

I often look up the meaning of a key word so that I clearly understand my

subject. At that time I also locate related words and check their meanings.

I probably refer to the dictionary least while I carry out the

actual writing. At that time my writing so absorbs my thoughts that I

overlook spelling and, when I can't think of the right word, I use any word

that comes close in meaning. I place a mark in the margin as a reminder

to myself that I need to find a different word later.

After I affix my last period, I prepare to dig in to my dictionary.

Then I ask myself if each word I use is appropriate for my meaning. If I have any doubt, I look up the word and check its meaning. At that point, I also investigate other words given as synonyms; if they seem better than the ones I have, I use them instead. As I revise, I also check the spellings of words I'm not sure about.

My final use for the dictionary occurs when I am writing the final draft. I need to know how to divide words at the ends of lines. My dictionary has little dots between syllables to tell me where the syllables divide.

Because my dictionary is so useful to me while I write, I keep it handy all the time.

TENSE

Tense is the quality of a verb that shows the time of its action. The **simple tenses** indicate present, past, and future. The **perfect tenses** indicate action that was or will be completed before another action or time.

SIMPLE TENSES	REGULAR VERB	IRREGULAR VERB
Present	I *use*	I *run*
Past	I *used*	I *ran*
Future	I *will use*	I *will run*

PERFECT TENSES		
Present perfect	I *have used*	I *have run*
Past perfect	I *had used*	I *had run*
Future perfect	I *will have used*	I *will have run*

Another form, the **progressive**, sometimes called the **progressive tense**, uses the *-ing* form of the verb and indicates continuing action.

PRESENT PROGRESSIVE	We *are waiting.*
PAST PROGRESSIVE	They *were stalling.*
PRESENT PERFECT PROGRESSIVE	Others *have been fleeing.*

To ask questions, to make negative statements, and to show emphasis, we use *do* (*does*) or *did* as a helping verb with the infinitive.

> *Do* you *know* what you're asking? [Question.]
> I *do*n't *know* what I'm asking. [Negation.]
> I *do know* what I'm asking. [Emphasis.]

7e | Use the appropriate tense to express your meaning.

Even though native speakers of English usually have little trouble using the appropriate tenses of verbs, it is a good practice when editing a piece of writing to read it once, checking only for appropriate tense. Usually only a few special uses present problems.

1 | Observe the special uses of the present tense.

The present tense indicates action occurring in the present. But it can also be used in several other situations.

TO DESCRIBE HABITUAL OR RECURRING ACTION

I *vote* for Democrats.

TO STATE A GENERAL TRUTH

Oak *is* a hardwood.

TO DISCUSS THE CONTENT OF A BOOK, MOVIE, OR OTHER CREATIVE WORK

Michael Corleone *is* the Godfather's favorite son.

We *leave* for Europe next Monday.

2 | Observe the uses of the perfect tenses.

The perfect tenses indicate action completed before another action or time. The present perfect tense also indicates action begun in the past and continued into the present.

PRESENT PERFECT

Hosea *has written* a letter of thanks to his grandmother. [Action is completed at the time of the statement.]

The sun *has shone* every day this week. [Action began in the past and is still continuing.]

PAST PERFECT

The bus *had* already *left* by the time our cab arrived. [Action of the verb *had left* is completed before the action of the verb *arrived*.]

FUTURE PERFECT

If the sun shines again tomorrow, it *will have shone* eight days straight. [The future perfect *will have shone* indicates action that began in the past and will be continuing at a future time.]

7f | Use the appropriate sequence of verb tenses.

The **sequence of tenses** is the relation between the verb in a main clause and the verbs or verbals in a subordinate clause or verbal phrase. Sometimes the correct sequence calls for the same tense, but, as the following sentence indicates, the verbs in the different constructions need not always have identical tenses to be in sequence.

Glenna *will explain* why she *is* so unhappy. [Action of the present verb *will explain* occurs after that of the present verb *is*.]

1 | Generally, the verb in the subordinate clause may be in any tense required by meaning.

The tenses need not be identical as long as they indicate differences in actual or relative time, as the following sentences illustrate.

He *hopes* that his boss *will give* him a raise. [Action of the present verb *hopes* precedes the future action of *will give*.]

I *have sat* through that movie more times than I *care* to admit. [Action of the present perfect verb *have sat* brings past action up to the time of the present verb *care*.]

We *know* that the doctor *meant* well. [Action of the present verb *know* follows that of the past verb *meant*.]

The only requirement in using tenses in the proper sequence is that the tenses be logical. For example, it would be illogical to say *He hoped his boss will give him a raise.*

vb

7

2 | The verb in a subordinate clause must be past or past perfect if the verb in the main clause is past or past perfect.

> She *thought* the dog *had spoken*. [The past perfect verb in the subordinate clause, *had spoken*, indicates action before that of the past main verb, *thought*.]
>
> Judith *had* already *called* when I *arrived*. [The past verb in the subordinate clause, *arrived*, indicates action occurring after that of the past perfect main verb, *had called*.]
>
> After we *posted* announcements, the opening *attracted* a large crowd. [The action of both verbs takes place in the past.]

EXCEPTION: A subordinate clause that expresses a general truth, such as *people are funny*, can be stated in the present tense even though the verb in the main clause is past tense.

> She *said* that people *are* funny. [Past and present.]
>
> She *thought* that dogs *can speak*. [Past and present.]

3 | Observe the appropriate tense sequence with infinitives.

The tense of an infinitive is determined by the tense of the verb in the predicate. The **present infinitive** is the infinitive preceded by *to: to kick, to write*. It shows action occurring at the same time as or later than that of the verb.

> I *prefer to stay* right here. [The action of the present infinitive *to stay* occurs at the same time as that of the present verb *prefer*.]
>
> She *would have liked to join* you. [The action of the present infinitive *to join* occurs at the same time as that of the present perfect verb *would have liked*.]

The **perfect infinitive** combines *to have* with the verb's past participle: *to have kicked, to have written*. It shows action that occurred earlier than that of the verb.

> We now *know* what *to have studied* for the test. [The action of the perfect infinitive *to have studied* occurs before that of the present verb *know*.]
>
> My father *would like to have been* an actor. [The action of the perfect infinitive *to have been* occurs before that of the verb *would like*.]

4 | Observe the appropriate tense sequence with participles.

Like the tense of an infinitive, the tense of a participle is determined by the tense of the verb in the predicate. The present participle shows action occurring at the same time as that of the verb.

> *Walking* into the house, I *greeted* each of my relatives in turn. [Action of the present participle *walking* occurs at the same time as that of the verb *greeted*.]

The past participle and the present perfect participle show action occurring earlier than that of the verb.

Fanned by strong breezes, the fire *swept* through the brush. [Action of the past participle *fanned* occurs earlier than that of the verb *swept*.]

Having seeped through the walls, the water *left* large orange stains in the wallpaper. [Action of the present perfect participle *having seeped* occurs earlier than that of the verb *left*.]

|Writing verb tenses

Underline the verbs in the following sentences. Then rewrite each sentence twice, changing the verb to the tenses indicated in parentheses.

Example: I have repaired refrigerators for twenty years.

(*past*) *I repaired refrigerators for twenty years.*

(*past perfect*) *I had repaired refrigerators for twenty years.*

1. Because of his upbringing, Jack will never be late.

   (*past*)

   (*present perfect*)

2. The computer salesperson will travel frequently to the main office.

   (*present*)

   (*past*)

3. We were expecting a large response to our letter.

   (*present progressive*)

   (*past perfect*)

4. My brother Peter feels inadequate for his job.

   (*past*)

   (*present perfect*)

5. As a result of his shyness and lack of acquaintances, Charlie was getting bored at parties.

   (*present*)

   (*present perfect*)

6. On the recommendation of its officers, the union has finally terminated the agreement.

   (*past*)

   (*future*)

7. With an increasing use of research, the science of linguistics is still developing.

   (*present perfect progressive*)

   (*future*)

8. Ethel has just discovered a wart on her knee.

   (*past*)

   (*past perfect*)

9. The radio next door was playing too loudly for the rest of us in the building.

   (*present progressive*)

   (*present perfect progressive*)

10. The people next door have finally turned off their radio.

    (*past*)

    (*present progressive*)

Using the correct sequence of tenses

EXERCISE **7-5**

vb

7

Rewrite the following paragraphs to read as if Suki has already departed this life. Your first sentence should read:

Suki always knew precisely how to annoy someone.

As you rewrite, change the rest of the verbs so that they are in the appropriate sequence.

Suki always knows precisely how to annoy someone. Suki is a cat, a regal blend of Siamese and Persian, two breeds that guarantee snobbery. This particular cat knows exactly when to come asking for food — just when the other cats have already been fed and the food has been put away. She understands precisely when to want to go into a room — just when the door has been closed. She is uncanny at knowing exactly where to sit — right where you want to dust-mop the floor or, more unerringly annoying, right on the dirt you have already swept together.

Suki has a way of meowing that is meant to be especially irritating. The sound she makes is not a sweet little "mew" or a lusty "meow"

193

or a pitiful "oh-h-h." Her utterance is more of a noisy complaint, a loud

"ow-ow-ow!!" She makes this sound only when she thinks there's no one

in sight. Her other complaint, which comes when someone bumps her off

the pile of dirt she's sitting on or won't open a door for her, is a cat sound

that in human terms comes out something like "Everybody hates me."

Suki obviously thinks she is queen of the house and whatever

she does is her right and privilege.

MOOD

The **mood** of a verb indicates the writer's or speaker's attitude toward what he or she is saying. The **indicative mood** states a fact or opinion or asks a question (*The trees are changing color. What makes the colors change?*). The **imperative mood** expresses a command or direction and omits the understood subject *you* (*Turn left at the light*). The **subjunctive mood** expresses a requirement, a desire, a suggestion, or a condition contrary to fact (*We insisted that she come; if she were present, we could finish the job faster*). Because the indicative and imperative moods are used so commonly, they cause very little problem to writers. The subjunctive, however, is used less commonly in speech and consequently is sometimes troublesome in writing.

7g | Use the subjunctive verb forms appropriately.

The subjunctive mood uses distinctive verb forms. All verbs in the subjunctive use the plain form of the verb for the present tense, regardless of the subject: *They suggested that he step outside. Be* uses *be* (rather than *am, is,* or *are*) for the present tense with all subjects: *The dean requested that we be patient.* The past subjunctive form of *be* is *were* for all subjects: *I wish I were somewhere else.* These subjunctive forms are used in only a few kinds of constructions.

1 | Use the subjunctive form *were* in contrary-to-fact clauses beginning with *if* or expressing a wish.

If you *were* well, you would not have a fever.
I wish my brother *were* happier.

2 | Use the subjunctive in *that* clauses following verbs that demand, request, or recommend.

The rules required that she *start* over.
The counselor suggested that I *be* more self-confident.

3 | Use the subjunctive in some set phrases and idioms.

Far *be* it from me to interfere.
If that's the way you want it, then so *be* it.

VOICE

Verbs can indicate whether their subjects are acting or are acted upon. When the subject is the actor, or doer, of the action, the verb is in the **active voice:** *John opened three presents.* When the subject is the recipient of the action, the verb is in the **passive voice:** *Three presents were opened by John.* A verb in the passive voice consists of the verb's past participle and a form of *be.* Only transitive verbs — verbs that take objects — can form the passive voice.

To change a sentence from active to passive voice, move the

direct object or indirect object to the subject position; if you want to say who performed the action, use a *by* prepositional phrase, making its object the doer of the action. Change an active verb to passive by using the past participle and the form of *be* that is appropriate for the tense of the sentence.

	S **V** **DO**
ACTIVE	A foul ball *struck* a fan.
	S **V** **OP**
PASSIVE	A fan *was struck* by a foul ball.
	S **V** **IO** **DO**
ACTIVE	My dad *will send* me some money.
	S **V** **DO** **OP**
PASSIVE	I *will be sent* some money by my dad.

To change a sentence from passive to active voice, find out who or what is performing the action (either expressed in a *by* phrase or omitted) and make that noun or pronoun the subject of the sentence; the subject from the passive sentence becomes the direct object or indirect object in the active sentence. In changing the verb, omit *be* and change the past participle to the appropriate tense form.

	S **V** **OP**
PASSIVE	The toy *was crushed* by the car.
	S **V** **DO**
ACTIVE	The car *crushed* the toy.
	S **V**
PASSIVE	Fifty blue shirts *have been ordered*.
	S **V** **DO**
ACTIVE	Somebody *has ordered* fifty blue shirts.

7h | Generally, prefer the active voice. Use the passive voice when the actor is unknown or unimportant.

Use the passive voice with caution. It is wordier and less direct than the active voice, and often omits the important information of who or what is performing the action, as illustrated in the following sentences.

WEAK PASSIVE	If budget allocations for this fund are *to be generated* solely by federal income tax, a sixfold increase *would be required*. [The passive infinitive *to be generated* puts the doer of the action in the *by* phrase; the passive verb *would be required* avoids saying that taxes must increase.]
STRONG ACTIVE	If federal income tax alone is *to generate* budget allocations for this fund, taxes *will have to increase* sixfold.

There are times, however, when the passive is appropriate, most commonly when the reader does not need to know who performed the action or when the actor is not known. Here are examples:

The back window *was broken* during the night. [Nobody knows who broke the window.]

The pamphlets *will be printed* in color. [It is not important to know who will print the pamphlets.]

| *Using subjunctive verb forms*   EXERCISE **7-6**

Rewrite the following sentences, changing each italicized verb to a subjunctive form.

Example: If that *was* the case, he would have protested.

> *If that were the case, he would have protested.*

1. If I *was* you, I would pay less rent.

2. The assignment sheet requires that each student *writes* a research paper.

3. If she *was* smart, she would take a mathematics course this term.

4. If the storm *was* to cause a blackout, we would be in trouble.

5. The requirement is that he *pays* before entering.

6. If the tax *was* repealed, the city would go bankrupt.

7. Requesting that we *are* seated, the instructor passed out the tests.

8. His mouth moved as if he *was* speaking.

9. If I *was* certain I could get a job in the space industry, I would major in engineering.

10. If the President *was* elected by popular vote instead of by the electoral college, the country would be more of a democracy.

Using the active
and passive voices

EXERCISE **7-7**

vb

7

Identify each of the following sentences as active or passive by writing an *A* for active or a *P* for passive on the blank to the left. Rewrite each passive sentence into the active voice and each active sentence into the passive. In rewriting sentences that are passive you will sometimes need to supply a subject because the doer of the action is not mentioned; in rewriting active sentences you can decide whether the doer of the action should be mentioned in a *by* phrase.

Example: ___*P*___ The police chief was fired.

The mayor fired the police chief.

___*a*___ The chairperson called the meeting to order.

The meeting was called to order.

_____ 1. The secretary distributed the ballots at the opening session.

_____ 2. The question was not understood by the students.

_____ 3. The shop was closed down a year ago.

_____ 4. Her car was parked in the public lot yesterday.

_____ 5. A heavy rain prevented us from arriving on time.

_____ 6. The costs of continued environmental damage have been ignored by toxic chemical industries.

201

_____ 7. Each student was given a subscription to *Time*.

_____ 8. The package has been mailed.

_____ 9. The posting of grades has been delayed for two more days.

_____ 10. The suspect has been identified by two witnesses.

_____ 11. We were never introduced.

_____ 12. The sparrow snatched a crumb from the sidewalk.

_____ 13. A fleet of cars was owned by the corporation.

_____ 14. A week later the room had been rented.

_____ 15. The building was razed on schedule.

Verb forms, tense, and mood: Review

In the following paragraph cross out any errors in verb forms, tense, or mood. Then write the correct verb above the error.

Nothing went right in my attempt to have a job interview last week. The interviewer had written me a letter requesting that I was on time; he also give me directions on how to get to his company. But I lost the directions, so when I was near the city, I begun looking for a service station where I could ask the way. Suddenly I heard a grinding noise coming from the right wheel. Since I knew something was broke or was about to break, I pull off the road. I knew I should of had the car inspected before the trip, but I had chose to put off the inspection so I will have money for the trip to the city. A police officer called a tow truck for me. Fortunately, I had brung along a credit card and so could pay for the repair. When I was ready to leave, I ask the mechanic for directions. I

found the company easily, but I was three hours late. The interviewer had

vb

7

went home, so I had drove all that way for nothing.

8 | *Agreement*

Self-test

Underline the correct choice in each of the following sentences.

Example: We (*was*, *were*) pleased by the election.

1. Neither Jeff nor Paula (*is*, *are*) willing to work hard.
2. Someone abandoned (*his*, *their*) cat on my doorstep.
3. The herd moved to (*their*, *its*) winter feeding area.
4. If anyone has (*his*, *their*) umbrella here, lend it to me.
5. Two parrots and a cat (*is*, *are*) my pets.
6. No one should leave (*his*, *their*) valuables in the locker.
7. Either the Smiths or John (*is*, *are*) responsible.
8. Three apples in a basket (*was*, *were*) set on the table.
9. She (*ask*, *asks*) that we join her.
10. Physics (*was*, *were*) the field she chose.

      Agreement is something we have come to expect of our language: our verbs agree with their subjects and our pronouns agree with the nouns or pronouns they refer to. Most of the time we have little trouble making these elements of our sentences agree. This chapter discusses the few ways in which sentences sometimes lack agreement.

8a | Make subjects and verbs agree in number.

      Subjects and verbs can be singular or plural depending on whether they are referring to one of something or more than one. The subject always determines the number of the verb, and the number of the subject is decided by what the writer wants to say.

1 | **Use the verb ending -*s* or -*es* with all third-person singular subjects. Use the noun ending -*s* or -*es* to make most nouns plural.**

      Adding -*s* or -*es* to a noun usually makes the noun **plural.** An -*s* or -*es* on a present-tense verb makes the verb **singular.**

SINGULAR	PLURAL
A tree grows.	Trees grow.
A car runs.	Cars run.
The house is green.	The houses are green.

The -s or -es ending often is not distinctly pronounced in speech and thus is wrongly omitted in writing:

> Elroy often asks the teacher for advice. [Singular verb.]
>
> The monkey passes his hat when the organ grinder finishes. [Two singular verbs.]
>
> The tests were more difficult than I thought they would be. [Plural noun.]

2 | Subject and verb should agree even when other words come between them.

When subjects and verbs come next to each other in a sentence, they usually agree because they sound right to us. But often modifiers come between subjects and verbs and throw off our sense of the sound of grammar. These modifiers, in fact, have no influence on the number of the verb.

> The problem with all of Riley's poems *is* that they are sentimental. [*Problem* is the subject, not *poems*.]
>
> The goals of this construction work *are* not clear. [*Goals* is the subject, not *work*.]

Sometimes we use expressions like *as well as, together with, along with*, and *in addition to* between the subject and verb, treating the object of the preposition as part of a compound subject. But even though it adds, in meaning, a second performer of the action, it is not a second subject and has no influence on the number of the verb.

> Mrs. Rapjohn, as well as the Zimmers, *goes* to Damascus often. [*Mrs. Rapjohn* is the subject of the sentence; *Zimmers* is the object of the preposition *as well as*.]

To avoid the awkwardness of such a sentence, a good writer would probably use the conjunction *and: Mrs. Rapjohn and the Zimmers go to Damascus often.*

3 | Subjects joined by *and* usually take plural verbs.

Even when one or more parts of a compound subject are singular, the entire subject takes a plural verb. The *and* that joins two subjects in effect adds things together, resulting in more than one — that is, plural.

> Howard and Emma *like* to go deer hunting together.
>
> The Zimmers and Mrs. Rapjohn *go* to Damascus often.

Occasionally a compound subject refers to a single person or thing or is preceded by *each* or *every*. Then the verb is singular.

> The wife and mother *was* proud of her work. [*Wife and mother* refers to one person.]
>
> Every log and stick *was* burned. [*Every* is grammatically singular.]

4 | **When parts of a subject are joined by *or* or *nor,* the verb agrees with the nearer part.**

Unlike compound subjects joined by *and,* compounds joined by *or* or *nor* are not added together. In effect, when all parts of a subject joined by *or* or *nor* are singular, the verb is singular. When all parts are plural, the verb is plural.

> Jones or Albertson *is* to be arrested on Monday.
> Neither the horses nor the cows *have* been sold.

The practice of this rule is most troublesome when one part of the subject is singular and the other plural. However, the rule is still the same: the verb agrees with the part closer to it.

> Either the roadbed or the curbs *are* scheduled for repair next week.
> Either the curbs or the roadbed *is* scheduled for repair next week.

5 | **Generally, use singular verbs with indefinite pronouns.**

Indefinite pronouns function very much like nouns except that they do not refer to specific persons or things. The common indefinite pronouns include *all, any, anybody, anyone, anything, each, either, everybody, everyone, everything, neither, nobody, none, no one, one, some, somebody, someone,* and *something.* Most take singular verbs.

Indefinite pronouns are similar to nouns in several ways. First, instead of having antecedents like other pronouns (for example, *she* or *this*), they function on their own to refer to persons or things in general. Another similarity is that, like mass nouns, they do not form plurals and are generally considered singular, taking singular verbs. (See 8b-3 for indefinites as antecedents of other pronouns.)

> No one *knows* the real danger.
> Everyone *has* caught the flu.

Many of these indefinites can function also as adjectives: *some news, any person, each one, either way, neither paper, one fence, every street.* The same agreement rules apply; that is, the nouns they modify usually take singular verbs.

A few of the indefinites — *all, any, none,* and *some* — may be either singular or plural depending on the noun or pronoun they refer to. If they refer to a plural noun (see 5a-2), they are plural; if they refer to a singular noun, they are singular.

> All of the gas *is* held in tanks. [*All* refers to the singular *gas.*]
> All of the people *are* eager to have some news. [*All* refers to the plural *people.*]

6 | **Collective nouns take singular or plural verbs depending on meaning.**

Collective nouns such as *committee, family,* and *team* have singular form but name groups of individuals or things. Collective nouns take singular verbs when the group is considered as a unit and plural verbs when the group's members are considered individually.

> The committee *has* the power to decide.
> The committee *have* argued over every decision.

As a practical matter, we very seldom use collective nouns in their plural sense because they sound awkward when used that way. Instead we phrase our sentences differently: *The members of the committee have argued over every decision.*

agr

8

The collective noun *number* takes a singular verb when preceded by *the* and a plural verb when preceded by *a*.

> The number of highway deaths *has* decreased.
> A number of officials *attribute* the decrease to the new speed limit.

7 | The verb agrees with the subject even when the normal word order is inverted.

> There *are* many reasons for voting in school elections. [The subject is *reasons*, not *There*.]
> Has the cause of Alzheimer's Disease been discovered yet? [The subject is *cause*.]
> On the floors *was* a clutter of toys. [The subject is *clutter*.]

8 | A linking verb agrees with its subject, not the subject complement.

Subject complements are sometimes different in number from the subjects they rename. When this occurs, we may be inclined to make our verb agree with the complement. But the rule is still that the verb *must* agree with its subject.

> The chef's selection *is* pork chops. [The verb agrees with *selection*, the subject of the sentence.]
> Pork chops *are* the chef's selection. [The verb agrees with *chops*, the subject of the sentence.]

9 | When used as subjects, *who, which,* and *that* take verbs that agree with their antecedents.

When a **relative pronoun** — *who, which,* or *that* — serves as a subject, the verb should agree with the noun or pronoun the relative pronoun refers to (its antecedent).

> The paintings that *were* on display have been sold. [*That* refers to *paintings*, a plural noun.]
> The painting that *was* on display has been sold. [*That* refers to *painting*, a singular noun.]
> Mary is the only one of the actors who *knows* her lines. [*Who* refers to *one*, a singular indefinite pronoun.]
> Mary is one of the actors who *want* to strike. [*Who* refers to *actors*, a plural noun.]

10 | **Nouns with plural form but singular meaning take singular verbs.**

Some nouns ending in -s, such as *news, athletics,* and *physics,* are generally regarded as singular in meaning and thus take singular verbs. Measurements and figures ending in -s may also be singular when the quantity they refer to is a unit.

> Economics *is* not being offered this spring.
> Politics *takes* patience and compromise.
> Two quarts *is* the capacity of each jar.

11 | **Titles and words named as words take singular verbs.**

Even though words in a title may be plural, the title is a single thing, and it takes a singular verb. The same is true when words are referred to as words.

> "Swans" *is* going to win the literature prize.
> *Ladies is* spelled wrong in your essay.

|*Subjects and verbs*

EXERCISE **8-1**

agr

8

Underline the subject of each sentence or clause below and locate the corresponding verb. If the verb does not agree with the subject, cross out the verb and write the correct form on the blank to the left. If the sentence is correct as given, write *OK* on the blank to the left.

Example: __*are*__ There ⨯ three <u>problems</u> to work out before we can proceed.

_____ 1. The difference between twins are often surprising.

_____ 2. Both the drinks and the dessert was left off the bill.

_____ 3. Each of the puzzles require thirty minutes to solve.

_____ 4. Neither of us enjoy the outdoors.

_____ 5. There is only three original songs in the band's repertoire.

_____ 6. The price of every one of the houses in our neighborhood is beyond reach.

_____ 7. The cabinet for the stereo components are made of oiled oak.

_____ 8. The subject I want to write about are the effects of acid rain on the environment.

_____ 9. Delaware's two senators and one representative is its only representation in Congress.

_____ 10. Among the crowd was three pickpockets.

_____ 11. Neither the ring nor the watch were stolen.

_____ 12. There are a little group of houses at the curve in the road.

_____ 13. The pieces of the grandfather clock was spread over the floor.

_____ 14. Three kinds of film is sold at the shop.

_____ 15. When are the committee members to meet?

_____ 16. If the audience fail to applaud, the play will close.

_____ 17. Either the motorcycle or the car is to remain uninsured.

_____ 18. The first thing that I saw at the festival were the cheerful faces of the crowd.

_____ 19. One of the students who rides to school with me falls asleep each morning in class.

_____ 20. Neither the books nor the record are his.

_____ 21. The number of students who favor the new dean are not large.

_____ 22. Some of the statistics released by the state shows that New Browntown has a high rate of murder.

_____ 23. He is one of the many students who plays basketball well.

_____ 24. The style of clothes that my roommates wear are now very popular.

_____ 25. The similarity in their clothes is just one of those things that make my roommates seem like one person.

_____ 26. All of our exported wheat is not enough for all of the people who is starving.

_____ 27. The top two teams in each division gets to go to the play-offs.

_____ 28. The family eat together every evening.

_____ 29. Neither the sofa nor the chairs needs recovering.

_____ 30. Only one of the houses that were sold has a garage.

Rewriting subjects and verbs   EXERCISE **8-2**

Rewrite each of the following sentences, changing the italicized words in the first group from singular to plural and those in the second group from plural to singular. Make all other changes that are necessary. Check your work by reading your rewritten sentences aloud.

Example: A good *grade* was her only goal.

Good grades were her only goal.

Singular to Plural

 1. A *star* is a giant *ball* of glowing gas.

 2. A *star* shines both day and night, even though *it* is visible only at night.

 3. A *meteor* looks like a falling *star* but is really a *piece* of rock or metal.

 4. A *double star* consists of a *pair* of stars.

 5. A *quasar* sends out strong radio waves.

 6. The *life* of a *star* is billions of years.

 7. An *astronomer* gets information about the *life* of a *star* by studying star clusters.

 8. After a *star* begins to shine, *it* starts to change slowly.

 9. The *speed* of this process depends on the mass of the *star*.

10. A *phonometer* measures the brightness of a *star*.

Plural to Singular

11. *Sounds* are caused by vibrations traveling through the air.

12. Sound *vibrations* travel in waves.

13. *Animals* hear sounds that *humans* do not hear.

14. *Pitches* affect the loudness of a sound.

15. *Echoes* are produced by sound waves striking reflecting *surfaces.*

16. *Bats* make high-pitched *sounds* as *they* fly in the dark.

17. *Microphones* change sound waves into an electric current.

18. Human *ears* hear sounds with frequencies ranging from 20 to 20,000 vibrations a second.

19. The highest *tones* on a piano have a frequency of about 4,000 vibrations a second.

20. *Sounds* travel faster through dense *substances* than through less dense *ones.*

8b | Make pronouns and their antecedents agree in person and number.

The **antecedent** of a pronoun is the noun or other pronoun it refers to. Pronouns and their antecedents agree in person — first (*I, we*), second (*you*), or third (*he, she, it, they*). They also agree in number — singular or plural.

1 | Antecedents joined by *and* usually take plural pronouns.

Two or more antecedents joined by *and* take a plural pronoun even when each individual antecedent is singular.

> Ann and Grace sold *their* textbooks.

Occasionally, a compound antecedent refers to a single person or thing or is preceded by *each* or *every*. Then the pronoun is singular.

> The chief cook and bottlewasher wanted *his* name on the menu.
> Every boy and man sang *his* loudest.

2 | When parts of an antecedent are joined by *or* or *nor*, the pronoun agrees with the nearer part.

In practice, when all parts of an antecedent joined by *or* or *nor* are singular, the pronoun is singular; when all parts are plural the pronoun is plural.

> Either Anne or Jane left *her* umbrella behind.
> Scientists do not know how either walruses or sea cows get *their* food.

The practice of this rule is most troublesome when the antecedents are not the same number. The pronoun agrees with the part of the antecedent that is closest to it.

> Neither the Smiths nor Ms. Hogan weakened in *her* determination.

The awkwardness of this sentence can be avoided by rephrasing.

> Neither Ms. Hogan nor the Smiths weakened in *their* determination.

3 | Generally, use a singular pronoun when the antecedent is an indefinite pronoun.

Unlike other pronouns, **indefinite pronouns** do not have antecedents; instead, they function on their own, like nouns, to refer to persons or things in general. And like nouns, indefinite pronouns can be antecedents for other pronouns. Like mass nouns, they do not have plural forms. Since the indefinites are usually singular, the pronouns referring to them are singular too.

> Neither of those two Boy Scouts paid *his* dues. [*Neither* is the antecedent.]
> Each of the women succeeded in *her* chosen career. [*Each* is the antecedent.]

Traditionally, the pronoun *he* has been used to refer to an indefinite pronoun even when the female gender is also intended. More and more writers, seeing the traditional usage as excluding females unfairly, are rewriting their sentences to avoid overreliance on *he*.

> Everyone took *his* seat.
> Everyone took *his or her* seat.
> All the students took *their* seats.

4 | **Collective noun antecedents take singular or plural pronouns depending on meaning.**

Collective nouns like *team* or *committee* are singular or plural depending on whether they refer to the group as a whole or to the individuals making up the group. Pronouns correspond to the intended meaning.

> The herd of wildebeests is too cramped in *its* small pasture.
> The couple divided *their* belongings evenly.

Pronouns and antecedents

Underline each personal pronoun in the following sentences and draw an arrow to its antecedent. If the pronoun does not agree with its antecedent, cross out the pronoun and write the correct form on the blank to the left. If the sentence is correct as given, write *OK* on the blank.

Example: ___*his*___ Neither Tom nor Bud enjoyed their vacation.

_____ 1. No one can know if they will get a job in June.

_____ 2. The growing complexity of economics has not lessened their appeal to students.

_____ 3. The teachers' union lost their right to bargain.

_____ 4. Anyone who turned in a late paper had their grade reduced.

_____ 5. The audience voiced its approval loudly.

_____ 6. The herd of sheep wandered in all directions from its pasture.

_____ 7. An elephant never eats a leaf or bark that has fungus growing on them.

_____ 8. Bettors tend to follow his or her own whims at the racetrack.

_____ 9. Every dog on the block barked themselves hoarse that night.

_____ 10. The College of Arts and Sciences changed their entrance requirements.

_____ 11. Neither of the two cars is known for their fuel economy.

_____ 12. The police could not anticipate the danger they would encounter.

_____ 13. The manager or the employees will get their raises, but not both.

_____ 14. The company planned to clear out the forests until a petition stopped them.

_____ 15. Ed told each of his coworkers to keep their sense of humor.

_____ 16. Someone had left his shoes in my locker.

_____ 17. The young boy and older man who shoplifted received stiff sentences for his act of shoplifting.

_____ 18. If a person has no pride in their appearance, others can always tell.

_____ 19. None of the engineers bidding on the contract thought his bid would be too high.

_____ 20. Families should install at least one smoke alarm in their homes.

| *Agreement: Review* | EXERCISE **8-4** |

Rewrite the following passage, changing each occurrence of *person* to *people*. Change corresponding verbs and pronouns, together with other related words as necessary. Underline all changes as you make them.

Example: (sentence 2)

> *One side says that terminally ill people should be allowed to die without having their lives extended with special treatments and equipment.*

An argument new to our modern age is that of the right to die. One side says that a terminally ill person should be allowed to die without having his or her life extended with special treatments and equipment. The other side says that a dying person should be kept alive by his or her doctor for as long as possible. In earlier days, before the advent of modern technology, a terminally ill person simply died in his or her bed. Now that life can be extended for weeks and months in a period of protracted dying, we have the problem of how much a person should have to say about his or her own death.

In many states, it is legal for a person who believes strongly in his or her right to die to draw up a "living will." With this document, a person can direct physicians not to extend his or her life by artificial means — that is, not to use any treatment whose sole purpose is to put off an inevitable death. A person draws up this living will while he or she is still in good health and of sound mind. And in the states where these documents are legal, physicians will abide by them.

There is still some opposition to such a practice, however. A person should be kept alive, so goes the argument, to leave the way open for a miraculous recovery or a new treatment or cure. The next step after allowing a person to die is to take that person's life in order to shorten his or her pain and suffering. Called *euthanasia* or *mercy killing*, this practice is less widely accepted than that of writing living wills, although there are many who say that a terminally ill, suffering person should be assisted in his or her death.

The problem is a difficult one that has no easy solution.

9 | Adjectives and Adverbs

Self-test

Circle the correct choice in each of the following sentences.

Example: The minister preached (*serious*, (*seriously*)).

1. The (*more, most*) successful of the three brothers is Dave.
2. We fought a (*real, really*) hard battle.
3. She felt (*bad, badly*) for a day after she fell.
4. The ice cream tasted (*good, well*) on a hot day.
5. I felt (*worse, worser*) than he did.
6. The person with the friendly smile is the (*nicest, nicer*) of the two.
7. We drove (*slow, slowly*) past the house.
8. Her ability came (*natural, naturally*).
9. The (*baddest, worst*) act won an award.
10. He set the vase (*careful, carefully*) on the table.

Adjectives and adverbs are modifiers that describe, limit, or restrict the words they relate to. An **adjective** modifies a noun or a pronoun. An **adverb** modifies a verb, an adjective, another adverb, or a group of words. (See 5b-1.)

9a | Don't use adjectives to modify verbs, adverbs, or other adjectives.

NOT	She speaks Spanish *good.*
BUT	She speaks Spanish *well.*
NOT	We played a *real* good game.
BUT	We played a *really* good game.
NOT	They watched the children *close.*
BUT	They watched the children *closely.*

221

9b | Use an adjective after a linking verb to modify the subject. Use an adverb to modify a verb.

A **linking verb** connects a subject and its noun or adjective complement. The linking verbs include *be, seem, become, appear, remain,* and verbs associated with the senses such as *look, sound, smell, feel,* and *taste.* When a linking verb connects a subject and a modifier, the modifier is an adjective, not an adverb. However, since some of these verbs may also function as nonlinking verbs, they are sometimes modified by adverbs. The only sure way to tell whether you need an adjective or an adverb is to look at how the individual word functions in its sentence.

He felt *tired.* [Adjective modifying *He.*]
He felt *tiredly* for her hand. [Adverb modifying *felt.*]

Chris appeared *calm.* [Adjective modifying *Chris.*]
Chris appeared *suddenly.* [Adverb modifying *appeared.*]

He felt *bad.* [Adjective modifying *He,* meaning "sorry" or "ill."]
The orchestra performed *badly.* [Adverb modifying *performed.*]

9c | After a direct object, use an adjective to modify the object and an adverb to modify the verb.

The only sure way to tell whether you need an adjective (object complement) or an adverb following a direct object is to look at how the individual word functions in its sentence.

The mayor considered the proposal *appropriate.* [Adjective; the proposal was appropriate.]
The mayor considered the proposal *appropriately.* [Adverb; the considering was done in an appropriate way.]

9d | When an adverb has a short form and an *-ly* form, distinguish carefully between the forms.

Some adverbs have both an *-ly* form and a short form without the *-ly;* these include *high, highly; late, lately; loud, loudly; near, nearly; quick, quickly; sharp, sharply; slow, slowly; wrong, wrongly.* Sometimes the meanings of the two forms are different, but with others the meanings are similar. When there is little difference in meaning, the short form is more often used informally and the *-ly* word is used for writing that is more formal.

DIFFERENCE IN MEANING

The ambulance arrived too *late.* [*Late* modifies *arrived.*]
He has been missing class *lately.* [*Lately* modifies *has been missing.*]

SIMILARITY IN MEANING

Drive *slow* around the corner. [Or *slowly; slow* is informal, modifying *Drive.*]
Slowly the clouds passed across the moon. [Appropriate usage; *Slowly* modifies *passed.*]

9e | Use the comparative and superlative forms of adjectives and adverbs appropriately.

Most adjectives and adverbs have three forms. The **positive form** describes without comparing (*small, quickly*). The **comparative form** is used to indicate a difference or similarity between two items (*smaller, more quickly*). The **superlative form** is used to indicate a difference or similarity among three or more items (*smallest, most quickly*). (Downward comparisons are formed with *less* and *least: quickly, less quickly, least quickly.*)

1 | When word length or sound requires, use *more* and *most* instead of the endings *-er* and *-est.*

Most adverbs longer than a syllable form the comparative and superlative with the words *more* and *most* instead of the endings *-er* and *-est* (*happily, more happily; nearly, more nearly*). Adjective usage is a little different: most one-syllable and many two-syllable adjectives can use either the *-er* and *-est* endings or the words *more* and *most* (*stealthy; stealthier* or *more stealthy; stealthiest* or *most stealthy*). Adjectives longer than two syllables use only *more* and *most.*

2 | Use the correct form of irregular adjectives and adverbs.

Irregular adjectives and adverbs change the spelling of their positive form to show comparative and superlative. Many of the following irregular forms can be used as both adjectives and adverbs.

POSITIVE	COMPARATIVE	SUPERLATIVE
good/well	better	best
bad/badly	worse	worst
little	littler, less	littlest, least
many, some, much	more	most

3 | Don't use double comparatives or double superlatives.

Don't use the *-er* and *-est* endings in conjunction with the words *more* and *most.*

This is the *sharpest* (not *most sharpest*) knife I have.

4 | In general, use the comparative form for comparing two things and the superlative form for comparing three or more things.

This is the *longer* of the two plays.
The *longest* play we ever performed was *shorter* than this one.

5 | In general, don't use comparative or superlative forms for modifiers that cannot logically be compared.

Absolute modifiers like *unique, dead, perfect,* and *impossible* cannot logically be compared because their positive forms describe their only state.

| NOT | That was the *most impossible* trick I ever tried. |
| BUT | That trick was *almost impossible*. |

9f | Avoid overuse of nouns as modifiers.

Overuse of nouns as modifiers can cause writing to be wordy or confusing.

| NOT | The device is a wind speed measurement instrument. |
| BUT | The device measures wind speed. |

Using adjectives and adverbs I

EXERCISE **9-1**

ad

9

In each sentence below, circle the appropriate form of the modifier from the pairs in parentheses, underline the word or words it modifies, and identify the modifier as an adjective (*adj.*) or adverb (*adv.*) by writing the appropriate abbreviation on the blank to the left.

Example: ___*adj.*___ <u>Louisa</u> felt ((*bad*) *badly*) after eating the soup.

_____ 1. The radio played (*loud, loudly*).

_____ 2. The dessert tasted too (*sweetly, sweet*).

_____ 3. Oliver executed the pass play (*perfect, perfectly*).

_____ 4. She arrived too (*late, lately*) to see the show.

_____ 5. The jade ring is (*more expensive, expensiver*) than the opal ring.

_____ 6. The pool in the city park looks (*deeply, deep*).

_____ 7. The magnetic lock is the (*safer, safest*) of the three.

_____ 8. A (*special, specially*) designed mirror enabled him to drive.

_____ 9. The letter carrier pounded the door (*hard, hardly*).

_____ 10. Of the two, the second son is the (*smarter, smartest*).

_____ 11. My foot hurt so (*bad, badly*) that I could not walk.

_____ 12. Anne feels (*differently, different*) about Violet than she used to.

_____ 13. We played (*well, good*), but we didn't win.

_____ 14. Harry always takes arguments (*serious, seriously*).

_____ 15. Alex looked (*cautious, cautiously*) out the door.

_____ 16. Someone had treated the poor animal (*cruelly, cruel*).

_____ 17. The (*littlest, littler*) of the two boxes was damaged.

_____ 18. San Francisco's transportation system remains (*unique, uniquely*).

_____ 19. He stayed home because he felt (*bad, badly*).

_____ 20. Molly is a dog bred (*specific, specifically*) for obedience.

_____ 21. A (*normal, normally*) developed bicep is sufficient for this exercise.

_____ 22. The (*baddest, worst*) commercial got the most attention.

_____ 23. The milk tasted (*sour, sourly*).

_____ 24. Alice seems (*weak, weakly*) after her operation.

_____ 25. Mark was the (*better, best*) of the two guards.

_____ 26. The strength of a goat is (*considerable, considerably*).

_____ 27. A person should always drive (*safe, safely*).

_____ 28. Of all the snakes, Sinbad has the (*prettier, prettiest*) skin.

_____ 29. David cares for his brother (*happily, happy*).

_____ 30. That movie was the (*worse, worst*) one I have ever seen.

*Using adjectives
and adverbs II*   EXERCISE   **9-2**

In each sentence below, identify any incorrect form of a modifier by cross-ing it out and inserting the correct form on the blank to the left. If the adjectives and adverbs are correct as given, write *OK* on the blank.

Example: __worst__ July is the w~~o~~rse time to visit the Southwestern deserts.

_____   1. They never complained of being real lonely.

_____   2. The valley looked forbiddingly when winter came.

_____   3. She always comes dressed odd.

_____   4. Why should you feel angrily about something you cannot
                   control?

_____   5. We tourists located the hotel easy.

_____   6. The difference between male and female gorillas is clear
                   to anyone.

_____   7. Nancy has the more sharply defined features of all the
                   Mendoza girls.

_____   8. A more neater room you will never see.

_____   9. Greg is surely going to lose his job.

_____   10. Hot grits smell well in the morning.

_____   11. The Edsel was the most unique car of the 1950s.

_____   12. My father is the more open of my parents.

_____   13. Playing bad for one game was no reason to give up.

_____   14. The old man had a friendly look.

_____   15. The car turned the corner so slow that I hit it.

_____ 16. Keith was one of the most brightest students to graduate from this school.

_____ 17. She always greets me cheerfully.

_____ 18. The bus driver applied the brakes quick to avoid hitting the bicyclist.

_____ 19. Don't speak blunt to the dean.

_____ 20. Beating the Hartford tennis team is near impossible.

_____ 21. Of the two, Reggie has the highest average.

_____ 22. I could not find a scarier movie.

_____ 23. Max has the better grades in the class.

_____ 24. How sudden did he stop?

_____ 25. The customer smiled polite at the clerk.

III | Clear Sentences

10 | *Sentence Fragments*

Self-test

Circle the number of each incomplete sentence in the following paragraph.

¹Police shows usually start out rather predictably with the commission of a crime. ²Normally murder or robbery. ³Murder, the most common beginning, is usually premeditated and usually carefully planned; careful planning of a crime makes its solving at least somewhat complicated. ⁴Because the police have to look very carefully for clues. ⁵What can make a show dull, though, is lack of character development of the victim. ⁶Not to mention of the murderer. ⁷If the murder victim's character is not developed, then I do not care very much about the death. ⁸Only about how the crime is solved. ⁹Oddly, robberies are often more interesting than murders. ¹⁰There being no attempt, usually, to achieve anything in murder shows other than to attract the viewer by showing outrageous violence.

A **complete sentence** consists of both a subject and a predicate, a verb that asserts something about the subject. (See 5a.) A phrase or clause that lacks a subject or a predicate or both but is set off like a sentence (with a capital letter and a period) is a **sentence fragment.** A clause that begins with a subordinating word and is set off like a complete sentence is also a sentence fragment. These incomplete structures are generally avoided by careful writers because in most cases they represent incomplete thoughts. They are distracting to readers and often give the impression that the writer is not in control of his or her sentences.

FRAGMENT   For example, when I play the piano.

FRAGMENT   Especially in the rain.

FRAGMENT   Which is what I meant to say in the first place.

10a | Test your sentences for completeness, and revise any fragments.

The best test of sentence completeness is to rely on your own sense of grammar. To do this you must treat the word group between

229

periods as a separate entity, something that makes a complete statement on its own. Read the following group of words, and determine whether they are a sentence fragment.

> Because Carla had already registered for the class.

You probably had no trouble identifying this subordinate clause as a fragment, but that's because you read it as a separate entity. If you can manage to do the same with your own writing, you will probably be able to identify and revise any fragments. To offset the inclination of your mind to connect a fragment to the preceding sentence, you might do as some other writers do — read your essays or paragraphs backward during revision. Doing so will keep you from breezing along, reading for meaning rather than for errors. (*Note:* In looking for fragments, don't be distracted by pronouns; a sentence is not incomplete just because it has a pronoun without an antecedent. The following word group is a complete sentence: *He ran five miles before the sun came up.* But see Chapter 12 for pronoun reference.)

frag

10

While you're trying to develop your sense of sentence completeness, here are some tests you can apply to your sentences.

Test 1: Find a verb.

Look for a verb in the group of words. If there is none, the word group is a fragment.

> FRAGMENT   Five blocks down this street and to the right. [This word group has no verb. Compare: *The theater is five blocks down this street and to the right.*]

See Chapter 7 for a discussion of verb forms.

Test 2: Find a subject.

If you find a verb in your group of words, look for a subject by asking who or what is performing the action of the verb: Who or what *does?* Who or what *is?* If you do not have a subject and if the word group is not a command, you have a fragment.

> FRAGMENT   And consequently went six blocks in the wrong direction. [The group of words has a verb, *went*, but it does not state who performed the action.]

Test 3: Look for a subordinating word.

If you find a verb and a subject, look for a subordinating word at the beginning of the word group. These are words like *because, after, when, if, which,* and *where.* (See p. 137 for a list of subordinating conjunctions and relative pronouns.)

> FRAGMENT   Which is why the hostages weren't released sooner. [The relative pronoun *which* subordinates the entire clause.]

FRAGMENT   When twenty-four people were captured by the rebels. [The subordinating conjunction *when* makes the clause a fragment even though it is punctuated as a sentence.]

Revising sentence fragments

You can revise a sentence fragment in one of two ways: (1) by attaching it to a sentence, usually the one that goes before it, or (2) by adding whatever is necessary to make it a sentence. These two methods are illustrated below.

FRAGMENT   Music videos began to make their appearance in late 1980. *Some of them concert performances and some technological innovations.*

REVISED   Music videos began to make their appearance in late 1980, *some of them concert performances and some technological innovations.* [Fragment attached to the sentence, separated by a comma.]

REVISED   Music videos began to make their appearance in late 1980. Some of them were concert performances and some were technological innovations. [A verb, *were*, is added to the fragment, making it a sentence.]

FRAGMENT   Some people think the best time to have champagne is in the morning. *Or just before a meal.*

REVISED   Some people think the best time to have champagne is in the morning *or just before a meal.* [Fragment attached to the sentence with no separating punctuation.]

REVISED   Some people think the best time to have champagne is in the morning. *Some prefer it just before a meal.* [Fragment expanded to a sentence with the addition of a subject and a verb.]

FRAGMENT   Videocassette recorders are sold in a variety of stores. *Video specialty shops, supermarkets, hardware stores, and other mass-market outlets.*

REVISED   Videocassette recorders are sold in a variety of stores: *video specialty shops, supermarkets, hardware stores, and other mass-market outlets.* [Fragment attached to the sentence, separated by a colon.]

REVISED   Videocassette recorders are sold in a variety of stores — *video specialty shops, supermarkets, hardware stores, and other mass-market outlets.* [Fragment attached to the sentence, separated by a dash. The dash is less formal than the colon.]

REVISED   Videocassette recorders are sold in a variety of stores. *You might find them in video specialty shops, supermarkets, hardware stores, and other mass-market outlets.* [Fragment expanded to a sentence with a subject and a verb.]

10b | Don't set off a subordinate clause as a sentence.

A **subordinate clause** has both a subject and a predicate and begins with a subordinating conjunction (such as *after, although, because, since*) or a relative pronoun (*who, which, that*). (See 5c-4.) When set off from the main clause on which it depends for its meaning, a subordinate clause is a sentence fragment.

FRAGMENT	The return on the investment was 20 percent. *Which was higher than he expected.*
REVISED	The return on the investment was 20 percent, which was higher than he expected. [Subordinate clause linked to main clause.]
REVISED	The return on the investment was 20 percent. The earnings were higher than he expected. [Subordinate clause rewritten as main clause.]

10c | Don't set off a verbal phrase as a sentence.

A **verbal phrase** consists of an infinitive (*to spend*), a participle (*spending, spent*), or a gerund (*spending*), along with its objects or modifiers. (See 5c-2.)

FRAGMENT	I went to the convocation for one reason. *To hear the architect speak.*
REVISED	I went to the convocation for one reason, to hear the architect speak. [Verbal phrase linked to main clause.]
REVISED	I went to the convocation for one reason. I wanted to hear the architect speak. [Verbal phrase rewritten as main clause.]
FRAGMENT	He has one purpose in life. *Spending money.*
REVISED	He has one purpose in life: spending money. [Verbal phrase linked to main clause.]
REVISED	He has one purpose in life. He wants only to spend money. [Verbal phrase rewritten as main clause.]
FRAGMENT	The trip cost $400. *Money well spent.*
REVISED	The trip cost $400, which was money well spent. [Verbal phrase linked to main clause.]
REVISED	The trip cost $400. The money was well spent. [Verbal phrase rewritten as main clause.]

10d | Don't set off a prepositional phrase as a sentence.

A **prepositional phrase** consists of a preposition (such as *by, on, to, with*) plus its object and the object's modifiers (see 5c-1). Since it has neither a subject nor a predicate, a prepositional phrase set off as a sentence is a sentence fragment.

frag

10

FRAGMENT	The accident occurred at the main intersection. *During the evening rush hour.*
REVISED	The accident occurred at the main intersection during the evening rush hour. [Prepositional phrase linked to main clause.]

10e | Don't set off any other word group as a sentence if it lacks a subject or a verb or both.

Fragments are created when a writer punctuates a noun plus its modifiers, an appositive, or the second part of a compound predicate as a sentence.

Nouns plus their modifiers are sometimes so long that they seem like sentences, but without verbs they cannot stand alone as sentences.

FRAGMENT	The flash flood warning that came on the television screen during the Dallas–Green Bay football game. It caused quite a stir in the family.
REVISED	The flash flood warning that came on the television screen during the Dallas–Green Bay football game caused quite a stir in the family. [Fragment replaces *It* as the subject of the main clause.]

Appositives are nouns, plus any modifiers, that rename other nouns (see 5c-5).

FRAGMENT	The car was a gift from her eccentric uncle. *Hubie Crumbacher.*
REVISED	The car was a gift from her eccentric uncle, Hubie Crumbacher. [Appositive linked to main clause.]
REVISED	The car was a gift from her eccentric uncle. Hubie Crumbacher was his name. [Appositive rewritten as main clause.]

A **compound predicate** consists of two or more verbs and their objects, if any (see 5d).

FRAGMENT	The rescuers loaded their backpacks with food and bandages. *And struck out for the woods.*
REVISED	The rescuers loaded their backpacks with food and bandages and struck out for the woods. [Second part of compound predicate linked to main clause.]
FRAGMENT	We accepted their congratulations. *And the reward money.*
REVISED	We accepted their congratulations and the reward money. [Second part of compound object linked to main clause.]

10f | Be aware of the acceptable uses of incomplete sentences.

We omit the sentence subject in commands and some exclamations.

> (*You*) Learn these rules.
> (*You*) Forget it!

We also use incomplete sentences for question-and-answer patterns in speech and sometimes in writing, and we may use them to make a transition from one idea to another:

> Got it? Sure.
> First a word of explanation.

Experienced professional writers sometimes use sentence fragments that do not fit any of these patterns and that violate the rules for avoiding fragments discussed above. For such writers, sentence fragments can be effective structures. Most inexperienced writers, however, use fragments unintentionally, and these accidents are distractions to the communication of a thought. In most academic writing you show control of your sentences by avoiding fragments.

Understanding sentence fragments

To increase your understanding of what a fragment is, copy each of the sentences plus fragments that appears below. Then write an imitation of the same pattern, using your own ideas. *You will be writing sentence fragments.* Finally, revise your sentence, using punctuation and grammatical structure appropriate for academic writing.

frag

10

Example: While writing, I like to have my headset tuned to the classics. Mendelssohn. Beethoven. Bach.

Exact copy: While writing, I like to have my headset tuned to the classics. Mendelssohn. Beethoven. Bach.

Imitation: While running, Maria watches for birds. Cardinals. Redheaded woodpeckers. Cedar waxwings.

Revision: While running, Maria watches for birds: cardinals, redheaded woodpeckers, cedar waxwings.

1. After doing his laundry, John found that all his clothes had something in common. Pink shirts. Pink underwear. One red sock.

   Exact copy:

   _____

   _____

   Imitation:

   _____

   _____

   Revision:

   _____

   _____

2. We finally settled the argument by staying home. Which was what I wanted to do in the first place.

Exact copy:

_____

_____

Imitation:

_____

_____

Revision:

_____

_____

3. At the bookstore I bought three new novels. Just because I wanted to.

Exact copy:

_____

_____

Imitation:

_____

_____

Revision:

_____

_____

4. When Luis got his first paycheck, he was intoxicated with the thought of money in his pocket. For buying record albums and getting new clothes.

Exact copy:

_____

_____

Imitation:

_____

_____

Revision:

_____

_____

5. The house had clear signs of abandonment. Overgrown shrubs. Broken
   windows. Loose clapboards.

   Exact copy:

   _____

   _____

   Imitation:

   _____

   _____

   Revision:

   _____

   _____

Identifying and revising sentence fragments

EXERCISE **10-2**

frag

10

Each of the following word groups is either a sentence fragment or a complete sentence. Rewrite each sentence fragment as a complete sentence by changing word forms, omitting words, or adding new words. If the word group is a complete sentence, write *OK* in the space below it.

Example: After the flood waters receded.

The flood waters receded.

Or:

People were rescued after the flood waters receded.

1. When the ice destroys the pavement.

2. There being many extra features without extra cost.

3. And it was rejected.

4. A former editor, who has a sharp, critical eye.

5. On a snowy slope far from any shelter.

6. Taking the time to check.

7. Come and see our apartment.

8. Which was slimy but cool.

9. The fox looking for its mother.

10. From behind and all around.

11. But is not honest.

12. A resident of Toledo.

13. Although it was a gory film.

14. Food prices were soaring.

15. Based on historical fact.

16. Puzzled by poor sales.

17. Which looked like a passageway.

18. Afterward, the answer was challenged.

19. Having joined a band of gypsies.

20. During a tornado alert.

Revising sentence fragments

EXERCISE **10-3**

Most of the following passages contain a sentence fragment. Identify each fragment by writing the number preceding it on the blank to the left. Then rewrite the passage to correct each fragment by making it a complete sentence, adding, changing, or deleting words as necessary. If there is no fragment in the passage, write *OK* on the blank.

Example: ____2____ ¹After studying French for three years, I tried to translate a poem. ²Without much success.

After studying French for three years, I tried to translate a poem. But I didn't have much success.

_____ 1. ¹The contrast between the two women is great. ²One of them, Roberta, being arrogant, and Patrice being shy.

_____ 2. ¹They moved into a condominium in a quiet neighborhood. ²Quiet being all they wanted.

_____ 3. ¹The National Geographic specials have been very popular. ²Sponsored in part by an oil company. ³PBS has shown several.

_____ 4. ¹The river was polluted with insecticides. ²Funds for cleaning it up were not available. ³The chemical company had gone bankrupt.

_____ 5. [1]Chris has one quality that her roommate doesn't have. [2]Patience. [3]Chris is so patient that she is boring.

_____ 6. [1]Riding the subway, I always read the advertisements above the windows. [2]Trying to figure out what gimmicks the advertisers use.

_____ 7. [1]I tried to be gentle with the old woman. [2]Who had insulted me the day before but now needed my help.

_____ 8. [1]Perry can be loudmouthed and overbearing. [2]For example, his saying he should be in a dorm with "better-quality people."

_____ 9. [1]The salary starting at $10,000 a year. [2]The job failed to attract qualified applicants. [3]The advertisement ran for three weeks.

_____ 10. [1]Mike seems to be a good father. [2]For example, taking his children to ball games or on trips, or just staying around the house teaching his children new games.

Sentence fragments: Review

In each passage below, circle the number preceding any word group that is a sentence fragment. Then revise each fragment by linking it to a main clause or by rewriting it as a main clause.

A.   [1] The so-called Gothic romances are criticized unfairly. [2] Just because they do not conform to some critics' ideas of what makes "literature." [3] To me the best poetry or fiction uses colorful writing and takes my mind off everyday events. [4] Making me experience things I wouldn't ordinarily encounter. [5] Or leading me to think of ideas that might not have occurred to me. [6] Gothic romances treat romantic subjects in the context of historical events. [7] Imaginary characters in real settings. [8] In Gothic romances I learn about how different people deal with different situations. [9] For example, how a poor person responds to an heiress. [10] Or how a man forgives his spendthrift grandson. [11] But I also learn about the history of our country. [12] One book was set in the South after the Civil War and told of the suffering experienced by those who lost the war. [13]Another book gave me insights into early twentieth-century Texas. [14]Where Mexican immigrants, cattle ranchers, cowboys, and drifters all came together. [15]On the other hand, I find that works of "literature" deal with dull people in

dull places and situations. [16]Such as those I experience daily. [17]"Literature" does nothing for my imagination or my curiosity. [18]Leaving me cold and bored. [19]The snobbish critics would probably enjoy reading even more. [20]If only they would stop worrying about what others think.

Name _____ Date _____ Score _____

B. ¹In the African nation of Dahomey. ²A man's wives were put to death at his funeral. ³Their spirits being supposed to keep him company in the afterlife. ⁴When a king died, many attendants and wives were put to death. ⁵The people believed that a dead person had desires and emotions. ⁶Such as anger. ⁷The dead person could take revenge on the living if his desires were not satisfied. ⁸Thus a king remained very powerful even after death. ⁹With as much power as he had had when he was alive. ¹⁰Since the dead were so powerful, the survivors had to prevent the dead from becoming envious. ¹¹As well as angry. ¹²So the survivors often sacrificed possessions. ¹³Along with attendants and wives. ¹⁴Appropriate possessions for sacrifice being cattle, food, and jewelry. ¹⁵Such sacrifices guaranteeing continual poverty for the people. ¹⁶War frequently resulted. ¹⁷Because through war the people renewed their wealth. ¹⁸The additional result, however, was the destruction of even more lives. ¹⁹Only in this

frag

10

245

century did these mourning sacrifices disappear. [20]And now the people

seem to live in a state of spiritual uneasiness.

frag

10

11 | Comma Splices and Fused Sentences

Self-test

For each sentence below, circle the letter preceding the option that correctly fills in the blank.

Example: "We waited in line for an hour," she _____ we went home."
   a. said, "then   b. said "then   ⓒ said; "then

1. We will certainly be able to identify Bob's boat during the _____ is the only one with red and purple sails.
   a. races it   b. races, it   c. races; it

2. My morning ritual includes listening to the news while I _____ morning, however, I was in too much of a hurry to turn the radio on.
   a. shave, this   b. shave; this   c. shave this

3. He is an outstanding _____ is also a fair athlete.
   a. student he   b. student, he   c. student. He

4. She felt happy after the test was _____ and went home smiling.
   a. returned, however,   b. returned; however,   c. returned however

5. After calling the roll, my history professor tells a _____ he begins his lecture.
   a. joke then   b. joke, and then   c. joke, then

6. The car stopped _____ policeman got out.
   a. abruptly, a   b. abruptly; a   c. abruptly a

7. He is one of the kindest men I _____ will certainly help you.
   a. know he   b. know; he   c. know, he

8. The child's musical talent was _____ she was considered a musical prodigy.
   a. amazing indeed   b. amazing. Indeed,   c. amazing, indeed,

9. During the last song she pushed her way through the _____ wanted to get a closer look at the band.
   a. crowd, she   b. crowd she   c. crowd. She

10. In the summer I had to do manual _____ I have to overtax my brain.
   a. labor, now   b. labor now   c. labor; now

Two problems commonly occur in linking main clauses in a single sentence. The first, the **comma splice,** occurs when two or more main clauses are separated only by a comma, with no coordinating conjunction between them. (*The car was bright red, its interior was black*). The second, the **fused sentence** or **run-on sentence,** occurs when two or more main clauses are joined with no punctuation or conjunction between them (*The car was bright red its interior was black*).

COMMA SPLICES

11a | Separate two main clauses with a comma *only* when they are joined by a coordinating conjunction.

COMMA SPLICE   The mattress caught fire, the flames spread quickly.

REVISED   The mattress caught fire, *and* the flames spread quickly.

A comma splice can be corrected in various ways, each one establishing a different relation between the clauses.

1. Insert a coordinating conjunction (*and, but, or, nor, for, so, yet*) after the comma that separates the two main clauses (see 5d-1). This method is illustrated above.
2. Make separate sentences of the two main clauses: *The mattress caught fire. The flames spread quickly.*
3. Insert a semicolon rather than a comma between the main clauses: *The mattress caught fire; the flames spread quickly.*
4. Make one of the main clauses into a subordinate clause by using a subordinating conjunction such as *although, since,* or *when* or a relative pronoun (*that, which, who*) (see 5c-4): After *the mattress caught fire, the flames spread quickly.*
5. Reduce one of the main clauses to a subordinate phrase (see 5c): *The mattress having caught fire, the flames spread quickly.*

11b | Use a period or semicolon to separate main clauses connected by conjunctive adverbs.

Conjunctive adverbs include *also, consequently, however, then, thus,* and *therefore* (see 5d-2 for a more complete list). Because these words are not conjunctions, the two main clauses that they connect must be separated by a semicolon or a period. The words are themselves often set off by commas (see 5d-2).

COMMA SPLICE   The house looked run down, however the inside was in beautiful shape.

REVISED   The house looked run down; however, the inside was in beautiful shape.

REVISED   The house looked run down. However, the inside was in beautiful shape.

| REVISED | The house looked run down. The inside, however, was in beautiful shape. [A conjunctive adverb may be placed at the beginning, middle, or end of its clause.] |

FUSED SENTENCES

11c | **Don't combine two main clauses without using an appropriate connector or punctuation mark between them.**

A **fused,** or **run-on, sentence** joins two or more main clauses with no connecting word or punctuation between them. It can be corrected in the same ways as a comma splice.

| FUSED | Dr. Ling is director of the hospital he also maintains a private practice. |

| REVISED | Dr. Ling is director of the hospital, *but* he also maintains a private practice. [Comma and coordinating conjunction.] |

| REVISED | Dr. Ling is director of the hospital. He also maintains a private practice. [Separate sentences.] |

| REVISED | Dr. Ling is director of the hospital; he also maintains a private practice. [Semicolon.] |

| REVISED | Dr. Ling is director of the hospital, *although* he also maintains a private practice. [Subordinating conjunction.] |

| REVISED | Dr. Ling is director of the hospital and also maintains a private practice. [Coordinating conjunction joining second verb phrase.] |

cs / fs

11

Identifying and revising comma splices and fused sentences

Most of the following word groups are either comma splices or fused sentences. Correct each error in one of five ways: (1) by inserting a coordinating conjunction or a comma and a coordinating conjunction; (2) by forming separate sentences; (3) by using a semicolon; (4) by subordinating one of the clauses; or (5) by reducing one of the main clauses to a subordinate phrase. If an item contains no error, write *OK* on the blank.

Example: _____ We installed a wood-burning stove, it heated the kitchen.

We installed a wood-burning stove that heated the kitchen.

_____ 1. The fireworks had deteriorated they had not been stored properly.

_____ 2. The visitor came to the door, however, it was too late for him to get in.

_____ 3. Bret Harte's works had great appeal to Easterners, they appreciated his attitude toward his rural characters.

_____ 4. They chattered and daydreamed the serious issue was not discussed.

_____ 5. She planned to be a chemist, but instead she wound up in advertising.

_____ 6. The reunion was in St. Louis, I could not attend.

_____ 7. The waiter piled the glasses, then the plates fell.

_____ 8. I wanted to chair the committee, however, I did not have a chance.

_____ 9. Having climbed the stairs, she rested on her suitcase.

_____ 10. Blending your own tea, however, does not take much time it saves money, too.

Revising comma splices and fused sentences

The following word groups are either comma splices or fused sentences. Correct each error in two ways, as specified. (To make a clause subordinate, you will have to add a subordinating conjunction or a relative pronoun.)

Example: _____ The wedding gifts had to be returned, the wax grapes were no loss.

Add coordinating conjunction:

The wedding gifts had to be returned, but the wax grapes were no loss.

Add semicolon and conjunctive adverb:

The wedding gifts had to be returned; however, the wax grapes were no loss.

_____ 1. The factory once employed 500 persons now there is a parking lot in its place.

Add comma and coordinating conjunction:

Add semicolon and conjunctive adverb:

_____ 2. She moved to Florida, however, she found the summers too sultry.

Add semicolon:

Make separate sentences:

253

_____ 3. Frederick Douglass had been an illiterate slave, he became a famous speaker and writer.

Add coordinating conjunction:

Make one clause subordinate:

_____ 4. Stevie Wonder has been a professional entertainer since the age of twelve, he was the first black Motown artist to perform overseas.

Add coordinating conjunction:

Add semicolon:

_____ 5. The airline gave a discount on the Atlanta flight, the number of passengers continued to decline.

Add semicolon and conjunctive adverb:

Make one clause subordinate:

_____ 6. The band was formed in 1971 its first hit came the same year.

Make separate sentences:

Add semicolon:

_____ 7. Some vitamins may reduce the risk of certain diseases, in high doses the vitamins are toxic.

Add coordinating conjunction:

Make one clause subordinate:

_____ 8. In the morning there was a rumor that the president of the company had suffered a heart attack by noon stock prices had dropped sharply.

Make separate sentences:

Add comma and coordinating conjunction:

_____ 9. Muhammad Ali associates with people of all races and religions, that is why he is respected worldwide.

Add semicolon:

Make separate sentences:

_____ 10. The movie got mostly positive reviews some critics found the acting unconvincing.

Add comma and coordinating conjunction:

Make one clause subordinate:

| *Understanding comma splices and fused sentences* | EXERCISE **11-3** |

Each of the following sentences is a compound sentence with correct punctuation between two main clauses. Copy each one as it is, and then, using your own ideas, write a sentence that imitates the pattern.

Example: Deficiency diseases result from a diet lacking certain elements; for example, a lack of vitamin A results in night blindness.

Exact copy: Deficiency diseases result from a diet lacking certain elements; for example, a lack of vitamin A results in night blindness.

Imitation: Our library has several features to help the new students; for example, a librarian is always seated at the information desk.

1. The official language of Djibouti, a small country in eastern Africa, is Arabic, but most of the people speak Afar or Somali.

   Exact copy:

   Imitation:

2. The bottle-nosed dolphin has a keen sense of hearing, good eyesight, and an excellent sense of taste; however, it has no sense of smell.

   Exact copy:

   Imitation:

3. A dormouse is about three inches long; its tail is another three inches.

   Exact copy:

   Imitation:

4. Werewolves exist in stories of the supernatural; according to legend, they are people who somehow change into threatening wolves.

   Exact copy:

   Imitation:

5. The ancient Egyptians wrote on a paperlike material called papyrus; in fact, they may have been its inventors.

   Exact copy:

   Imitation:

6. The Monroe Doctrine was intended to protect the Latin American countries from European colonialism; however, it more often these days is seen as U.S. imperialism.

   Exact copy:

   Imitation:

7. One week after the Normandy invasion, Hitler sent the first V-1 rockets over London; the British called them "buzz bombs."

Exact copy:

Imitation:

8. Yams look very much like another root vegetable, the sweet potato, and many people mistakenly confuse the two.

Exact copy:

Imitation:

9. The large country in Africa's midsection is called Zaire; however, until its independence in 1971 it was known as the Belgian Congo.

Exact copy:

Imitation:

10. Approximately 97 percent of the earth's water is in the oceans, and another 2 percent is in glaciers and icecaps.

Exact copy:

Imitation:

Comma splices and fused sentences: Review

In the following paragraph, circle the number preceding any sentence that is a comma splice or a fused sentence. Then revise each faulty sentence in the most appropriate way.

¹ From the office window I could see the cars lined up along the bridge, the muddy river ran beneath it. ² Traffic was backed up for several blocks on the three roads they converged at the foot of the bridge. ³ Rain started falling, the cars' lights came on. ⁴ Across the river was the city shrouded in fog. ⁵ The traffic moved even more slowly, the commuters must have hated having one more thing to delay them. ⁶ A few brightly colored dots gradually moved across the bridge, six pedestrians, carrying red and yellow umbrellas, moved with quickening paces. ⁷ Soon the traffic began to thin. ⁸ A gray and yellow band of sky began to show as the rain

eased. [9] The sun was coming up, the rain was subsiding, the fog was dissi-

pating. [10] Rush hour over, the morning sky brightened the workers were

at their jobs.

cs / fs

11

262

12 | *Pronoun Reference*

Self-test

In each of the following sentences, underline any pronoun whose antecedent (the noun or pronoun it refers to) is not clear, specific, or definite. If the sentence is already correct, write *OK* to the left of it.

Example: John told Dennis that <u>he</u> had a problem.

1. When I saw my teachers greeting my friends, I said hello to them.
2. The man's shadow loomed against the wall, which alarmed John.
3. After Hilda's snake escaped, Martha would not go into her room.
4. As long as the council members refused to meet the developers, there would be no end to their frustration.
5. When he saw how much the parts cost for the repairs, he decided to obtain them elsewhere.
6. Once the man met his nephew, he knew the boy was missing something in life.
7. It says on the bottle not to drink its contents.
8. In Agnes's glove compartment, she kept a revolver.
9. After my roommate insulted my father, he refused to speak to him.
10. Alice told Karen that Esther found her purse.

    A **pronoun** is a substitute for a noun and has no meaning by itself. The pronoun takes its meaning from the noun it stands for and refers to, called its **antecedent.** Thus the antecedent must be clear.

CONFUSING	When my mother stopped speaking to my aunt, *she* rewrote *her* will. [Antecedent of *she* and *her* unclear.]
CLEAR	My mother rewrote *her* will when *she* stopped speaking to my aunt. [Antecedent of *her* and *she* is clearly *mother.*]
CLEAR	My aunt rewrote *her* will when my mother stopped speaking to *her.* [Antecedent of *her* both times is clearly *aunt.*]

    Most pronoun reference problems occur because the pronoun could refer to more than one antecedent (as in the example above), because the pronoun is so far from its antecedent that its meaning is unclear, or because the antecedent is not specific or cannot be located at all.

12a | Make a pronoun refer clearly to one antecedent.

A plural pronoun may refer to a compound antecedent:

Smith and *Bean* doubled *their* profits.

But a pronoun will be unclear if it can refer to *either* of two antecedents.

CONFUSING	Mort told Anna that Hildy lost *her* money.
CLEAR	Mort told Anna that Hildy lost *Anna's* money. [Pronoun replaced with appropriate noun.]
CLEAR	Mort told Anna, "Hildy lost your money." [Sentence rewritten to quote Mort directly.]

12b | Place a pronoun close enough to its antecedent to ensure clarity.

Avoid separating a pronoun and its antecedent with other nouns that the pronoun could refer to.

CONFUSING	Maria almost lost her watch during a scuffle with a mugger on the subway. Fortunately, she only sprained her toe. *It* was a gift from her fiancé.
CLEAR	Maria almost lost her *watch, which* was a gift from her fiancé, during a scuffle with a mugger on the subway. Fortunately, she only sprained her toe.

A clause that begins with a relative pronoun (*who, which, that*) is generally placed immediately after the noun it modifies.

CONFUSING	The article pointed out that the spaceships on the surface of Mars, *which* can never be recovered, form the beginning of a garbage dump on the planet.
CLEAR	The article pointed out that the spaceships, *which* can never be recovered, form the beginning of a garbage dump on Mars.

12c | Make a pronoun refer to a specific antecedent rather than to an implied one.

1 | Use *this, that, which,* and *it* cautiously in referring to whole statements.

In **broad reference** a pronoun such as *this, that, which,* or *it* refers to an entire phrase, clause, sentence, or even paragraph instead of to a single noun. Such references are generally unclear. Unless the meaning of the pronoun is unmistakable, avoid making a broad reference. Think of *this* (or *that* or *which*) as an adjective: *this something.* By filling in a noun after *this* you will first of all clarify your own thinking (broad references often result when writers themselves don't really know what they mean). By clarifying your own thinking you also make your meaning clear to your readers.

CONFUSING	In an apparently bloodless coup, a group of military officers seized governmental power. *This* happened just eight days after the country's president died.
CLEAR	In an apparently bloodless coup, a group of military officers seized governmental power. *This coup* happened just eight days after the country's president died.
CONFUSING	As we watched, the two men began hitting each other and yelling for help. *This* started the riot.
CLEAR	As we watched, the two men began hitting each other and yelling for help. *This fight* started the riot.
CLEAR	We saw the riot start when the two men began hitting each other and yelling for help.

2 | Don't use a pronoun to refer to a noun implied by a modifier.

Modifiers — adjectives, nouns used as modifiers, and the possessives of nouns and pronouns — do not provide specific antecedents for pronouns.

WEAK	In the teacher's desk, *she* kept a paddle and a pint bottle.
REVISED	The teacher kept a paddle and a pint bottle in her desk.
WEAK	The sick man claimed he caught *it* from a cow at the 4-H fair.
REVISED	The sick man claimed he caught *his illness* from a cow at the 4-H fair.

3 | Don't use a pronoun to refer to a noun implied by some other noun or phrase.

UNCLEAR	After Albert studied accounting techniques, he decided to become *one*.
REVISED	After Albert studied accounting techniques, he decided to become *an accountant*.

4 | Don't use part of a title as an antecedent in the opening sentence of a paper.

TITLE	A Shortage of Locksmiths
NOT	*This* is responsible for the increase in burglaries.
BUT	Since the town's last locksmith closed his shop, the number of burglaries has doubled.

12d | Avoid the indefinite use of *it* and *they*. Use *you* only to mean "you, the reader."

The use of *it* and *they* with no clear antecedent, though well established in conversation, is generally unacceptable in writing because such pronouns are vague and lead to wordiness.

WEAK	*It* says in the directions that the small box should be opened first.
REVISED	The directions say that the small box should be opened first.
WEAK	On the television advertisement *they* said that science had finally conquered the common cold.
REVISED	The television advertisement said that science had finally conquered the common cold.

You is acceptable when it is used to mean "you, the reader": *You can see that I had no choice.* But *you* should not be used indefinitely in other contexts.

WEAK	Citizens of Mudburg know that *you* can have *your* car towed away for illegal parking.
REVISED	Citizens of Mudburg know that *people* can have *their* cars towed away for illegal parking.

12e | Avoid using the pronoun *it* more than one way in a sentence.

We use the pronoun *it* correctly in a number of ways. First, we have seen it as a personal pronoun standing for many nouns. We also use the word in certain set expressions like *It's raining* and *It's almost two o'clock.* Still another acceptable use occurs in sentences where we want to delay the subject or direct object.

It's no secret that John wants to move. [The real subject is *that John wants to move,* a noun clause.]

Fred's financial situation made it important that he look for a job. [The real direct object is *that he look for a job.*]

While all these uses of *it* are correct, using this pronoun in more than one way in a sentence can confuse the reader.

CONFUSING	*It* was an inaccurate forecast: *it* predicted rain, but *it* is snowing.
CLEAR	The forecast was inaccurate: it predicted rain, but instead we have snow.

12f | Be sure the relative pronouns *who, which,* and *that* are appropriate for their antecedents.

We commonly use *who* to refer to persons and to animals that have names:

My dog Carly, *who* ran away last spring, turned up yesterday at the high school.

Which refers to animals and things:

I'd hoped to inherit the diamond stickpin, *which* my father wore at his wedding.

That refers to animals and things and occasionally to persons:

> The book *that* I bought was missing seventy pages.
> He studies babies *that* are just beginning to see.

(See also 21c-1 for the use of *which* and *that* in nonrestrictive and restrictive clauses.)

ref

12

Unclear or remote antecedents of pronouns

EXERCISE **12-1**

ref

12

Circle each pronoun in the following sentences. Then revise the sentences so that all pronouns refer clearly to their antecedents.

Example: After the sick man tended (his) ailing brother, (he) developed a goiter.

After the sick man tended his ailing brother, the brother developed a goiter.

Or:

The sick man, after tending his ailing brother, developed a goiter.

1. After the tail pipe fell off Linda's car, Helen knew she would have to take a bus.

2. The conservationists sent the senators a petition to repeal the laws, and the newspaper published an editorial on them.

3. As long as a group of technocrats made regulations for the students, frustration was going to plague them.

4. When my father was young, my grandfather regularly rubbed onions on his skin.

5. When I saw that the dogs had knocked down two elderly people, I ran toward them.

6. The salesman thought that the commission his partner received would make him look bad.

7. I finally paid the bill for dental work that had been lying around for several months.

8. Solar power promises relief from the energy shortage, just as synthetic fuel does, but it would be more practical for northern climates.

9. The misspelling on the placard was unintentional, but it was not noticed anyway.

10. Small foreign cars and small domestic cars are different: they have a solid feel and good acceleration.

Implied or indefinite antecedents of pronouns

EXERCISE **12-2**

Circle each pronoun in the following sentences. Then revise the sentences so that all pronouns refer to definite, stated antecedents.

Example: Television networks show such violent programs that people want to try ⓘt in real life.

Television networks show such violent programs that people want to try violence in real life.

1. After being depressed for two weeks, she decided to get over it and resume her routine.

2. When you lived in the nineteenth century, your feet and your horses were your only private means of transportation.

3. Some toothpastes contain abrasives that whiten teeth. However, it warns on the label that the abrasives may wear down tooth enamel.

4. They say that trouble comes in threes.

5. After discussing the repair for the car, we knew it was time it was taken care of.

6. The exam was scheduled for Tuesday, which was not in my plans.

7. Many people shy away from the word *old* because they think of it as being ugly and withered.

ref

12

8. The soldiers' orders in the war games left them unclear about where they were supposed to go.

9. The buses need more gasoline to run to distant places, they put on more miles, and they break down more often. This makes people's taxes higher.

10. He saw how expensive the supplies were for the art courses, which made him decide not to take them.

Pronoun reference: combining sentences

EXERCISE **12-3**

Make a single sentence of each of the following sentence groups, omitting unnecessary words and being careful not to alter meaning. Use pronouns where you can, but avoid faulty pronoun references.

Example: Susan's book bag is better than mine. Susan bought her book bag on sale. Susan paid less for her book bag than I paid for mine.

Susan's book bag is better than mine, but, because she bought hers on sale, she paid less for it than I paid for mine.

1. It is only two hundred miles to Minneapolis. I could drive this distance easily.

2. It rained last night. I left my sleeping bag outside. Now the lining of my sleeping bag is soaking wet.

3. By *streetwise* I mean having common sense. Common sense can't be learned from a book.

4. I admire Gwendolyn Brooks's poetry. So I am choosing Gwendolyn Brooks as the subject of my paper.

5. The weather finally turned warm. We painted the porch. Painting the porch was a big job.

6. Rachel takes violin lessons. Rachel was seven years old when she started. Rachel hopes to become a professional violinist.

7. The children were on the playground. The children were watching the demonstrators move down the street. Suddenly the demonstrators began to run.

ref

12

8. My supervisor told me something this morning. I would get a raise. What he told me came as a surprise.

9. I wanted to back my car out of the driveway. I had to remove the snow from the driveway.

10. We finally came to an understanding. The understanding was over which book we should read. Coming to the understanding was difficult for all of us.

Pronoun reference: Review   EXERCISE **12-4**

In the following paragraph, circle any pronoun whose antecedent is unclear, remote, implied, or indefinite. Then revise the sentences as necessary so that all pronouns refer clearly and appropriately to a definite and stated antecedent.

The three-story building, which had been constructed in 1935, was used for many years as a dormitory. Its wooden stairs were badly worn by the feet of thousands of students. It is a wonder that they never broke while they were hauling their heavy suitcases up to the third floor. Nothing had been repaired in it because it was deemed too costly. Then two years ago the building was turned into offices for the Arts and Sciences faculty. This causes less wear and tear on it. However, no refurbishing has ever been done to them. Recently, however, Professor Pines told Doctor Wiley that because of her efforts some funding might soon be allocated to redecorate them. I hope she is right. That will certainly please many faculty members who have found the rooms depressing.

13 | *Shifts*

Self-test

In the following sentences, underline any unnecessary or confusing shifts in person, number, tense, mood, subject, voice, or form of quotation. If a sentence is already correct, write *OK* to the left of it.

Example: They had already left when the taxi <u>arrives</u>.

1. We entered the museum not knowing you were supposed to pay.
2. She wanted to know whether to take the job and did it pay well.
3. We planned to commute by car, but bus was found to be cheaper.
4. Oliver had no way of knowing we were there until he walks through the door.
5. The intensity of a person's feelings can cause you to act foolishly.
6. The waiter scowled at the diners, who had left a small tip.
7. A person should always have professional playing experience before they coach.
8. To revise a paper, read it through for errors, and then you should examine its structure.
9. All the members of the squad looked on me as their leader.
10. I had to decide whether to go on the trip and could I afford it?

To be clear, a sentence, paragraph, or essay should be consistent in such grammatical elements as person, number, and tense unless grammar or meaning requires a shift. The following guidelines deal with each of these elements.

13a | Keep sentences consistent in person and number.

In speaking and writing, we deal with persons (and things) in three ways: (1) we can *be* one, (2) we can talk or write *to* one, and (3) we can talk or write *about* one. In grammar these ways of dealing with people and things are given numbers: (1) first person (*I*), (2) second person (*you*), and (3) third person (*he, she, it*). We also indicate whether we are referring to one or more than one (*I, we; he, she, it, they*).

Writing that shifts unintentionally from one person to another, say from writing *about* someone to writing *to* someone (from third person to second), or that shifts in number, using a singular noun but referring to that antecedent with a plural pronoun, is difficult for readers to follow.

INCONSISTENT	*We* learned before going on the desert tour that *you* should leave *your* itinerary with the park rangers. [Shift from first person to second person.]
REVISED	*We* learned before going on the desert tour that *we* should leave *our* itinerary with the park rangers.
INCONSISTENT	A football *player* should be in good condition even before *they* begin training. [Shift from singular to plural.]
REVISED	A football *player* should be in good condition even before *he* begins training.

Consistency sometimes requires that words other than the pronouns — usually nouns — agree in number.

INCONSISTENT	All the countries represented at the convention displayed their *flag*.
REVISED	All the countries represented at the convention displayed their *flags*.

The consistency in the number of the nouns in the revised sentence is called **logical agreement.**

13b | Keep sentences consistent in tense and mood.

By their forms, verbs tell time of action (tense) and mood (7d and 7f). Unintentional shifts in either tense or mood distract a reader from understanding the writer's meaning.

INCONSISTENT	Doctors *had* no way to prevent polio until Salk *develops* the vaccine. [Shift from past tense to present tense.]
REVISED	Doctors *had* no way to prevent polio until Salk *developed* the vaccine.
INCONSISTENT	Teachers first insist that we *be* quiet in class and then that we *are supposed* to participate in discussions. [Shift from subjunctive to indicative mood.]
REVISED	Teachers first insist that we *be* quiet in class and then that we *participate* in discussions.

13c | Keep sentences consistent in subject and voice.

Within a sentence, we sometimes change from active to passive voice, or vice versa, to keep our subjects consistent, and sometimes we change subjects from one part of the sentence to another while keeping our voice consistent (see 7f).

| SHIFT IN VOICE | If the *petition had been signed* by all of us students, *it would have won* reduced fees. [Shift from passive to active; subject is consistent.] |
| SHIFT IN SUBJECT | If *all of us students had signed* the petition, *it would have won* reduced fees. [Shift from *all* to *it,* meaning "petition"; voice is consistently active.] |

But inconsistency with both voice and subject in the same sentence can cause confusion.

| SHIFT IN VOICE AND SUBJECT | If the *petition had been signed* by all of us students, *we would have won* reduced fees. [Shift in subject from *petition* to *we* and in voice from passive to active.] |
| NO SHIFT | If *all of us students had signed* the petition, *we would have won* reduced fees. |

shift

13

13d | Don't shift unnecessarily between indirect and direct quotation.

Direct quotation reports the exact words of a speaker or writer, in quotation marks. **Indirect quotation** also reports what someone said or wrote, but not in the exact words and not in quotation marks.

INCONSISTENT	Jack asked why the Cubs kept losing and is there going to be a management change? [Shift from indirect quotation to word order of direct quotation.]
REVISED	Jack asked why the Cubs kept losing and whether there would be a management change. [Consistent indirect quotation.]
REVISED	Jack asked, "Why do the Cubs keep losing? Is there going to be a management change?" [Consistent direct quotation.]

| *Revising for consistency*   EXERCISE **13-1**

Examine each sentence below for any unnecessary shifts in person (*P*), number (*N*), tense (*T*), mood (*M*), subject (*S*), voice (*V*), or form of quotation (*Q*). If a sentence is inconsistent, identify each shift by writing the appropriate letter or letters on the blank to the left. Then rewrite the sentence to achieve consistency.

Example: __S, V__ The meeting was to be attended by representatives from three colleges, but they could not agree on where to meet.

Representatives from three colleges were to attend the meeting, but they could not agree on where to meet.

_____ 1. He said he bought the recorder without asking would it work.

_____ 2. A person should stay clear of credit cards because they encourage you to spend more money than you have.

_____ 3. To have it printed, take it to the shop on Wednesday, and then you should call the next day.

_____ 4. Although the poet's words are fascinating, I do not know what they meant.

_____ 5. She wanted to buy flannel, but it was learned by her that she was allergic to flannel.

_____ 6. If one wants to get the most from college, you must work hard, ask questions, and keep an open mind.

_____ 7. The two countries had had peaceful relations for a decade when suddenly a border dispute erupts into a war.

_____ 8. An American going to a Japanese bath for the first time should have left his or her modesty at home.

_____ 9. He said my face was red and was I embarrassed?

_____ 10. When someone receives repeated nuisance phone calls, they have no choice but to change their number.

_____ 11. After a mugger attacked the elderly woman, she was taken to the hospital by police.

_____ 12. To get the dog to swallow the pill, place it in the dog's mouth, and then one should stroke the dog's throat.

_____ 13. A person should be aware that poor night vision can endanger your life.

_____ 14. The crowding one experiences at a beach can make you wish you had stayed home.

_____ 15. The characters in the movie are average people, but they had more than average problems.

Shifts: Review

In the following paragraph, underline any unnecessary or confusing shifts in person, number, tense, mood, subject, voice, or form of quotation. Then revise the paragraph to achieve appropriate consistency both within sentences and from sentence to sentence.

shift

13

Our trip to the beach got off to a bad start when the car has two flat tires a mile from home. You can always count on some trouble with our car, but usually nothing this annoying. We arrived at the motel late, but fortunately our reservations had not been canceled by the manager, who remembers us from last time. He asked how long we would be staying and did we want the seafood special for dinner. We checked into our room, and our luggage was unpacked. Everything was going smoothly. Then we went to dinner and turned in for the night. One would have expected that the rest of the vacation should be routine if not fun. But that night each one of us gets sick from their seafood dinner. The next morning the rain came, and for the next three days we just sat in the room playing cards

until it was time that our trip home had to be made.

14 | Misplaced and Dangling Modifiers

Self-test

In the following sentences, underline any words or phrases that do not clearly modify the words intended or that relate nonsensically to other words. If a sentence is already correct, write *OK* to the left of it.

Example: The man said he thought the car was in good condition <u>during his sales pitch.</u>

1. Art only walked to the campus once last month.
2. Looking in the mirror, the new suit was very becoming.
3. She kept the dog in the closet that was housebroken.
4. After calling the repairman, the furnace started working.
5. He kept the marble cups that he bought in Taiwan during his tour last spring in the closet.
6. Having hired an attorney, the lawsuit was under way.
7. Never again in his life did he want to travel by boat.
8. Two teams were in the play-offs that were undefeated.
9. To gain entry, a special pass is necessary.
10. Six of us ordered drinks at the bar that tasted like after-shave lotion.

MISPLACED MODIFIERS

A **misplaced modifier** does not clearly modify the word intended by the writer.

14a | Place prepositional phrases where they will clearly modify the words intended.

Prepositional phrases function as adjectives and as adverbs. As adjectives they generally come directly after the nouns or pronouns they modify:

> The house *across the street* is being repainted. [The prepositional phrase functions as an adjective, modifying the noun *house.*]

As adverbs they may directly follow the words they modify, or, like single-word adverbs, they may appear elsewhere in the sentence if their function is clear:

The house is being repainted *despite the weather.*
Despite the weather, the house is being repainted.

Faulty placement of prepositional phrases can lead to confusion.

CONFUSING	The teacher said that she expected us to do well on the exam *during her lecture.* [The prepositional phrase seems to modify *exam* instead of *said,* as intended.]
CLEAR	*During her lecture,* the teacher said that she expected us to do well on the exam.
CONFUSING	I heard that Mayor Miller was accused of slander *on the evening news.* [Does *on the evening news* modify *heard* or *was accused*?]
CLEAR	I heard *on the evening news* that Mayor Miller was accused of slander.
CLEAR	I heard that *on the evening news* Mayor Miller was accused of slander.
CONFUSING	The house is being repainted *across the street.* (The prepositional phrase seems to modify *repainted* instead of *house,* as intended.)
CLEAR	The house *across the street* is being repainted.

14b | Place subordinate clauses where they will clearly modify the words intended.

Like phrases that function as adjectives and adverbs, adjective clauses directly follow the words they modify, and adverb clauses can stand next to the words they modify or at the beginning or end of the sentence. (See 5c-4.)

CONFUSING	The house was in the woods *that burned last night.*
CLEAR	The house *that burned last night* was in the woods.
CONFUSING	I like the blue shirt with the white egrets *that Jack is wearing.*
CLEAR	I like *Jack's* blue shirt with the white egrets. [If the subordinate clause can't be made clear, you can recast the sentence.]

14c | Place limiting modifiers carefully.

Limiting modifiers such as *almost, even, just, only,* and *simply* modify the word or word groups that immediately follow them.

Aaron sold *only* one car today. [He sold no more than one.]
Only Aaron sold one car today. [No one else sold one car.]
Aaron *only* sold one car today. [He did nothing else but sell one car.]

14d | Avoid squinting modifiers.

A **squinting modifier** could modify either the word preceding it or the one following it. Since modifiers can perform only one modifying function, the reader will read it either the way the writer intended or the other way. It's the writer's job to see that the modifier modifies the right word.

SQUINTING	People who walk *normally* are healthier than those who don't.
CLEAR	People who walk are *normally* healthier than those who don't.
CLEAR	*Normally,* people who walk are healthier than those who don't.

14e | Avoid separating a subject from its verb or a verb from its object or complement.

We frequently interrupt a subject and its predicate or a verb and its object or complement with modifiers relating to one of the parts.

> The people *who take that attitude* deserve to be friendless. [The italicized clause separates the subject, *people*, from the verb, *deserve*.]

However, a long modifier in such a position may make a sentence awkward or confusing, especially if it precedes the word it modifies or relates to the whole sentence.

| AWKWARD | The old papers were, *just as I had suspected when I found them in the attic*, valuable. |
| REVISED | The old papers were valuable, *just as I had suspected when I found them in the attic*. |

14f | Avoid separating the parts of a verb phrase or the parts of an infinitive.

It is normal practice to separate parts of a verb phrase with single-word modifiers, as in *had surely known* or *hasn't entirely seen*. However, dividing these parts with a long modifier can create awkwardness.

AWKWARD	Charles has, *whether he admits it or not*, known about the exam. [Verb phrase *has known* split.]
REVISED	*Whether he admits it or not*, Charles has known about the exam.
REVISED	Charles has known about the exam, *whether he admits it or not*.

It is sometimes natural and acceptable to split an infinitive with a single-word modifier when the alternative would be awkward: *To openly shun younger students is not only arrogant but also rude.* However, dividing infinitives with a long modifier is usually unacceptable.

| AWKWARD | The aides are expected *to,* whether they want to or not, *do* whatever the nurses ask. [Infinitive split.] |
| REVISED | The aides are expected *to do* whatever the nurses ask, whether they want to or not. |

DANGLING MODIFIERS

14g | Avoid dangling modifiers.

A **dangling modifier** is a modifier that does not relate sensibly to any word in its sentence.

| DANGLING | To win the marathon, the weather should be cool. [The modifying phrase *To win the marathon* seems, illogically, to describe *weather*.] |

mm / dm

14

A dangling modifier usually appears at the beginning of a sentence, and it is usually a participial phrase (*screaming for help*), an infinitive phrase (*to arrive on time*), a prepositional phrase in which the object of the preposition is a gerund (*after riding the subway*), or an elliptical clause in which the subject is understood (*while in school*). (See 5c.)

All of these modifiers imply that somebody is performing the action they describe (somebody is screaming, somebody arrives on time, somebody rides the subway, somebody is in school). Readers generally understand that the doer of the action is the person or thing named in the subject of the main clause.

Screaming for help, the woman ran out of the burning house. [The woman was screaming.]

To arrive on time, I'll have to leave soon. [I want to arrive on time.]

After riding the subway, Cleo walks six blocks to school. [Cleo rides the subway.]

While in school, Karen tries to forget her troubles at home. [Karen is in school.]

If the implied subject of the modifier is different from the subject of the main clause, the modifier dangles.

Dangling modifiers can be corrected in two ways: (1) by expanding the modifier into a clause and naming the subject or (2) by revising the main clause so that its subject is the same as the subject implied in the phrase.

DANGLING	*After riding the subway,* Cleo's wallet was missing. [Prepositional phrase appears to modify *wallet,* so that the wallet rather than a person appears to have been riding the subway.]
REVISED	*After Cleo had ridden the subway,* his wallet was missing. [The phrase is expanded into a clause to include the subject.]
REVISED	*After riding the subway,* Cleo discovered that his wallet was missing. [The subject of *discovered* is the same as that of *riding.*]

|*Revising misplaced modifiers I*   EXERCISE   **14-1**

In the following sentences identify each misplaced modifier by underlining it. Then rewrite the sentence, placing the modifier where it belongs.

Example: I entered the frog that can jump sixteen feet <u>in the contest</u>.

> *In the contest, I entered the frog that can jump sixteen feet.*

1. Tobacco companies suggest that cigarettes are good for us in their ads.

2. Those of us who expect to get raises soon will be surprised.

3. They just bought gasoline before starting for the mountains.

4. Those who get average grades occasionally drop out of school.

5. Students only were allowed one helping at the dinner.

6. Mary wanted to have lunch in the park under the trees.

7. The rude woman blew smoke in our food that smelled like burning tires.

8. The man who committed the theft recently was caught.

9. The bus driver walked away from the accident with a freight train.

10. To get the costumes done in time for tonight's taping, help is needed in the costume department.

mm / dm

14

| *Revising misplaced modifiers II* EXERCISE **14-2**

In the following sentences underline the modifiers that cause awkwardness or confusion because they separate subject from predicate, verb from complement or object, parts of a verb phrase, or parts of an infinitive. Then rewrite each sentence, placing the modifier where it belongs.

mm / dm

14

Example: Maria had ever since junior high school planned to be a teacher.

Ever since junior high school, Maria had planned to be a teacher.

1. His goal is to have, with energy to spare, the ability to run as far as the courthouse.

2. The bicycle hit at high speed, with the front wheel wobbling crazily, the curb, throwing the rider into the hedge.

3. People drive ten miles hoping to, at the rate of a few cents a gallon, save themselves money.

4. Henry chose to, after a great deal of consideration, buy a violin that cost $2000.

5. The law requires, for the safety of the drivers behind you, that your brake lights be in working order at all times.

6. They held, on nearly any issue of importance, a difference of opinion.

7. You will see that the new building, after the ceremonies have ended and the bills have been paid, was absurdly expensive.

8. Arthritis tends to slowly and painfully swell a person's joints.

9. I always found she made, whenever asked to do something, excuses and objections.

10. The players were able to expertly and for several minutes stall the game.

|Revising dangling modifiers EXERCISE **14-3**

Most of the following sentences contain dangling modifiers. Rewrite each incorrect sentence by changing either the phrase or the main clause. When you keep the verbal phrase, make sure that its implied subject (the person or thing performing the action) is the same as the subject of the sentence. If a sentence is already correct, write *OK* in the space below it.

mm / dm

14

Example: To operate a citizen's-band radio, the fee is no longer required.

> *To operate a citizen's-band radio, one no longer needs to pay a fee.*

1. When reading poetry, rhythm often contributes to meaning.

2. After selecting an entrée, a wine should be ordered.

3. To recover from the surgery, the vet recommended leaving our puppy overnight.

4. When painting the walls, care should be taken to protect the floor from dripping brushes.

5. After adding three cups of ground chickpeas, the pot should be heated.

6. Taking a look at the gifts, the smallest box was the one the child selected.

7. Going for a touchdown, the quarterback lofted the ball.

8. Being a nonconformist, a multicolored wig was what she chose to wear.

9. With no concern that the audience was bored, the lecture continued for two hours.

10. To get the employer's attention, your résumé should be attractive and informative.

Misplaced and dangling modifiers: Review

Underline any misplaced or dangling modifiers in the following paragraph. Then revise the paragraph by moving modifiers, adding words, or rewriting sentences as necessary.

mm / dm

14

To successfully and calmly wait at a dentist's office before having your teeth drilled, a little preparation can make a great difference. First, select for taking along to the dentist's office your own book. Never plan to read old magazines dentists set around their waiting rooms that are always dog-eared, dated, and boring. Such magazines cannot provide you any escape from anticipating the pain that awaits you. Second, because you only by arriving early can increase your anxiety, arrive exactly on time and hope your wait will be brief. Third, have a good joke that you can tell the dentist in mind, because a dentist will be less likely to hurt you who is not feeling tense. By keeping the dentist at ease, the most important step will be achieved. A big pain, however, comes when the

dentist finishes. It is then that you must pay the bill.

15 | Mixed and Incomplete Sentences

Self-test

Write *M* on the blank to the left of any sentence that has mixed structure (parts that do not fit together in grammar or meaning). Write *I* on the blank if the sentence has an illogical or incomplete comparison. If a sentence is already correct, write *OK* on the blank.

Example: _____*M*_____ Getting a puppy is when you are up all night.

_____ 1. The reason we lost was because of a weak center.

_____ 2. Physics is where you apply mathematics to theory.

_____ 3. Joyce likes Sam better than Carol.

_____ 4. The Civil War era was a period of economic strain.

_____ 5. Cigars are more dangerous to inhale than any tobacco product.

_____ 6. Some kinds of gasoline have higher octane.

_____ 7. By seeing the accident made us start wearing seat belts.

_____ 8. The ones who are opposed or uninterested in participating stayed away from the rally.

_____ 9. A problem that came up was my stereo when the speaker blew out.

_____ 10. The catcher dropped the ball is why the runner is safe.

MIXED SENTENCES

A **mixed sentence** is a sentence whose parts do not fit together, either in grammar or in meaning.

15a | Be sure that the parts of your sentences, particularly subjects and predicates, fit together grammatically.

A **mixed sentence** will occur if you begin a sentence with one grammatical construction and end it with another.

MIXED	During the worst part of the storm frightened all of us. [Prepositional phrase used as a subject.]
REVISED	During the worst part of the storm, all of us were frightened. [Main clause revised to include a subject.]
REVISED	The worst part of the storm frightened all of us. [Preposition omitted; its object, *part*, becomes the subject of the sentence.]

Here is another example of a mixed construction in which there is no grammatical subject.

MIXED	By doing these things has made me a better person.
REVISED	By doing these things, I have become a better person. [Main clause revised to include a subject.]
REVISED	Doing these things has made me a better person. [Preposition omitted.]

15b | Be sure that the subjects and predicates of your sentences fit together in meaning.

The mixed constructions in 15a are faulty because they have no element that can function as the grammatical subject. Other mixed constructions result from **faulty predication,** in which the subjects and predicates do not fit together, especially when they are joined by a linking verb. While such constructions are common in speech, they are generally unacceptable in formal writing.

MIXED	A prank that irks me is my brother when he jumps out from behind corners. [The prank is not the brother.]
REVISED	A prank that irks me is my brother's jumping out from behind corners. [The prank is the jumping.]

Another common mixed construction occurs when the linking verb is followed by a *when, where,* or *because* clause. Such clauses are adverbial, but the linking verb requires a noun or a phrase or clause that can function as a noun.

MIXED	Happiness is when you know what you want from life. [The *when* clause is an adverb; the construction requires a noun.]
REVISED	Happiness is knowing what you want from life. [The gerund phrase beginning with *knowing* functions as a noun.]
MIXED	The reason for her failure is because she was ill. [The *because* clause is an adverb; the construction requires a noun.]
REVISED	The reason for her failure is that she was ill. [The *that* clause functions as a noun.]

INCOMPLETE SENTENCES

15c | **Be sure that omissions from compound constructions are consistent with grammar or idiom.**

Writers commonly omit unnecessary or repetitious words from their sentences, and such omissions are entirely acceptable. Here is an example of an acceptable omission:

COMPLETE   My mother graduated from both high school and college, my father only from high school. [The verb *graduated* can be omitted in the second part of the sentence.]

Sometimes, however, we omit words that only seem unnecessary, when in fact they are needed for grammatical completeness.

INCOMPLETE   My grandparents' generation was indoctrinated in conventional morality and strong-minded as a result.

REVISED   My grandparents' generation was indoctrinated in conventional morality and *was* strong-minded as a result. [The first *was* is part of a passive construction; the second is a linking verb.]

INCOMPLETE   Most of us lack knowledge or comfort with science.

REVISED   Most of us lack knowledge *of* or comfort with science. [Idiom requires different prepositions with *knowledge* and *comfort*. (See also 31b-3.)]

15d | **Be sure that all comparisons are complete and logical.**
1 | **State a comparison fully enough to ensure clarity.**

UNCLEAR   Mars is nearer to us than Pluto.

CLEAR   Mars is nearer to us than *it is to* Pluto.

CLEAR   Mars is nearer to us than Pluto *is*.

2 | **Be sure that the items being compared are in fact comparable.**

UNCLEAR   The chimpanzee's thumb is smaller than a *human*.

CLEAR   The chimpanzee's thumb is smaller than a *human's*.

3 | **In comparing members of the same class, use *other* or *any other*. In comparing members of different classes, use *any*.**

ILLOGICAL   The Pacific is larger than *any* ocean in the world.

LOGICAL   The Pacific is larger than *any other* ocean in the world.

ILLOGICAL   Toyotas are more popular than *any other* American car.

LOGICAL   Toyotas are more popular than *any* American car.

4 | Avoid comparisons that do not state what is being compared.

NOT   That restaurant is *better*.

BUT   That restaurant is *better than the other one we went to*.

15e | Be careful not to omit articles, prepositions, or other needed words.

Writers sometimes omit necessary words because of inattentive proofreading.

INCOMPLETE   She sat moodily in front the fireplace.

REVISED   She sat moodily in front *of* the fireplace.

Writers often omit *that* when it introduces a noun clause: *We realized* (*that*) *Joe was responsible.* But sometimes such an omission may cause an initial misreading: *Karen knew the flower vendor on the corner would leave by dark.* (At first reading we think that Karen knew who the flower vendor was rather than what time the vendor would leave.)

|*Revising mixed sentences*   EXERCISE **15-1**

Revise each mixed sentence below by changing, adding, or deleting words as needed to make its parts fit together in grammar and meaning.

Example: The team that won was the result of bad refereeing.

The team's winning was the result of bad refereeing.

mixed / inc

15

1. While bargaining for a discount was how she made the clerk angry.

2. Just because you took a course in computer programs doesn't mean you're an expert.

3. Hesitation is when you lose your chance.

4. For someone who knows that fighting and sports are not necessarily related could be very disturbed at a hockey game.

5. The hardware store that burned down on First Street was caused by an arsonist.

6. The reason he was lonely was because he had a quick, violent temper.

7. When you have a college education means that you have more skills for the job market and a better knowledge of the world.

8. By being obedient to the rules of my parents has kept me out of trouble.

9. Psychology is where people study behavioral characteristics.

10. The use of a little mustard in egg salad improves the flavor.

Revising
incomplete sentences

Adding or changing words as necessary, rewrite the following sentences to provide any carelessly omitted words or to complete the compound constructions and comparisons.

mixed / inc

15

Example: The apartment was as roomy as any other house.

The apartment was as roomy as any house.

1. We suspect that Judy is more devoted to music than Andy.

2. The administration claims to believe and plan for the college's future.

3. Some brands of vodka contain more alcohol than any beverage.

4. I was going seventy miles per hour and stopped for speeding.

5. The Hilton's room service is as good as the Astor.

6. They were fond and totally devoted to their grandchild.

7. The second-night audience found the play more impressive than the opening-night audience.

8. He left the art book in the car or the basketball practice.

9. Aspirin does more good and less harmful to you than some other nonprescription drugs.

10. Faulkner's novels are more complex than any author's.

11. He fears death more than his sister.

12. Fruit juice stains are harder to remove than grass.

13. All the voting members are consulted regularly and present at every meeting.

14. The living room was larger than any other house she had ever seen.

15. All those opposed or in favor of the resolution raised their hands.

Mixed and incomplete sentences: Review

EXERCISE **15-3**

Circle the number preceding any mixed or incomplete sentence in the following paragraph. Then revise the paragraph by changing, deleting, or adding words as necessary.

mixed / inc

15

¹During the first day at college was somewhat frightening for me. ²I was unsure of my ability to meet new people and do well in my classes. ³I began feeling more secure when I met my roommate, who was friendlier than any student I had met so far. ⁴The second day I met my classes and found that the professors and my classmates were all human. ⁵Most seemed nice. ⁶When I got the assignments and heard what was expected of me gave me even more security. ⁷By the third day, I felt relaxed. ⁸I knew my schedule very well, and I was beginning make friends. ⁹Although I had planned to go home on the first weekend, I stayed on campus. ¹⁰Now I do not plan to home until Thanksgiving.

IV | Effective Sentences

16 | *Using Coordination and Subordination*

Self-test

In each set of sentences below, circle the letter preceding the sentence that most effectively establishes relations among ideas in the sentence.

Example: a. The 3:30 plane had engine problems and crashed on the runway.
b. The 3:30 plane, which had engine problems, crashed on the runway.

1. a. Because the doctor had moved from the town, 325 persons had nowhere to go for emergency treatment.
   b. The doctor moved from the town, and 325 persons had nowhere to go for emergency treatment.
2. a. The islanders once practiced cannibalism and infanticide, and they now operate hospitals.
   b. The islanders, who once practiced cannibalism and infanticide, now operate hospitals.
3. a. Roland, an accomplished pole-vaulter, won three national championships.
   b. Roland was an accomplished pole-vaulter, and he won three national championships.
4. a. The box had a locked, blue lid, and he carried it with him everywhere.
   b. He carried the box, which had a locked, blue lid, with him everywhere.
5. a. I had read twenty reports of rabies, and I was quite wary of the raccoon.
   b. Having read twenty reports of rabies, I was quite wary of the raccoon.
6. a. As he was missing the ball game, the child hunched angrily over the keyboard.
   b. Because he was missing the ball game, the child hunched angrily over the keyboard.
7. a. The donation went to refugee orphans who were suffering from malnutrition.
   b. The donation went to refugee orphans, and they were suffering from malnutrition.

8. a. We finally finished rehearsing the song, but the polls had already closed, so I didn't have a chance to vote.
   b. Because the polls had already closed by the time we finished rehearsing the song, I didn't have a chance to vote.
9. a. The woman decided to rake the leaves even though they were blowing against the fence.
   b. The woman decided to rake the leaves, and they were blowing against the fence.
10. a. The test, which I failed and which made me want to quit school, was given on Monday.
    b. Because I failed the test on Monday, I wanted to quit school.

Use **coordination** to give equal emphasis to the meanings contained in two or more sentence elements: *The conductor fainted, but the orchestra played on.* Use **subordination** to emphasize the meaning in one element over that in another: *Even though the conductor fainted, the orchestra played on.*

16a | Coordinating to relate equal ideas

Coordination is achieved by linking sentence elements with the coordinating conjunctions *and, but, or, nor,* and sometimes *for, so,* and *yet* (see 5d-1); by linking elements with conjunctive adverbs such as *however* and *therefore* (see 5d-2); or by expressing elements in the same grammatical construction (see Chapter 17 on parallelism). By linking ideas, coordination shows a relation between them that simple sentences alone rarely can.

> Men in the Middle Ages granted women few political rights. Men idolized women in literature. [No relation established.]
> Men in the Middle Ages granted women few political rights, *but* they idolized women in literature. [Coordinating conjunction.]
> Men in the Middle Ages granted women few political rights; *however,* they idolized women in literature. [Conjunctive adverb.]
> Men in the Middle Ages *excluded women from politics* but *idolized them in literature.* [Parallelism and coordinating conjunction.]

Punctuating coordinated words, phrases, and clauses

A comma is conventionally used between two main clauses joined by a coordinating conjunction. The comma is *not* used between other sentence elements joined by the conjunction.

> Some varieties of sweet alyssum grow about nine inches high, and others are much shorter. [Two main clauses joined by *and* are separated by a comma; 21a.]
> The alyssum plant has clusters of tiny lavender or white flowers. [The two adjectives *lavender* and *white* are joined by the conjunction *or* but are not separated with a comma.]
> The alyssum is a hardy plant and starts easily from seed. [The two verbs *is* and *starts* are joined by the conjunction *and* but are not separated with a comma; 21j-2.]

Two main clauses that are not joined by a coordinating conjunction should be separated with a semicolon, whether or not the second clause contains a conjunctive adverb.

> Some varieties of sweet alyssum grow about nine inches high; others are much shorter. [Two main clauses not joined by a conjunction; 22a.]
>
> Some varieties of sweet alyssum grow about nine inches high; however, others are much shorter. [The second main clause begins with a conjunctive adverb, and the semicolon is required; 22b.]

Commas are used for separating two kinds of coordinate elements: (1) coordinate adjectives not joined by a conjunction and (2) items in a series.

> Sweet alyssum is a low, spreading plant. [The coordinate adjectives *low* and *spreading* are not joined by a conjunction, so they are separated by a comma; 21f-2.]
>
> Sweet alyssum is a popular plant for borders because it *grows low, spreads broad,* and *flowers profusely*. [The series of three verbs plus their modifiers are separated by commas; 21f-1.]

1 | Avoiding faulty coordination

Faulty coordination occurs when two ideas that are coordinated do not seem related in fact.

> FAULTY   The crash occurred at night, and all the passengers were rescued.
>
> REVISED   Because the crash occurred at night, the rescuers had a difficult job. However, they rescued all the passengers.

2 | Avoiding excessive coordination

Though coordination can establish relations between ideas, it does not do so as effectively as subordination does. Since strings of compounded elements may blur relations, use subordination to clarify relations and to vary sentence structure.

> EXCESSIVE COORDINATION   I spent Easter vacation at the beach, and I met my future wife, and three months later we were married.
>
> REVISED   During Easter vacation at the beach, I met my future wife. Three months later we were married.

16b | Subordinating to distinguish main ideas

As the preceding example shows, subordination allows you to play down less significant information and to stress important points by placing them in main clauses. Subordinate information may be conveyed in a subordinate clause (introduced by a subordinating conjunction such as *although* or *when* or a relative pronoun — *who, which,* or *that*), in a phrase, or in a single word.

The dog snarled at me, and it ran toward the fence. [Compound sentence gives equal emphasis to both ideas by placing both in main clauses.]

The dog snarled at me as it ran toward the fence. [Subordinate clause reduces emphasis on the dog's running and shows how the running relates to the snarling.]

Running toward the fence, the dog snarled at me. [Participial phrase further subordinates the dog's running.]

Snarling at me, the dog ran toward the fence. [Participial phrase subordinates the dog's snarling and emphasizes its running.]

The snarling dog ran toward the fence. [Adjective gives minimum emphasis to the dog's snarling.]

How do we decide which clauses should be subordinate? Generally as writers we don't have any trouble knowing what our main ideas are. If you do at times have some trouble, you might consider this rule of thumb: details of time, cause, condition, concession, purpose, and identification are usually subordinate; that is, they are details that can serve adjective or adverb functions.

Punctuating subordinate constructions

A modifying word, phrase, or clause that introduces a sentence or clause is usually set off with a comma (21b).

Islamic law influenced Turkish life for nearly a thousand years; *however,* the new republican government outlawed many Islamic practices. [The conjunctive adverb that introduces the second clause is set off with a comma.]

The Turkish Ottoman Empire ended in 1922; *the next year*, Turkey became a republic. [The phrase *the next year* introduces the second clause and is set off with a comma.]

Although in landmass Turkey is little larger than Texas, it has more than three times as many people. [The introductory clause is set off with a comma.]

An interrupting or concluding modifier that restricts the meaning of the word it modifies is not set off with commas (21c).

Leaves *of various species of trees* differ in size and shape. [The prepositional phrases are essential to the meaning of the sentence.]

The trunks of trees are made up of four layers of plant tissue *wrapped around one another*. [The participial phrase is essential to the meaning of the sentence.]

Some tree buds contain a shoot *that develops into a leaf-bearing twig*. [The italicized clause is essential to the sentence.]

When interrupting subordinate constructions do not restrict meaning, they are set off with commas (or sometimes with dashes). (See also 21c and 5c-4.)

A tennis ball may be hit either on the fly, *which is called a volley*, or after the first bounce, *which is called a ground stroke*. [Both *which* clauses are not essential to the meaning of the sentence.]

Adverb clauses are usually set off when they come at the beginning of the sentence and are usually not set off when they follow a main clause. (See 21c and 5c-4.)

1 | Avoiding faulty subordination

Faulty subordination occurs when the idea expressed in a subordinate clause or a phrase seems more important than the idea expressed in the main clause.

FAULTY   Elephants and their ancestors have ruled the plains for millions of years, although they are now being squeezed out by humans.

REVISED   Although elephants and their ancestors have ruled the plains for millions of years, they are now being squeezed out by humans.

2 | Avoiding excessive subordination

Excessive subordination occurs when too many subordinate constructions, containing details only loosely related, are strung together in a single sentence. The result is not only awkward but confusing. A common kind of excessive subordination occurs with the use of a succession of modifying *which* clauses. Use other modifying structures to simplify the sentence.

EXCESSIVE SUBORDINATION   The internal structure of minerals was shown by X-ray studies, the first of which occurred in 1912, at which time scientists did not really understand crystals, which is what minerals are.

REVISED   In 1912, before scientists really understood what crystals are, X-ray studies showed that the internal structure of minerals is made up of crystals.

16c | Choosing clear connectors
1 | Avoiding ambiguous connectors: *as* and *while*

Because the subordinating conjunction *as* can indicate a relation of time or cause (as well as comparison), its meaning in a sentence may be unclear.

UNCLEAR   *As* I was awaiting a visitor, the telephone's ringing surprised me.

CLEAR   *When* I was awaiting a visitor, the telephone's ringing surprised me.

CLEAR   *Because* I was awaiting a visitor, the telephone's ringing surprised me.

Similarly, the subordinating conjunction *while* can indicate a relation of time or concession. If the meaning of *while* is not unmistakably clear, use a more precise connector.

UNCLEAR	*While* the downtown stores were renovated, customers flocked to the shopping malls.
CLEAR	*Until* the downtown stores were renovated, customers flocked to the shopping malls.
CLEAR	*Although* the downtown stores were being renovated, customers flocked to the shopping malls.

2 | Avoiding misused connectors: *as, like,* and *while*

As is a nonstandard substitute for *whether* or *that.*

| NONSTANDARD | Jim didn't know *as* he wanted to play his guitar. |
| REVISED | Jim didn't know *whether* he wanted to play his guitar. |

Like used as a subordinating conjunction is common in everyday speech but is avoided in writing and standard speech. Use *as, as if,* or *as though* instead.

| INFORMAL | The singer sounded *like* she was getting tired. |
| REVISED | The singer sounded *as if* she was getting tired. |

Avoid using the subordinating conjunction *while* when you mean *and* or *but.*

| FAULTY | Jack wanted to go to the theater, *while* his wife preferred to stay home and watch television. |
| REVISED | Jack wanted to go to the theater, *but* his wife preferred to stay home and watch television. |

|Using coordination

Combine each pair of simple sentences below into one sentence, using the coordinating conjunction that is most appropriate for meaning. Choose from *and, but, or, nor, for, so,* and *yet.* Try to use each conjunction at least once.

Example: The novels have richly varied characters. The philosophy contained in all the novels is the same.

> *The novels have richly varied characters, but they all contain the same philosophy.*

coord / sub

16

1. Television announcers want to look appealing on color sets. They usually wear bright clothing.

2. Gretzky broke the record for the number of goals in a single season. He is also likely to break the lifetime record.

3. She exercises for several hours a day. She sleeps well at night.

4. Winter driving is hazardous. More accidents occur in summer than in winter.

5. Rush hour is my favorite time to drive. I enjoy the challenge of heavy traffic.

6. You should go to sleep now. You won't be able to play in the game tomorrow.

7. I do not enjoy physics. I do not enjoy the other sciences either.

8. The reporter was fired from the newspaper. She has now been unemployed for a year.

9. Woody Allen is our favorite film director. We have seen all of his films.

10. A set of tennis gives me ample exercise. The running burns off hundreds of calories.

| *Using subordination*

Combine each pair of simple sentences below into one sentence by placing the less important information in a subordinate clause, a phrase, or a single word, as specified in parentheses.

Example: Many Americans favor handgun control. Congress has not enacted any laws requiring it. (Subordinate clause beginning with *although*.)

Although many Americans favor handgun control, Congress has not enacted any laws requiring it.

coord / sub

16

1. His shoulders are slightly stooped. He still looks energetic. (Subordinate clause beginning with *although*.)

2. Tonight he played his greatest role. It was Lothario. (Single word.)

3. We were nearly at the end of our trip. Then we were stopped by the state police. (Phrase beginning with *nearly*.)

4. The meeting ended. The hall was again deserted. (Subordinate clause beginning with *after*.)

5. Sparrows are unwelcome pests. They may eat as much as 6 percent of a grain crop. (Phrase beginning with *unwelcome*.)

6. She wore jogging shoes. The waiter refused to seat her. (Subordinate clause beginning with *because*.)

7. The patient was recovering. He was depressed and irritable. (Single word.)

8. He felt embarrassed. He could not get a word out. (Phrase beginning with *feeling*.)

9. German stereo components are often of high quality. They are usually more expensive than Japanese components. (Subordinate clause beginning with *although*.)

10. I did not know how to interpret the question. It had four possible answers. (Subordinate clause beginning with *because*.)

Using coordination and subordination

EXERCISE **16-3**

Revise each passage below to use both coordination and subordination effectively in establishing relations among ideas and in distinguishing main ideas from less important ones.

1. A good example of corruption occurred in the U.S. Navy. The event occurred recently. A Washington columnist told the story. An officer was demoted. He had reported some of his fellow officers. The officers were responsible for training recruits. The officers had sold the recruits uniforms. The uniforms were supposed to be issued free.

coord / sub

16

_____

_____

_____

_____

_____

_____

_____

_____

_____

2. A triangle was tattooed on the back of his hand. He got the tattoo when he was sixteen. It was a symbol of the instrument he had played. He had played in a rock band. His instrument had been a brass triangle.

_____

_____

_____

_____

_____

_____

_____

_____

_____

_____

3. The night was black, and the road was slippery, and the car, which ran up an embankment, rolled over twice, an action that caused the occupants to be thrown out, while no one was injured. The car was a total loss.

_____

_____

_____

_____

_____

_____

_____

_____

_____

17 | *Using Parallelism*

Self-test

Some of the following sentences could be made more effective if words and phrases with parallel importance and function were given parallel grammatical form. If a sentence seems ineffective because of a lack of parallelism, underline those words or phrases that should be given parallel form. If a sentence uses parallelism effectively, write *OK* to the left of it.

Example: I spent the evening reading and with my friends.

1. Going to a professional football game is better than to watch one on TV.
2. The Episcopalians and those who are Catholics have more ritual in their services than Methodism has.
3. In the spring I took economics, and in the fall I took statistics.
4. Men's clothing styles and the clothes that women wear have grown similar in recent years.
5. In both the campus and in the town, sentiment for drug control was strong.
6. Field trips are required not only for biology but also for geology.
7. The seniors, juniors, and the sophomores all helped raise money.
8. To coach professional baseball and coaching professional football were both career possibilities for him.
9. Listening to records and attendance at live concerts are both enjoyable.
10. In many aspects of technology, the Japanese excel over England.

      Parallelism is the duplication of grammatical form between two or more coordinate elements.

I was beckoned by	the	broad	blue	horizon
and	the	straight	open	road.

Parallelism gives the same grammatical form to elements with the same function and importance. It also emphasizes important points and gives a sentence coherence.

17a | Using parallelism for coordinate elements

1 | Using parallelism for elements linked by coordinating conjunctions

The coordinating conjunctions (*and, but, or, nor,* and *yet*) should link words and word groups with parallel structures. The very term *coordinating* implies equivalence — balanced ideas and balanced grammatical structures.

<table>
<tr><td>FAULTY</td><td>A commercial should be of interest and informative. [Prepositional phrase is paired with an adjective.]</td></tr>
<tr><td>REVISED</td><td>A commercial should be interesting and informative. [Two adjectives.]</td></tr>
<tr><td>FAULTY</td><td>The rookie pitched an uneven game, allowing only three hits but he walked seven batters. [Participial phrase is paired with a clause.]</td></tr>
<tr><td>REVISED</td><td>The rookie pitched an uneven game, allowing only three hits but walking seven batters. [Two participial phrases.]</td></tr>
</table>

//

17

Although the two elements that are coordinated must be parallel in structure, they need not be matched word for word.

<table>
<tr><td>PARALLEL</td><td>Mosquitoes lay their eggs in marshes, swamps, and other pools of quiet water. [Three nouns coordinated as objects of the preposition in; only the third noun is modified by an adjective and another prepositional phrase.]</td></tr>
</table>

2 | Using parallelism for elements linked by correlative conjunctions

Correlative conjunction (such as *not only . . . but also, either . . . or, both . . . and*) should always link parallel elements. Be sure that the element after the second connector matches the element after the first connector.

<table>
<tr><td>FAULTY</td><td>The poet wrote not only of Greece but also Asia Minor.</td></tr>
<tr><td>REVISED</td><td>The poet wrote not only of Greece but also of Asia Minor.</td></tr>
<tr><td>FAULTY</td><td>He said either to wait or go without him.</td></tr>
<tr><td>REVISED</td><td>He said either to wait or to go without him.</td></tr>
<tr><td>FAULTY</td><td>You can either pay by cash or by check.</td></tr>
<tr><td>REVISED</td><td>You can pay either by cash or by check.</td></tr>
</table>

3 | Using parallelism for elements being compared or contrasted

<table>
<tr><td>FAULTY</td><td>Riding in a parade is better than to watch one.</td></tr>
<tr><td>REVISED</td><td>Riding in a parade is better than watching one.</td></tr>
</table>

4 | Using parallelism for items in lists or outlines

FAULTY The most dangerous forms of transportation are *riding motorcycles, cars,* and *riding a bicycle.*

REVISED The most dangerous forms of transportation are *motorcycles, cars,* and *bicycles.*

17b | Using parallelism to increase coherence

Parallelism helps strengthen the relation between elements in a sentence.

WEAK The brightest object in the night sky is the moon, although it gives off no light of its own.

PARALLEL The moon is the brightest object in the night sky, but it gives off no light of its own. [The contrast is emphasized through parallel grammatical structure — two main clauses joined by the pivotal coordinating conjunction *but* — and with the same subject, *moon* and *it,* for both clauses.]

Parallelism also makes it possible for writers to reduce wordiness and repetition while strengthening the focus of their statements.

WORDY A few moon craters are located on the tops of small mountains. Craters have also been seen in the centers of low, rounded hills.

PARALLEL A few moon craters are located on the tops of small mountains or in the centers of low, rounded hills.

//

17

Identifying parallelism   EXERCISE **17-1**

Underline the parallel elements in each sentence below. Circle coordinating conjunctions.

Example: Fitzgerald was a novelist of the 1920s (and) 1930s who wrote colorful short stories (and) romantic novels.

1. The people crowded the main street, pouring from cars, trucks, buses, and subways.

2. In the lawn, in the garden, in the orchard — gypsy moths were everywhere she looked.

3. The Baptists and the Methodists have similar doctrines.

4. Some patients played checkers, others played cards, and still others played shuffleboard.

5. One bit of old-fashioned advice warns against baths in the morning and urges baths in the evening instead.

6. I think that self-help books, which not only peddle common sense but also inflate expectations, do more harm than good for their readers.

7. The kitchen doors squeaked on their hinges, plates clattered on the tables, and diners chattered throughout the small room.

8. Cigarette smoking is unhealthful not only for the smokers themselves but also for the nonsmokers around them.

9. Her clasped hands, her taut shoulders, and her tense face showed her concern.

10. I will go out of my way to see an old movie or to watch a puppet show.

//
17

11. Peering into the room and pushing against the windows, the children stared eagerly at the Christmas display.

12. Looking both at the exam paper and at the assignment sheet, she threw up her hands.

13. Last week I claimed that I would never again take an English course, but this week I find that I enjoy English.

14. His cheerful face — caked, chapped, and hardened — revealed not only the nature of his work but also the strength of his character.

15. Grease spots and tobacco stains made a curious design on his pink tie.

//

17

Name _____ Date _____ Score _____

|*Achieving parallelism*   EXERCISE **17-2**

The following sentences are weakened by a lack of parallelism for coordinate elements. Locate the coordinate elements and revise each sentence to make the elements parallel.

Example: I would much rather have an older Corvette than a new one because of the older one's body style and the engine is more powerful.

> *I would much rather have an older Corvette than a newer one because of the older one's better body style and more powerful engine.*

11

17

1. Replacing Chevrolet engine parts costs more than replacing the parts of an Oldsmobile.

2. With a lack of cash and not having a credit card, we could not fill the gas tank.

3. Neither a paper clip nor should a knife be used for cleaning a stereo needle.

4. She left the thermostat on high, took long showers, and she was a waster of energy.

5. Either by entering the side gate without paying or stealing tickets, they get in for free.

6. The bill could have been determined either at the hourly rate or determined at the job rate.

7. The corporation agreed to recall the cars and make the repair or is refunding the cost of replacement.

8. Different persons respond to different types of music, such as folk, rock, or they like to listen to blues.

9. The statistics were either unavailable or they were inaccurate.

10. There are many sports in which Americans excel over Europe.

Parallelism: Review

Combine each set of sentences below into a single sentence, using parallel structures where appropriate.

Example: Cattle management is being mechanized. Strip-mining consumes the rangelands. The rangelands are also being consumed by housing developments.

> *Because cattle management is being mechanized and the rangelands are being consumed by strip-mining and housing developments, cowboys are becoming an endangered species.*

1. Our school has put on several musicals. In May we put on *Godspell*. We put on *Hello, Dolly* in February. Two months before that, we did *Jesus Christ, Superstar*.

2. We paid $30 for steaks. The drinks cost $3.60. We spent $40 for the picnic.

3. The heat was stifling. Also stifling was the humidity. Thus we stayed indoors.

4. He often read aloud from Robert Frost's poetry. He also read from novels by Ernest Hemingway. He also read from plays written by Harold Pinter.

5. Elizabeth collected only commemorative stamps. Foreign stamps were all her father collected. They both collected only canceled stamps to keep their hobbies inexpensive.

6. During the summer easterly trade winds make the air feel pleasant. The air during the winter feels chilly because of dampness.

7. Civil defense may be a good use of our money. Or the money we spend on it may be wasted.

8. Sunlight reflected off the glass sides of the building. Drivers had difficulty seeing the traffic lights. The Walk/Don't Walk signs were hard for the pedestrians to see.

9. Many of the pictures were underexposed. A few of the pictures were exposed too much. Only one was exposed properly.

10. On his first trip to New York, he was mugged. He was hit by a taxi on his second trip. Someone stole his camera on his third trip.

18 | Emphasizing Main Ideas

Self-test

In each set of sentences below, circle the letter of the sentence that better emphasizes the main point.

Example: a. Crime affects thousands of people each day, and few crimes are solved.

(b.) Although crime affects thousands of people each day, few crimes are solved.

1. a. Because of a heavy snow and icy roads, the delivery truck did not make its rounds.
   b. The delivery truck did not make its rounds because a heavy snow fell and the roads were icy.
2. a. The first year his batting average was .220, the second year it was .300, and the third year it was .200.
   b. The first year his batting average was .220 and the third year it was .200, but the second year it was .300.
3. a. The manager forgot the cash box in the desk.
   b. The cash box in the desk was forgotten by the manager.
4. a. It is her desire to run her own architectural firm.
   b. She wants to run her own architectural firm.
5. a. When the city legalized pornography, the tax revenue increased and the population doubled.
   b. The population doubled when the city legalized pornography, and the tax revenue increased.
6. a. It is probable that the telephone company will introduce inexpensive telecopiers for residential customers.
   b. The telephone company will probably introduce inexpensive telecopiers for residential customers.
7. a. A man should seek to know in order to live instead of seeking to live in order to know.
   b. A man should seek to know in order to live, not seek to live in order to know.
8. a. Some spectators were angry, some were disappointed, but all wanted refunds.
   b. All the spectators wanted refunds, some were disappointed, and some were angry.

9. a. The defendant left the building by a rope ladder, according to a witness who testified on the first day of the trial.
   b. According to a witness who testified on the first day of the trial, the defendant left the building by a rope ladder.
10. a. Hovering around me, his brother watched everything I did by looking over my shoulder.
   b. His brother watched everything I did, hovering around me and looking over my shoulder.

18a | Arranging ideas effectively

Use sentence construction to emphasize your main ideas.

1 | Using sentence beginnings and endings

The most emphatic positions in a sentence are the beginning and the ending. Don't bury an important idea in the middle of a sentence.

emph

18

UNEMPHATIC   Because its winds sometimes exceed 500 miles per hour and it has more energy than an atomic bomb, *the tornado is one of the most destructive forces on earth*, and it can strike without warning.

REVISED   *The tornado is one of the most destructive forces on earth* because its winds sometimes exceed 500 miles per hour, it has more energy than an atomic bomb, and it can strike without warning.

REVISED   Because its winds sometimes exceed 500 miles an hour, because it has more energy than an atomic bomb, and because it can strike without warning, *the tornado is one of the most destructive forces on earth*.

The first revision above is a **cumulative,** or **loose, sentence:** The main point comes first and is followed by explanation. The second revision is a **periodic sentence:** All the explanation comes first, and the main point comes at the end. Since the main clause is withheld until the end of the sentence, the periodic sentence creates suspense.

2 | Arranging parallel elements effectively

Elements in a series using parallel constructions (see Chapter 17) should be arranged in order of increasing importance.

UNEMPHATIC   The friends he had, the life he led, the books he read, the sports he played — all brought him satisfaction.

REVISED   The books he read, the sports he played, the friends he had, the life he led — all brought him satisfaction.

A balanced sentence — one made up of directly parallel clauses — can be very emphatic.

The screen filled with color; the hall filled with music.
The climb was painfully difficult; the descent was refreshingly simple.

18b | Repeating ideas

Needless repetition will weaken a sentence, but careful repetition of a key word or phrase can effectively emphasize that word or phrase.

> Cholera, which kills by dehydration, should be treated *by giving* the victim huge amounts of water, *not by giving* food intravenously and *not by giving* a drug.

18c | Separating ideas

Setting a statement off from the ideas to which it relates emphasizes it. In the following sentences the emphasis increases as the separation becomes stronger, from coordinating conjunction to semicolon to period.

> The bill of the marabou stork is long and wedge-shaped, and its head is nearly bald.
> The bill of the marabou stork is long and wedge-shaped; its head is nearly bald.
> The bill of the marabou stork is long and wedge-shaped. Its head is nearly bald.

A revision using dashes to set off a part of a sentence is another way to gain emphasis.

> The bill of the marabou stork is long and wedge-shaped — its head nearly bald.

18d | Preferring the active voice

In the active voice the subject acts; in the passive voice the subject is acted upon. (See 7h.) Active constructions are usually more direct and emphatic than passive constructions.

> PASSIVE   The game was watched with great interest by the scout.
>
> ACTIVE   The scout watched the game with great interest.

18e | Being concise

Unnecessary words weaken sentences. Concise sentences convey the essential meaning in as few words as possible and thus help emphasize ideas. (See also 31c.) Examine your sentences for empty phrases as well as for needless repetition.

> WEAK   It is unlikely that a complete resolution of the conflict between the Arabs and Israelis will be achieved.
>
> EMPHATIC The Arab-Israeli conflict probably will not be resolved.
>
> WEAK   She behaved in such a way as to alienate her friends.
>
> EMPHATIC She alienated her friends.

emph

18

331

WEAK	A problem of communication arose between the room-mates, who did not speak to each other.
EMPHATIC	The roommates did not speak to each other.

| Revising for emphasis

Rewrite each sentence or group of sentences below to emphasize the main idea, following the instructions in parentheses. Make your sentences as concise as possible.

Example: Sea gulls quarrel frequently over food. They quarrel noisily. But they are graceful in flight. (Make one sentence with the main idea at the end of the sentence.)

Though they quarrel frequently and noisily over food, sea gulls are graceful in flight.

emph

18

1. The prize will probably be awarded by the foundation for the first time in fifty years. (Use the active voice.)

2. Legal gambling can increase tax revenues. It can increase tourism. It can also increase crime. (Make two sentences with the main idea in a separate sentence.)

3. The kitchen contains poisons that can kill instantly. It is a room filled with perils. It also contains appliances that can be heated to 500 degrees. (Make one sentence with the main idea at the end.)

4. He had only six dollars left for his heart medicine, to buy food for his cat, and for his dinner. (Use parallelism for series elements and arrange them in order of importance.)

5. It was the winning point that was scored by Shank. (Use normal word order and the active voice.)

6. Carrying its prey in its beak, the hawk swooped upward. The hawk was flapping its wings. (Make one sentence with the main idea at the beginning of the sentence.)

emph

18

7. A lock was placed on the warehouse door by the guard, who was afraid of theft. (Use the active voice and place the main idea at the beginning or end of the sentence.)

8. Because of the steady downpour, the ball could not be held on to by the players, three players tore ligaments, and the uniforms were ruined by the players. (Use parallelism for series elements and arrange them in order of importance. Change passive voice to active.)

9. For three hours the speaker discussed nutrition in a monotonous voice. (Place the main idea at the beginning of the sentence.)

10. There is some likelihood this year that raises may be withheld by management. (Use normal word order and the active voice.)

|Combining sentences

Combine each group of sentences below into one or two sentences that emphasize the main idea of the group. Make your sentences effective with an appropriate combination of beginnings and endings, parallelism, arrangement of elements in order of increasing importance, careful repetition, separation, and the active voice. Be concise.

Example: She does not own a crystal ball. She does not understand sports. She won the baseball pool. A four-leaf clover was not found by her.

> *She does not own a crystal ball or a four-leaf clover, and she does not understand sports. Yet she won the baseball pool.*

emph

18

1. The largest bank cut its lending rate. The other large banks followed. The experts thought the rates would keep dropping. The rates held steady.

2. My telephone does not work during a rain. I receive calls for wrong numbers. I got twenty-seven calls for an ice-cream shop one rainy afternoon. I was trying to study.

3. Summer jobs were hard to find. There was no construction work in town. The gas stations were going broke. No businesses were hiring.

4. A policeman has to keep his car keys handy. He has to know how to drive at high speed. A policeman needs special driving skills and habits. He has to know how to drive with caution. He must always remember to park facing an exit.

5. The old woman had white hair. Her face had many wrinkles. She pulled a revolver and took my wallet. Her blue eyes twinkled. She looked innocent.

6. A visit to a nursing home can be depressing. It does not have to be. Taking time to smile and say hello cheers up the residents. Bringing along a small child cheers up the residents.

7. *Breakout* by Ron LeFlore is an inspiring story. It describes his life in prison. It is my favorite biography. He used his skill at baseball to rejoin society.

8. Twelve head of cattle died in the fire. Gasoline spread across the highway and ignited a field. The tanker truck overturned.

9. The last issue of the magazine described Leon Spinks. He could have been a champion for several years. He seemed to lose faith in himself.

10. Dachshunds shed very little. They are great pets. They are obedient. Dachshunds are gentle with children.

19 | *Achieving Variety*

Self-test

Below are two pairs of paragraphs. Circle the letter preceding the paragraph in each pair that conveys its meaning more clearly by varying the lengths or structures of sentences.

1.   a. Backpacking in the wilderness is a gratifying experience, but it can also be dangerous. Besides contending with rough terrain and watching out for predatory animals, the backpacker must be self-sufficient because the wilderness by definition contains few people. Minimum survival equipment includes food, a canteen filled with water, a knife, a compass and maps, wooden matches in a watertight container, extra woolen clothes, and a poncho or tarpaulin. In addition, a first-aid kit can save a life in an emergency.

     b. Backpacking in the wilderness is a gratifying experience, but it can also be dangerous. The backpacker must contend with rough terrain, and he or she must also watch out for predatory animals. The wilderness by definition contains few people, so the backpacker must also be self-sufficient. Minimum survival equipment includes food, a canteen filled with water, a knife, a compass and maps, wooden matches in a watertight container, extra woolen clothes, and a poncho or tarpaulin; and a first-aid kit can save a life in an emergency.

2.   a. Crossword puzzles have been around since early in this century. They were introduced as space filler in newspapers, and they were primitive at first. Now they are more complex; some can be completed only by experts. The typical square puzzle with blank and darkened boxes and numbered clues is still most common. A more sophisticated puzzle is one with numbered clues but no diagram, and another sophisticated puzzle has a diagram but unnumbered, scrambled clues.

     b. Crossword puzzles have been around since early in this century. Introduced as space filler in newspapers, the puzzles were primitive at first. Now some are so complex that they can be completed only by experts. The typical square puzzle with blank and darkened boxes is still most common. More sophisticated are the puzzles with numbered clues but no diagram or with a diagram but unnumbered, scrambled clues.

Sentences work together to convey your meaning. A string of similar sentences is not only dull but also potentially confusing because important ideas do not stand out. To enhance your ideas, you should vary your sentences in length, emphasis, and arrangement of elements to reflect the importance and complexity of your thoughts.

19a | Varying sentence length and emphasis

A paragraph filled with sentences of the same length lacks variety, especially if the sentences are all very short (say, ten or fifteen words) or very long (thirty or more words). Check your sentences to be sure you have not relied primarily on similar lengths.

1 | Avoiding strings of brief and simple sentences

A series of brief, simple sentences can be choppy and dull. Use connecting and subordinating words to combine sentences, emphasizing important ideas and de-emphasizing lesser ones.

WEAK	The lab is modern and bare. It is almost frightening. It has fluorescent lights. The walls are green. The floors are gray. The equipment is shiny. All these produce a cold atmosphere. They remind the visitor of the work done here.
REVISED	The lab is modern, bare, and almost frightening. Its fluorescent lights, green walls, gray floors, and shiny equipment produce a cold atmosphere that reminds the visitor of the work done here.

2 | Avoiding excessive compounding

A string of compound sentences can be just as monotonous as a string of simple sentences. Vary the sentences and emphasize important ideas by changing some main clauses into modifiers and varying their positions.

WEAK	I opened the door, and a salesman stood on the porch. He began his pitch, but he seemed drowsy. His voice was expressionless, and it finally trailed off in midsentence. I was startled, but I did not know what to do. He clearly was not going away, so I just shut the door on him.
REVISED	I opened the door to a salesman on the porch. Though he began his pitch, he seemed drowsy, and his expressionless voice finally trailed off in midsentence. I was startled. Not knowing what to do and seeing that he was not going away, I just shut the door on him.

19b | Varying sentence beginnings

Most English sentences follow the standard pattern of subject followed by verb followed by object or complement. But a series of sentences all beginning with their subjects can be dull. Vary the pattern by beginning some sentences with elements other than subjects. An adverb modifier can postpone the subject.

> *Mercilessly,* the loan shark's agents pursued her. [Adverb.]
> *Because she had no money,* she could not pay the interest on the loan. [Adverb clause.]

A participial phrase can postpone the subject.

> *Sitting on the bench,* Oscar plucked his guitar.

A coordinating conjunction or transitional expression (see 3b-6) not only varies a sentence beginning but also links two sentences containing related ideas.

> Meteors rarely burn for more than a few seconds. One occasionally leaves a shining trail that lasts several minutes. [No connector.]
> Meteors rarely burn for more than a few seconds. But one occasionally leaves a shining trail that lasts several minutes. [Coordinating conjunction as connector.]
> Meteors rarely burn for more than a few seconds. However, one occasionally leaves a shining trail that lasts several minutes. [Conjunctive adverb as connector.]

Occasionally, you may want to vary sentence beginnings by using an expletive construction such as *there is* or *it is* (see 5e-4), although frequent use of expletives will make your writing wordy and vague. One of the best uses of the expletive *there* is to announce something.

> *There were* nine invitations in the mail.

> *There are* two ways for a student to register for classes in this school.

19c | Inverting the normal word order

Normal word order for English sentences is subject, verb, and complement or object. Occasionally reversing this order can provide sentence variety and sometimes emphasize an idea.

> Near the center of town stood a large orange sculpture. [Prepositional phrase, verb, subject.]

> Our question we asked without hesitation. [Direct object, subject, predicate.]

19d | Mixing types of sentences

Since most sentences we use in writing are statements, a question, command, or exclamation can introduce variety if used sparingly. Questions, especially, can raise the central issue of a discussion or emphasize an important point.

> Visitors appreciate the warmth of Homer's hotel. But why, they wonder, is it called the Hairless Raccoon? Legend has it that Homer once demonstrated a hair-growth tonic of his own invention on the back of a raccoon. The raccoon lost its hair, and Homer lost his business. In his next venture, operating a hotel, Homer immortalized his victim.

|*Varying sentence beginnings*   EXERCISE **19-1**

Rewrite each sentence or pair of sentences as specified in parentheses to practice postponing sentence subjects.

Example: The union remained on strike after the votes were counted. (Begin with *After.*)

After the votes were counted, the union remained on strike.

1. Penicillin can cure the disease she has. She is allergic to penicillin, though. (Begin one sentence with a coordinating conjunction or a transitional expression.)

2. The bamboo basket, which looks frail, is really quite sturdy. (Begin with *Although.*)

3. The speech was priced at one dollar a copy, and not one copy was sold. (Begin with *Because.*)

4. The crane crashed five stories to the street and smashed a truck. (Begin with a participial phrase.)

5. The party invitations omitted the address. Just a few people came. (Begin one sentence with a transitional expression.)

6. He never became a great architect, but he was not obscure. (Begin with *Even though*.)

7. Johnson won the game by sinking a shot from thirty feet. (Begin with a participial phrase.)

8. Money for travel is in the budget. (Begin with *There*.)

9. Being a good photographer certainly requires skill. It also requires money. (Begin one sentence with a transitional expression.)

10. We were swimming in the pond when we heard a shot from across the meadows. (Begin with *While*.)

Varying sentences
in paragraphs

The following paragraphs lack sentence variety. Rewrite each paragraph to stress main ideas by changing some main clauses into modifiers and by varying sentence lengths and beginnings.

Example: Almost everyone is afraid of something. Some people are paralyzed by multiple phobias, however. They cannot leave the house for fear of an emotional collapse. Treating such people is a slow process. They have to become comfortable with each feared object or situation. The treatment may occur in a laboratory. It may also occur in natural surroundings. The phobias are eliminated one at a time. The patient can often resume a normal life at the end of treatment.

var

19

> Although almost everyone is afraid of something, some people are so paralyzed by multiple phobias that they cannot leave the house for fear of an emotional collapse. Treating such people is a slow process, for they have to become comfortable with each feared object or situation. The treatment, which may occur in a laboratory or in natural surroundings, eliminates the phobias one at a time. At the end of the treatment, the patient can often resume a normal life.

1.   The army has spent over $3 million to evaluate the intelligence of its recruits. The results were satisfying in some respects. They were disappointing in other respects. The army discovered that it was recruiting many people of above-average intelligence. It was also recruiting many people with below-average intelligence. The army is planning to spend another $15 million this year to educate recruits. Its education programs have not had much success in the past.

2.   Almost 4 billion domesticated chickens exist in the world today, and they produce almost 400 billion eggs every year. The modern chicken descends from a wild Southeast Asian bird. Humans first tamed the wild bird over five thousand years ago, and they were breeding and raising them some time later. Spanish explorers first brought domesticated chickens to the New World, and later the Pilgrims also brought them. Chicken meat and eggs are a staple of the diet throughout the world, but Americans eat more of both than anyone else. A disproportionate share of the world's chickens are in the United States. Chicken farming is a major U.S. business.

var

19

V | Punctuation
20 | *End Punctuation*

Self-test

Add periods, question marks, or exclamation points wherever needed in the following sentences, and circle any punctuation marks that are not needed. If a sentence is already punctuated correctly, write *OK* to the left of it.

Example: What points should I consider before I make my decision **?**

1. The sign on the mailbox read, "William Morris, Esq.."
2. He asked whether I had played varsity
3. UNESCO is quite active in Africa.
4. "Did you return the package?," she asked.
5. They think the legislative delay is intolerable.
6. Hiram P Luce, BA, edited the anthology.
7. Her former home is Washington, D.C..
8. "Ready!!!" he shouted.
9. The talk was titled "When Will We Have Rights"
10. The report will be available at noon

. ? !

20

THE PERIOD

20a | **Use the period to end sentences that are statements, mild commands, or indirect questions.**

STATEMENT	The crisis resolved itself.
MILD COMMAND	Turn to the illustration on the next page.
INDIRECT QUESTION	They asked whether I intended to vote.

20b | **Use periods with most abbreviations.**

Dr., Mr., Mrs., B.A., A.M., B.C., p., George H. Packer

Periods are commonly omitted from abbreviations for organizations and agencies (CBS, FDA). They are always omitted from **acronyms,** which are pronounceable words made from the first letters of the words in a name (UNESCO, NATO). (See Chapter 28 for a discussion of abbreviations that are or are not acceptable in most writing.)

Use only one period when an abbreviation comes at the end of a sentence: *Our speaker was G. Maurice Dunning, M.D.*

THE QUESTION MARK

20c | **Use the question mark after direct questions.**

Do we know what caused the fire?

After indirect questions, use the period: *He asked whether I knew what caused the fire.* (See 20a.)

NOTE: Never use a question mark with another question mark, a period, or a comma.

FAULTY   He asked, "Which way to the dance hall?."

REVISED   He asked, "Which way to the dance hall?"

20d | **Use a question mark within parentheses to indicate doubt about the correctness of a number or date.**

At the time of Chaucer's birth in 1340 (?), only a few people could read.

THE EXCLAMATION POINT

20e | **Use the exclamation point after emphatic statements and interjections and after strong commands.**

EMPHATIC INTERJECTION   Oh! I wish I had my camera.

EMPHATIC STATEMENT   We must not allow it!

EMPHATIC COMMAND   Stop talking!

NOTE: Never use an exclamation point with another exclamation point, a period, or a comma.

FAULTY   "He stole my wallet!," I yelled.

REVISED   "He stole my wallet!" I yelled.

20f | **Avoid overusing exclamation points.**

Don't use exclamation points to express amazement or sarcasm or to stress important points. Avoid using multiple exclamation points (!!!).

FAULTY   These facts prove that women office workers are discriminated against in this city!

REVISED   These facts prove that women office workers are discriminated against in this city.

| *Using end punctuation* EXERCISE **20-1**

Circle the place in each sentence where punctuation should be added or is used incorrectly, and write the correct punctuation, along with the adjacent words, on the blank to the left. If the sentence is already punctuated correctly, write *OK* on the blank.

Example: _address ?" he_ "Why must I have an address⊙" he asked.

_____ 1. She screamed, "Get it right!!!"

_____ 2. A cloud of dust from the track settled on the crew from NBC.

_____ 3. We puzzled over the question of how to find the square root of 1109?

_____ 4. Stay away from the quarry.

_____ 5. Did he say, "Never"??

_____ 6. The lecture was titled "Why Are Citizens Alienated from Government."

_____ 7. I do not understand why the applause was so weak

_____ 8. Mr Schmidt got a new wig after Christmas.

_____ 9. The dean said the dorms would be painted, but we knew better!

_____ 10. Covered with mud, the dog made a horrible mess

_____ 11. Did he ask, "When?"

_____ 12. They wanted to see if there had been an accident?

. ? !

20

347

_____ 13. The snow continues to fall throughout May

_____ 14. We called to ask whether the snowstorm had closed the airport?

_____ 15. NATO is not in danger of collapse.

_____ 16. I demand to see him in person!!!

_____ 17. The physician studied what causes lycanthropy to strike the aged?

_____ 18. "Get out of my yard!," screamed the woman to the costumed children.

_____ 19. Sgt Meyer changed his tactics.

_____ 20. She asked, "Why are you late?."

_____ 21. The Greek philosopher Aristippus died in 356 (?) B.C..

.?!

20

_____ 22. Always take a good knife on a camping trip

_____ 23. The governor told the demonstrators to clear out of his path!

_____ 24. The Future Farmers of America formed a chapter here in 1953; since then the FFA has been quite active.

_____ 25. A one-armed man built this chair!

_____ 26. A nutritionist with an MS degree selected the school menu.

_____ 27. Is there a single reason why I have to tolerate my neighbor's late-night parties? No!

_____ 28. Does Dr Felson charge reasonable fees?

_____ 29. The speaker came all the way from Washington, D.C..

_____ 30. Her autobiography was published in 1903 by the St James Press.

21 | *The Comma*

Self-test

Add commas wherever they are needed in the sentences below, and circle any commas that are not needed. If a sentence is already punctuated correctly, write *OK* to the left of it.

Example: The owners preferred to negotiate with Zusky**,** who had broken his contract.

1. Some walls in the old house were painted yellow and others were covered with dark paneling.
2. Before the mail arrived this morning we were waiting impatiently for word.
3. Tuition of course is high this year.
4. He claimed that the lawn mower was defective.
5. The vandalized dilapidated building was the gym.
6. At sixty workers are eligible for retirement.
7. "I can't" she said, looking apologetic.
8. The voters elected a woman who had served three terms in Congress.
9. The time to act, is now.
10. The rally ended with the familiar song, "We Shall Overcome."

The comma is often essential to separate parts of a sentence and to provide clarity.

> **COMMA NEEDED**   Seventy stories below the basement caught fire.
>
> **REVISED**   Seventy stories below, the basement caught fire.

However, overuse of the comma can also make writing unclear.

> **UNNEEDED COMMA**   My father and I, began collecting the sap when snow was still on the ground.
>
> **REVISED**   My father and I began collecting the sap when snow was still on the ground.
>
> **UNNEEDED COMMA**   My sister and I decided, that we would not go to the game.
>
> **REVISED**   My sister and I decided that we would not go to the game.

∧
,

21

21a | Use a comma before a coordinating conjunction linking main clauses.

The coordinating conjunctions are *and, but, or, nor,* and sometimes *for, so,* and *yet.* When one of them links main clauses, it should be preceded by a comma. Do *not* use a comma before a coordinating conjunction that joins sentence elements other than main clauses. (See 21j-2.)

> I had three accidents, *and* my insurance costs doubled.
> The book listed poisonous plants, *but* it did not mention poison ivy.
> My high school teachers did not help me learn to write, *nor* did they encourage me to read extensively.
> The movie went way over budget, *for* the director insisted on shooting most of it in the jungle.
> I bought the text secondhand, *yet* it cost over $20.
> The book included all the information I could use, *so* I didn't need to consult other sources.

Exceptions: Some writers prefer to use a semicolon before *so* and *yet.*

> I bought the text secondhand; *yet* it cost over $20.
> The book included all the information I could use; *so* I didn't need to consult other sources.

A semicolon may clarify the division between long main clauses that contain internal punctuation (see 22c).

> The trip was six hours long, involving three plane changes, two hours waiting in airports, and two taxi rides; *but* I arrived feeling fresh.

A comma may be omitted between main clauses when the clauses are short and closely related in meaning, although the comma is always correct.

> We give little *and* we expect much.

21b | Use a comma to set off most introductory elements.

Grammatical elements that begin sentences — such as modifying verbal phrases, long prepositional phrases, and subordinate clauses — should be set off with commas.

> Although the bank offered "free checking," it tripled the charge for printing checks.
> Expecting a green and tree-filled campus, I was shocked to find it surrounded by highways and parking lots.
> Singing, he skipped down the hall.

If the introductory element is short, especially if it is a short prepositional phrase, the comma is often omitted.

> At times it seems the children have little in common.

Remember, however, that clarity may require the comma.

COMMA NEEDED	At three thoroughbred horses are eligible to run in the Kentucky Derby.
REVISED	At three, thoroughbred horses are eligible to run in the Kentucky Derby.

Although *modifying* phrases or clauses are often set off with commas, *noun* phrases and clauses are not.

What the reporter said may be wrong.
Walking to work gives me needed exercise.

$\wedge$
,

21

Using commas between main clauses and after introductory elements

Place a caret (∧) at each place in the following sentences where a comma is required. (Some sentences may require more than one comma.) If the sentence is already punctuated correctly or if an introductory element does not need to be set off, write *OK* to the left of the sentence.

Example: The snow was so deep that I could not get to class∧nor could I even get out the front door.

1. Shaking his head in amazement Jessup headed for the bench.
2. The hamburger was extended with oatmeal and the oatmeal seemed to be made of sawdust.
3. Lacking rating symbols the guidebook was difficult to follow.
4. If something is upsetting you might dream about it.
5. After witnessing Jones's third slam-dunk the crowd had new respect for him.
6. President Coolidge was not a great speaker nor was he a wise administrator.
7. As the light turned yellow the accident flashed through my mind.
8. The audience was receptive but the comedian made a poor effort.
9. In the old days a woman could be suspended for coming in a half-hour past curfew.
10. On the hood of the dragster the trophy gleamed in the sunshine.
11. If more people become unemployed housing prices will fall.
12. When the council changed the zoning law the mayor resigned in protest.
13. The pianist played a medley of Cohan tunes after the applause subsided.
14. Margaret had not yet learned about the theft for she had not yet been home.
15. If I had to bet I would place my money on the Yankees but it is a tough choice.
16. Paying a dollar for a bottle of water will always seem ridiculous to me.
17. Showing up late for practice the coach looked exhausted.

∧
,

21

18. The estate was not for sale but it remained unoccupied for many years.

19. A new set of luggage and a camera were stolen but the jewelry was overlooked.

20. In a single season attendance at professional hockey games dropped 15 percent.

21. Since it takes at least a week to obtain a passport you should get one in advance.

22. The beagle discovered the rabbit's hole and cornered the animal before we caught up.

23. Having taught for thirty years Professor Whitbeck looks as if he could use a rest.

24. Receiving a gift certificate to Woody's would make her happy.

25. When you go to sleep after intense mental activity your dreams may carry on with that activity and allow you to rest at the same time.

26. With winter coming everyone wants to get away.

27. About a month before school started in the fall I got a letter from the college.

28. Once a week the subway has broken down and I have been on it every time.

29. Not everyone who uses a pesticide reads the directions on the label and the result is a large number of preventable deaths and illnesses.

30. Four-wheel-drive vehicles have increased in popularity and also in price.

∧
,

21

21c | Use a comma or commas to set off nonrestrictive elements.

Restrictive elements limit the meaning of the word or words they refer to and thus cannot be omitted without changing meaning. They are not set off by commas or other punctuation. **Nonrestrictive elements** add information but do not limit meaning and thus are optional in the sentence. They are always set off by commas or other punctuation.

RESTRICTIVE | All the students *who graduated in June* found jobs. [The *who* clause cannot be omitted without changing meaning.]

NONRESTRICTIVE | The school library, *which now has 500,000 books,* is adequate for most undergraduates. [The *which* clause adds important information, but its omission would not change the meaning of the main clause.]

1 | Use a comma or commas to set off nonrestrictive clauses and phrases.

RESTRICTIVE | The car *that was stolen* was mine. [The *that* clause identifies which car and is essential to the meaning of the sentence.]

The police officers *on the case* didn't know me. [The prepositional phrase identifies the police officers, so it cannot be removed without obscuring the meaning of the sentence.]

NONRESTRICTIVE | The Guggenheim Gallery, *which opened two years ago,* has been very successful. [The *which* clause is useful information but can be omitted without altering the meaning of the main clause.]

Moline, Illinois, *located on the Mississippi River,* is known as the farm implement capital of the world. [The participial phrase, though important, can be removed from the sentence without changing the meaning.]

Adjective clauses introduced by *that* or an understood *that* are always restrictive and are not set off with commas.

NOTE: Most adverb clauses are restrictive and are set off only when they introduce or interrupt sentences (see 21b). Adverb clauses at the ends of sentences are set off only when they are truly nonrestrictive, adding incidental information.

RESTRICTIVE | I'll buy the rest of my books *when I get enough money.*
When I get enough money, I'll buy the rest of my books.

NONRESTRICTIVE | I didn't buy all my books, since I didn't have enough money.

2 | Use a comma or commas to set off nonrestrictive appositives.

RESTRICTIVE   The jazz pianist *Keith Jarrett* will perform here next year. [Without the appositive the sentence is meaningless.]

NONRESTRICTIVE   The concert will be held in Hadley Hall, *the place in which most music events are held.* [The meaning of the main clause doesn't change if the appositive is omitted. Appositives and modifiers following a proper noun are almost always nonrestrictive, since the name identifies the person or place.]

3 | Use a comma or commas to set off parenthetical expressions.

Parenthetical expressions interrupt a sentence to explain or make a transition or to add extra information. Brief parenthetical expressions are sometimes set off with commas. (See also Chapter 25 on the uses of dashes and parentheses to set off parenthetical elements.)

The cost of living, *believe it or not,* actually declined this month.
The bus, *for example,* has not been on time once in twenty days.
The tail, *almost twenty inches long,* acts as a fly swatter.

4 | Use a comma or commas to set off *yes* and *no,* tag questions, words of direct address, and mild interjections.

Yes, we would be willing to perform for the patients.
You went to the interview, *didn't you?*
Harriet, we appreciate your support.
Well, I didn't expect to receive an A.

21d | Use a comma or commas to set off absolute phrases.

An **absolute phrase** usually consists of a participle and the noun or pronoun performing the action of that verbal. (See 5c-3.) Because it includes the subject of its action, it modifies an entire sentence or main clause rather than a single word and can therefore function at different positions in the sentence. Wherever it appears, however, it is set off with commas.

The old car having refused to start, I am without transportation.
The meeting (being) over, the reporters called their papers. [When the participle is *being,* it is often omitted.]

21e | Use a comma or commas to set off phrases expressing contrast.

We saw the play, *not the movie.*

The use of the comma is optional for contrasting phrases that begin with *but.*

The dean invited faculty *but not students* to the reception.
The dean invited faculty, *but not students,* to the reception.

Using commas with nonrestrictive elements, absolute phrases, phrases of contrast

EXERCISE **21-2**

Place a caret (∧) at each place in the following sentences where a comma is required. (Some sentences may require more than one comma.) If the sentence is already punctuated correctly, write *OK* to the left of it.

Example: The poster∧a picture of a singer∧cost $4.98.

A. 1. The trial, which lasted for three days ended with a verdict of guilty.
2. No one who is related to a police officer would say police work is easy or safe.
3. The American director who may be most popular now is Steven Spielberg.
4. All the banks I hear, refuse to lend money to students.
5. Two men one of them wearing a ski mask robbed the small grocery store where I work.
6. The woman who called me claimed to work at the White House.
7. We are after all here to get an education.
8. There were few surprises I thought, in tonight's game.
9. Senator Cumo who chairs the finance committee voted against tax reform.
10. Her health failing Sarah called her children around her.
11. The audience becoming impatient the theater manager asked for a little more time to get the sound system working.
12. My dog whose name is Jasper eats two rawhide bones a day.
13. The tax forms six pages of figures were mailed yesterday.
14. The delay during which the pitcher's arm tightened up lasted an hour.
15. The famous New York restaurant Four Seasons has many imitators.
16. I replied, "Yes I would like to play music professionally."
17. Every morning I drink grapefruit juice which contains vitamins and eat a brownie which tastes good.
18. Hypnotism still not allowable in court testimony is a fertile method for developing one's memory.
19. The songs of birds are more complex than they sound.

∧
,

21

20. The music blaring next door I was unable to concentrate on my reading.

B. 1. We must report on three books one being a biography.

2. It was geometry not algebra that gave me the most trouble in high school.

3. Some local newspapers such as the *Times,* the *Enquirer,* and the *News* which is a weekly failed to carry the story.

4. We waited only two days before we walked on our new concrete steps.

5. Even then fifty years ago the house was run-down.

6. After defeating his opponent, who was much smaller than he, the wrestler retired.

7. Shakespeare's *Hamlet,* the world's best tragedy drew a record crowd at the college theater Saturday.

8. He answered, "Yes the price is reasonable isn't it?"

9. Mathematics which she believes is a pure science is her major.

10. Children under ten years old should not be exposed to violence.

11. My father reads only one magazine *The New Yorker* regularly.

12. We learned that a Dr. Allen microbiologist raises white mice for profit.

13. My cousin who has the same name that I do is in jail for bank robbery.

14. There is only one intersection in town that has a stoplight, and it is the scene of the most accidents.

15. Mrs. Kim who spoke little English wanted written directions.

16. When you wake up, remember to mail your application Richard.

17. He agreed, of course, that two more hours of play would be tiring.

18. Compared with the interstate highway, Route 460 is shorter not safer.

19. A specialist in fractures the physician studied the X rays.

20. Color photographs unlike black and white will fade in about ten years.

∧
,

21

21f Use commas between items in a series and between coordinate adjectives.

1 Use commas between words, phrases, or clauses forming a series.

A **series** consists of three or more items of equal importance.

> The sauce contained *mustard, ground cloves,* and *sherry.*

The last item in the series is usually preceded by a coordinating conjunction, most commonly *and.* Usage varies on including the comma before the conjunction, but most careful writers use it to prevent confusion over whether the last two items are coordinated separately from the other items.

> CONFUSING   The house had missing storm windows, shoddy plumbing and electrical outlets in inconvenient places.
>
> CLEAR   The house had missing storm windows, shoddy plumbing, and electrical outlets in inconvenient places.

When the elements in a series are long, grammatically complicated, or internally punctuated, they should be connected with semicolons (see 22d).

> Sylvia had three brothers: Jim, 16; Alfred, 14; and Billy, 2.

2 Use commas between coordinate adjectives not linked by conjunctions.

Coordinate adjectives are two or more adjectives modifying equally the same word. Such adjectives may be separated either by a coordinating conjunction or by a comma.

> The *rickety, old* swing could not support the child's weight.
> The *rickety* and *old* swing could not support the child's weight.
> The *old, rickety* swing could not support the child's weight.

As these examples show, two adjectives are coordinate (1) if they can be reversed without a change in the meaning and (2) if *and* can be inserted between them. (Note that a comma is not used between the final adjective and the noun.) If these changes cannot be made, then the adjectives are not coordinate and they should not be separated by a comma.

> FAULTY   My father owned a pair of unique, rubber boxing gloves.
>
> REVISED   My father owned a pair of unique rubber boxing gloves.

21g Use commas according to convention in dates, addresses, place names, and long numbers.

> August 23, 1943, is the day she was born. [The second comma is required to complete setting off the year.]
> She was born on 23 August 1943. [No commas are used when the day precedes the month.]
> She moved here from Axtel, Kansas, in 1975.

He lived at 1321 Cardinal Drive, Birmingham, Alabama 35223, for only a year. [No comma is used before the zip code.]

If a date is given only as month and year, no comma is necessary: *The battalion landed in April 1945.*

The comma separates long numbers into groups of three, starting from the right: *83,745,906.* The comma is optional in four-digit numbers: both *4,215* and *4215* are acceptable.

21h | Use commas with quotations according to standard practice.

1 | Ordinarily, use a comma to separate introductory and concluding explanatory words from quotations.

Ginott tells parents, "Resist the temptation to preach."
"Get out of my life," she said coldly.

Don't use a comma when the quotation ends in a question mark or exclamation point: *"Did they go?" I asked.* (See 20c and 20e.) Use a colon to introduce a quotation when the quotation is long or weighty (see 25a).

2 | Use a comma after the first part of a quotation interrupted by explanatory words. Follow the explanatory words with the punctuation required by the quotation.

"Our attitude toward money," Harvey Cox says, "is unrealistic in the extreme." [The explanatory words interrupt a sentence in the quotation.]
"We have been drifting for years," the speaker said. "It is almost too late." [The explanatory words fall at the end of a sentence in the quotation.]

3 | Place commas that follow quotations within quotation marks.

"No split infinitives," she muttered in her sleep.

For further guidance on punctuating quotations, see 24g.

21i | Use commas to prevent misreading.

Even when a comma is not required by a rule, it may be necessary to prevent words from running together in ways that cause confusion.

CONFUSING	Always before she had bought her tickets in advance. [The short introductory phrase does not require a comma, but clarity does.]
CLEAR	Always before, she had bought her tickets in advance.

| *Using commas with series, coordinate adjectives, dates, addresses, long numbers, quotations* | EXERCISE **21-3** |

Place a caret (∧) at each place in the following sentences where a comma is required. (Some sentences will require more than one comma.) If the sentence is already punctuated correctly, write *OK* to the left of it.

Example: Our team played tournaments last year in Canada∧Japan∧and Australia and lost only in Canada.

A.

1. A high-priced skimpy meal was all that was available.

2. After testing 33107 subjects, the scientist still thought she needed a bigger sample.

3. "Please, can you help me?" the old woman asked.

4. "I need fifty volunteers, now" the physical education teacher said ominously.

5. The excited angry bull was shot to death after it destroyed the garden.

6. The shop is located at 2110 Greenwood Street Kennett Square Pennsylvania 19348.

7. Many athletes believe that they are more important vital people than those who come to watch them.

8. The open mine attracted children looking for adventure couples needing privacy and old drunks seeking a place to sleep.

9. The aged exotic dancer gave the arresting police officer a phony address.

10. I bought a CB radio on July 2 1982 and I still have not received the missing warranty from the manufacturer.

11. The area around Riverside California has some of the most polluted air in the country.

12. The records disappeared from the doctor's office in Olean New York yesterday.

13. Seven lonely desperate people come to the neighborhood center for counseling every night.

14. The lantern has a large very heavy base.

∧
,
21

15. The town council designated the area's oldest largest house as a land-mark.
16. The evil day of 29 October 1929, when the stock market crashed, marked the beginning of the Great Depression.
17. The office is located at 714 W. Lincoln Harlingen Texas.
18. The November 17 1944 issue of the *Times* carried the submarine story.
19. The team lost its final games by scores of 72–66 72–68 and 72–70.
20. Through the wide-open door I could hear them by turns squabbling laughing and crying.

B.
1. The strangely spiced soup contained asparagus carrots and coriander.
2. The first line reads "I never said I wanted you to come."
3. In August 1982 over 36500 people saw the exhibit at the museum.
4. Dangerous experimental drugs are readily available in Europe.
5. Dozens and dozens of children lined up for lessons at the hot steamy poolside.
6. Squealing tires roaring engines yelling fans and black-and-white flags are my dominant images of the auto race.
7. I expected long classes lots of reading and difficult examinations when I entered college but not boring courses.
8. The 1982 team's record-breaking winning streak is unlikely to be matched.
9. We expected one more blanketing snow before spring.
10. The car's headlights were smashed its hood was badly dented and muddy and its convertible top was ripped.
11. "Hand in your tests" the examiner said "and then file singly out of the room."
12. The runner — fresh eager and well rested — took his starting position.
13. "What will happen if we lose the series?" the coach asked.
14. Only a foolish thoughtless person would leave the door unlocked.
15. He will never never agree to the proposal.
16. The *Journal* for September 28 1979 carried fourteen advertisements for adult movies.
17. She is young inexperienced and unfit for the position.
18. "Fertilizer" the consultant agreed "should have been applied in the fall."
19. Having old worn-out tires did not help the resale value of the car.
20. My mother yelled "Wash the sand off your feet!"

21j | Avoid misusing or overusing the comma.

1 | Don't use a comma to separate a subject from its verb, or a verb or a preposition from its object, unless the words between them require punctuation.

> FAULTY   The bearded man, was the one the police arrested. [Subject separated from verb.]
>
> REVISED   The bearded man was the one the police arrested.
>
> FAULTY   Washington quartered, his troops in the fields nearby. [Verb separated from direct object.]
>
> REVISED   Washington quartered his troops in the fields nearby.
>
> FAULTY   The city of Milwaukee is known for its variety of ethnic groups, such as, Germans, blacks, Irish, and Polish. [Preposition *such as* separated from its objects.]
>
> REVISED   The city of Milwaukee is known for its variety of ethnic groups, such as Germans, blacks, Irish, and Polish.

In the following sentence, the nonrestrictive appositive *my uncle* comes between the subject and verb and must be set off with two commas.

> The bearded man, my uncle, was arrested for demonstrating.

(See also 21c for use of commas with nonrestrictive elements.)

2 | Don't use a comma to separate words or phrases joined by co-ordinating conjunctions.

Although commas are conventionally used between two main clauses joined by a coordinating conjunction, they are *not* usually used between other sentence elements joined by a coordinating conjunction.

> FAULTY   The concerts in the chapel, and all other musical events are free. [Two subjects, *concerts* and *events*, are incorrectly separated.]
>
> REVISED   The concerts in the chapel and all other musical events are free.
>
> FAULTY   I found the book on Thursday, and returned it to the library on Friday. [Two verbs, *found* and *returned*, should not be separated.]
>
> REVISED   I found the book on Thursday and returned it to the library on Friday.
>
> FAULTY   My high school teachers did not help me learn to write, or to read extensively. [Two infinitives, *to write* and *to read*, the compound object of *learn*, should not be separated.]
>
> REVISED   My high school teachers did not help me learn to write or to read extensively.

∧
,

21

Do not use a comma directly following a coordinating conjunction unless the conjunction is followed by an interrupting clause or phrase that must be enclosed with commas.

FAULTY   Money can be anything that people agree to accept in exchange for goods and services, but, most nations today use metal coins, paper bills, and bank checks.

REVISED   Money can be anything that people agree to accept in exchange for goods and services, but most nations today use metal coins, paper bills, and bank checks.

REVISED   Most nations today use metal coins, paper bills, and bank checks, but, if a country wanted to do so, it could use beads or shells for money. [The interrupting *if* clause is set off with commas.]

3 | Don't use commas to set off restrictive elements.

FAULTY   The miner, who contracts black lung disease, is eligible for compensation.

REVISED   The miner who contracts black lung disease is eligible for compensation.

Adjective clauses beginning with *that* are always restrictive and should not be set off by commas.

FAULTY   Countries, that have completely socialized medicine, pay for all medical care with public funds.

REVISED   Countries that have completely socialized medicine pay for all medical care with public funds.

See also 21c.

4 | Don't use a comma before the first or after the last item in a series unless a rule requires it.

FAULTY   Tragedies, comedies, and tragicomedies, are represented in the text.

REVISED   Tragedies, comedies, and tragicomedies are represented in the text.

5 | Don't use commas to set off an indirect quotation or a single word unless it is a nonrestrictive appositive.

FAULTY   He asked, who was responsible.

REVISED   He asked who was responsible.

FAULTY   My roommate pronounces, "Washington," as, "Warshington."

REVISED   My roommate pronounces "Washington" as "Warshington."

Name _____ Date _____ Score _____

Correcting misused and overused commas

In the following sentences circle each comma that does not belong. Note that not all the commas are wrong. If a sentence is already punctuated correctly, write *OK* to the left of it.

Example: The characters in the novel,are not very believable.

A.
1. The dark clouds in the east, indicated the storm was near.
2. He declined the drink, saying he was sleepy.
3. The one who committed the crime, got away.
4. "What seems to be your problem?," the doctor asked.
5. The children, Oscar, and Bo, are cared for in the afternoons by their aunt.
6. The most valuable, beautiful stone in the world, is the diamond.
7. Architects, who design houses, should know better than to put the back and front doors on the same side of a house.
8. Anyone who earns honors, in this college has to work very hard.
9. She thought, that the old book was a valuable, first edition.
10. The first karate belt is white, and the next, is orange.
11. The Monte Carlo, is one of General Motors' most luxurious cars.
12. Our training exercises, consisting of wind sprints, push-ups, jumping jacks, and a three-mile run, leave us too tired to play.
13. Dressed in Navajo garb, he made a very, impressive entrance.
14. The new cars will not run as fast as the old ones because, they have too much pollution-control equipment.
15. I was one of two, unfortunate participants in the race, who had to drop out because of muscle cramps.
16. The sizes of the tanks used to make moonshine can vary, but, they usually hold fifty gallons.
17. Soon, there were six trout on the line.
18. I could not have a ruder, or meaner roommate.
19. The tourism bureau, it appeared, had closed for the summer.
20. At the end of our vacation, the refrigerator contained, two slices of salami, a bottle of soda, and half a jar of mustard.

$\wedge$
,

21

365

B. 1. We promote people on the basis of seniority, not merit.
2. The threat of aggression, is constant.
3. We were angry at the kid who yelled at us, but my friend said, to let him go.
4. Both of us qualified for the job, that only one of us could have.
5. We played, in a noisy, dark, café, for people who could not even see or hear us.
6. Hate derives from troubling experiences such as, an unhappy, strife-torn, home life.
7. The air, hazy and damp, drifted over the valley.
8. Divisive issues dominated the long, tedious, meeting.
9. Monkeys make bad pets because they have, bad tempers, long nails, and sharp teeth.
10. The best stories, in the literary magazine, are those by Muscante and Rowling.
11. The visitors' register, showed that our last call had been exactly, a year ago.
12. No one, of course, seeks humiliation, but some do ask for it.
13. Athletic shoes such as sneakers, which have been around for decades, seem more popular today than ever.
14. A dozen cats crowded eagerly, in front of the chipmunk's hole.
15. Just before the gun blast, the dove, wheeled sharply.
16. She said, that all of us would have to take the test over because one person cheated.
17. The, elusive, eccentric professor, usually kept his office door firmly shut.
18. In winter I do not have to cut the grass, or rake the leaves.
19. The word, *taco*, means different things to different people.
20. Buried 1000 years ago, the urn was unearthed in 1925.

∧
,
21

|Commas: Review I exercise **21-5**

The following sentences contain unneeded commas and omit needed ones. (They also contain commas that are used correctly.) Circle every unneeded comma and insert a caret (∧) where a comma is needed. If a sentence is already punctuated correctly, write *OK* to the left of it.

Example: For Sue∧Joe is a friend⊘that can be relied on.

1. Each time the train stopped the sudden, sharp, jolt awakened the, old, tired, porter.

2. People, who claim to feel sympathy for the poor but do not want to pay tax money to help the poor, are hypocrites.

3. Going back to school, is something that can frighten a veteran.

4. The competition scored a total of 1103 points against our 974 in 1982.

5. "Besides" he said "our success depends on our practicing."

6. *King Lear* the only tragedy we staged last fall, was a sellout.

7. A less successful effort, was that of the tennis team.

8. We know, however, that the markup on the car was 30 percent.

9. The movie, which was seen by the largest audience ever grossed millions of dollars.

10. Long an admirer of the actress, John, saw each of her pictures twice.

11. However long it may take you be certain to prepare thoroughly.

12. He said, that term insurance is the best buy.

13. If as predicted the storm had turned out to sea the trailer would still be in one, large piece instead of in two, smaller ones.

14. The main guest room, which is the largest room on the second floor, was once occupied by Mark Twain.

15. The photographs had double images so, we took them back to the store.

∧
,

21

16. After the plate went through the dishwasher the design faded.

17. ·Men's hats very popular in the 1930s are finally making a comeback.

18. The victim having been shoved inside the door the windows were nailed shut.

19. The third ship the *Aquinas* left three weeks later.

20. Cokes popcorn candy — that was her diet for two weeks.

21. The forms, that we were supposed to turn in on Friday, were not distributed until Thursday.

22. After a restless adolescence my sister has grown to be an active, responsible, concerned young woman.

23. We lost the tournament not the game.

24. Her address — 3004 Westcott, Brunswick Maine 04011 — was stenciled on the old leather bag.

25. Her duties which did not include making coffee did require skills in stenography and telex operation.

26. The poet Byron lived a romantic life to parallel a romantic age.

27. Our new neighbors moved from Reno Nevada to Columbia South Carolina to Atlanta Georgia to Davis California before arriving here.

28. The ledger — dated July 1 1946 — showed the city's finances to be in a condition, that many would envy today.

29. The one, Spanish-style house, is a refreshing change from the boxy houses that dominate the street.

30. Neither the class schedule, nor the examination schedule allows me to take all the courses I need and the registrar will not grant me special approval.

21

|*Commas: Review II*

The following paragraphs contain unneeded commas and omit needed ones. Circle every unneeded comma and insert a caret (∧) wherever a comma is needed.

Argentina, the second largest country in South America extends 2300 miles from north to south. It is about one-third the size of the United States not counting Alaska and Hawaii. The land was settled by people from many European countries but, most Argentines are descendants of early Spanish settlers, and Spanish and Italian immigrants. The official language of the nation is Spanish. The Argentine people, most of whom live in the cities are generally better educated than people in other South American countries. About 90 percent can read and write. Some Argentines live in large modern apartment buildings and others live in Spanish-style buildings with adobe walls, tile roofs and wrought-iron grillwork on the windows. The homes of the poorer people, of course are not so grand.

Argentina is a major producer of cattle, sheep, wool and grain. On the pampa which is a fertile grassy area covering about a fifth of the country, cowboys called *gauchos,* tend large herds of cattle and farmers raise sheep, hogs and wheat. Farther south, in the windswept region of Patagonia people raise sheep, and pump oil. Because the country has such a wide range of elevation, and distance from the equator, it has a climate,

∧
,

21

that varies greatly. For example the north has heavy rainfall, the central area has moderate precipitation and parts of Patagonia are desert. Being in the Southern Hemisphere Argentina has seasons just the opposite of those in North America the hottest days occurring in January and February and the coldest in July and August.

Since its first settlement in the 1500s, when early explorers hoped to find silver in the land Argentina has found, that its real wealth is in its fertile soil and its lively people.

∧
,

21

22 | *The Semicolon*

Self-test

In the following sentences add semicolons wherever they are needed or where they should replace commas and circle any semicolons that are not needed. If a sentence is already punctuated correctly, write *OK* to the left of it.

Example: Finley was quite popular; she was more popular than Alger.

1. A foreign coin jammed the vending machine, however, the coin was soon dislodged.
2. Although we found the atlas, the map of Iowa was missing.
3. She called to say she would arrive at noon, therefore, we ran out for groceries.
4. His face tightened with tension, he clenched his fists.
5. Hoping that he would be able to play the entire game, Smith practiced diligently.
6. They had met twice before, nevertheless, he did not remember her.
7. The horse, which was not used to a saddle, bucked, kicked, and shook its head; but still the rider stayed on.
8. The other driver offered an apology; then he sped off.
9. The following gave generously: E. E. Edwards, a broker, R. Zikowicz, a contractor, and L. Peters, a banker.
10. After repairing the carburetor, the mechanic worked on the transmission.

22a | Use a semicolon to separate main clauses not joined by a coordinating conjunction.

A main clause contains a subject and a predicate and does not begin with a subordinating word. When two main clauses in a sentence are not linked by a coordinating conjunction (*and, but, or, nor, for, so, yet*), they are separated by a semicolon.

> There are six museums in the city; the largest is the Museum of Fine Arts.
>
> The college motor pool has several cars; none is available for student activities.

Both clauses in these sentences could be written as separate sentences. If commas were used in place of the semicolons, the result would be a comma splice (see Chapter 11).

22b | Use a semicolon to separate main clauses joined by a conjunctive adverb.

The conjunctive adverbs include *however, indeed, moreover,* and *nonetheless.* (See 5d-2 for a more extensive list.) Since conjunctive adverbs are not conjunctions, clauses whose ideas they connect must be separated with semicolons.

> The reporters waited for an explanation of the policy change; *indeed,* they felt they were entitled to it.
> Manufacturers each year recall more cars with defects; the number of faulty and even dangerous cars on the road, *however,* is still alarming.

Notice that the conjunctive adverb, unlike a conjunction, may fall in several places in its clause. If it follows the semicolon, it is generally followed by a comma. If it falls elsewhere in the clause, it is generally preceded and followed by commas.

22c | Use a semicolon to separate main clauses if they are very long and complex or if they contain commas, even when they are joined by a coordinating conjunction.

Though a comma is normally sufficient to separate main clauses joined by a coordinating conjunction (see 21a), a semicolon signals a longer pause and can make the clauses easier to read when they are complicated or are punctuated by commas. Some writers prefer to use a semicolon to separate clauses joined by *so* and *yet,* even when the clauses are not complex or internally punctuated.

> The literacy rate in Indonesia, Malaysia, and Singapore is about 50 percent; *but* in Cambodia and Laos the rate is 70 and 80 percent, respectively.
> The caterer arrived on time, and the food she served was delicious; *but* the guests had to drink from plastic cups because she forgot to bring glasses.
> The announcement that classes were canceled had been posted all over campus; *yet* dozens of students missed it and showed up anyway.

22d | Use semicolons to separate items in a series if they are long or contain commas.

> The staff especially wishes to thank N. M. Matson, mayor; "Lima Bean" Horton, deputy mayor; Axel Garcia, police chief; and Norma Smith, school provost.
> Logan charged $370 for repairing the steps and the fence gate; Rogers charged $800 for painting the exterior of the house; and Morris charged $200 to replace the doors, $300 to fix the plumbing, and $250 to repair the patio.

22e | Avoid misusing or overusing the semicolon.

1 | Don't use a semicolon to separate a subordinate clause or a phrase from a main clause.

Many readers regard a phrase or subordinate clause that is set off with a semicolon as a fragment.

FAULTY	After he read the story; he gave his analysis of it.
REVISED	After he read the story, he gave his analysis of it.
FAULTY	I do not see how I can get good grades; with such a heavy course load.
REVISED	I do not see how I can get good grades with such a heavy course load.

2 | Don't use a semicolon to introduce a series.

FAULTY	Three of our team's players made the all-star team; the quarterback, the center, and the middle linebacker.
REVISED	Three of our team's players made the all-star team: the quarterback, the center, and the middle linebacker.

(See 25a and 25b for use of colons and dashes with lists.)

3 | Don't overuse the semicolon.

A series of sentences whose clauses are linked by semicolons often indicates repetitive sentence structure.

REPETITIVE	Several times they called to him; each time only their own echoes answered back. They had expected to rescue him before nightfall; now they hoped he could keep himself alive until morning.
REVISED	Several times they called to him; each time only their own echoes answered back. Although they had expected to rescue him by nightfall, they now hoped he could keep himself alive until morning.

;

22

| *Using the semicolon*   exercise **22-1**

Insert a caret (∧) in the following sentences where a semicolon is needed or where it should replace a comma. (Some sentences may require more than one semicolon.) If a sentence is already punctuated correctly, write *OK* to the left of it.

Example: I have not studied French, in fact, I have not studied any foreign languages.
                                      ∧

1. An ostrich is unable to fly, it can run at speeds of up to 40 miles per hour, however.
2. The town zoning laws are under the control of Mrs. Ida Balat, who owns much of the property in town, Mr. Luke Balat, her son and the town's mayor, Mrs. Ethel Goines, her daughter and a member of the town planning board, and Mr. Harold Goines, Ethel's husband and a member of the zoning board.
3. The telegram announcing his arrival on Tuesday was delivered Monday night, therefore, we had to scurry to have the house ready.
4. Most of the guests had left or fallen asleep from boredom, a few others read magazines, and one was cooking something in the kitchen, but the four remaining guests kept things going until three in the morning.
5. I do not understand why Mr. Nelson, for example, does not get tenure.
6. Never fix a leaky pipe if you can afford a plumber, that is my father's motto.
7. The chipmunk lived on crab apples, it stored them under the porch.
8. Horses prosper in our county because the soil has a high lime content.
9. In the 1950s many screenwriters were prevented from working because they were supposedly Communist sympathizers, some excellent scripts never got made into films as a result.
10. The advisory board comprised the manager, Martins, the foreman, and Travers, the engineer.
11. The two-day blackout of electricity affected three thousand houses, two hundred businesses, and thirty schools, yet no one can explain how it happened.

;

22

12. The trip was scheduled for Niagara Falls, I had been there, however, and so did not sign up.
13. The breakup of a marriage is usually upsetting, however it comes about.
14. My high school did not offer Latin, consequently, I am taking first-year Latin in college.
15. The doctor examined the child with great care, then he ordered additional tests.
16. The blueprints for the house showed a second bathroom the builders, apparently, had forgotten about it.
17. The police investigation was sloppy, several important leads were overlooked.
18. Oil exploration efforts are leveling off, however, energy shortages are worsening.
19. Brodhead has changed his open-shirt, chains-around-the-neck look and replaced it with a conservative, three-piece-suit look that makes him seem middle-aged.
20. I enjoy deep-sea fishing after trying it twice I could never go back to stream fishing again.
21. Japanese technology is superior to ours in several areas, including that of industrial robots.
22. The stores are refusing to accept credit cards, nevertheless, sales continue to grow.
23. I read the letter from my mother then I sent it on to my sister.
24. The three old brass keys, each at least six inches long, were found years ago in the attic, they have puzzled the family ever since, for no one can figure out what they open.
25. Reassuring though the promise sounded, few thought she could keep it.

The comma and the semicolon: Review I

EXERCISE **22-2**

Insert a comma or a semicolon, as appropriate, above each caret (∧) in the following sentences. If no punctuation is required at the caret, cross it out.

Example: When you drive into my hometown of Centerton, Nevada∧you see Dr. Ming's office first∧and then the Dairy Queen.

1. The museum∧which needs 300 visitors a day to meet costs∧will close in the spring∧no tax subsidy is available.
2. Dennison∧the former director∧and Ellis∧the current one∧were indicted for embezzlement.
3. The process consists of cutting the felt∧shaping it∧pressing it with steam∧and decorating the finished hat with a ribbon.
4. The pilot — angry∧nervous∧and tired — stood at the top of the ramp.
5. Moving in was annoying∧my roommate spent all morning hanging her favorite print∧while I rearranged furniture∧and carried heavy suitcases.
6. The computer system has been reliable∧however∧it will soon be obsolete.
7. The ceremony∧which started at ten o'clock∧was over∧before anyone thought to take pictures.
8. My roommates are my good friends∧and they are careful about sharing expenses.
9. The weather had been beautiful for four days in a row∧leading us to expect a perfect day∧for the season's biggest game∧instead∧we got rained out.
10. The Greek alphabet has one drawback∧to me∧it is incomprehensible.
11. The station∧which sold discount coupon books for $20∧raised its prices at the pump∧by 4¢ a gallon.
12. After searching through the atlas∧I located Bogotá∧Colombia∧ Caracas∧Venezuela∧and San Juan∧Puerto Rico.
13. The fire crackled noisily∧its glow and its warmth spread∧to the dark corners of the room.

;

22

14. The huge∧ornate∧carving∧which was made from cork∧rested on the top of the piano∧it overwhelmed the small room.

15. However∧only fifty∧unspirited∧people turned up.

16. My friend∧an insurance agent∧advised me∧to cut my car insurance back to the compulsory level∧and save the rest of the premium cost∧for statistics show that I would almost certainly save enough to replace the car∧before an accident ever occurred.

17. The new ignition shows major improvements∧however∧it still is not on the market.

18. They met eight times∧nevertheless∧they were no closer to agreement∧after the eighth meeting∧than they were after the first.

19. If we had been Plains Indians in our past lives∧we would more greatly appreciate∧understand∧and respect∧the natural world.

20. Spiders used to bother me until I learned∧that they keep down the populations of other insects∧that bother me more.

21. One can make fun of the overweight men and women∧who pay high fees∧for memberships in health spas∧but at least they are trying to help themselves.

22. Thousands∧who bought Stevie Wonder's first albums∧remain his faithful fans today.

23. Expecting to be elected president∧Mary Lou left the campaigning to her friends.

24. Whereas I feel∧that I can go in any direction∧when I graduate from college∧my mother felt∧that she had but one route to follow∧that of homemaker.

25. The students offered the dean a feeble∧halfhearted apology∧then they left to plot their next prank.

;

22

The comma and the semicolon: Review II

Insert a caret (∧) in the following paragraphs wherever a comma or semi-colon is needed, and then insert the appropriate mark above the caret.

The Aztec Indians inhabited the area around Mexico City from approximately A.D. 1200 until 1521 when they were conquered by Hernando Cortés. One of the most civilized groups of American Indians they lived in and around their capital city Tenochtitlán which was located at the site of the present Mexico City.

Families lived in simple adobe houses with thatched roofs. Some of their common foods were flat corn cakes which they called *tortillas* a drink called *chocolate* which they made out of cacao beans and corn beans tomatoes and chili. The men dressed in breechcloths capes and sandals the women wore skirts and sleeveless blouses.

Religion was central to the life of the Aztecs. They had many gods most of which they appeased with human sacrifices. As a consequence warfare was conducted largely for the purpose of taking prisoners who became objects of sacrifice. During the sacrificial rite the priests would often cut out the victim's heart with a knife made of obsidian. The Aztecs believed that human sacrifices were necessary to keep the sun rising every morning and to have success with the crops and warfare.

The Aztecs educated their children in history religious observances crafts and Aztec traditions. Outstanding boys and girls were trained in special schools so that some day they could perform religious duties.

Descendants of the Aztecs still live in the area around Mexico City still speaking their ancient language but practicing Spanish customs and religion.

;

22

23 | *The Apostrophe*

Self-test

Add apostrophes wherever they are needed in the following sentences. If a sentence is already punctuated correctly, write *OK* to the left of it.

Example: Alfred's dog has heartworms.

1. The princes reputations have been impugned.
2. At todays prices we cant afford to eat out.
3. The womens coats were left in the pew.
4. The child asked how many ss are in *Mississippi.*
5. Karen will graduate in the spring of 86.
6. The cat lost its collar.
7. The geometry texts are hers.
8. Students privileges are limited.
9. Childrens art will be featured.
10. "Its a big job," she said.

23a | Use an apostrophe to indicate the possessive case for nouns and indefinite pronouns.

The **possessive case** indicates the possession or ownership of one person or thing by another (see Chapter 6).

1 | Add -'s to form the possessive case of singular or plural nouns or indefinite pronouns that do *not* end in *s.*

The *men's* claim was honored.
That *person's* car was towed away.
Everyone's ears were ringing.
Dr. Hill's house is being painted.

2 | Add -'s to form the possessive case of singular words ending in -*s.*

Morris's career is prospering.
The *business's* files were confiscated.

EXCEPTION: Usage varies in a few nouns that end in *s* or *z* sounds, especially in names with more than one *s* sound (Cassius), names that sound like plurals (Gates), and other nouns when they are followed by a word beginning with an *s*. In these cases, some writers add only the apostrophe to show possession, while others use the apostrophe plus the *s*.

Cassius'   Cassius's
Gates'   Gates's
conscience' sake   conscience's sake

3 | **Add only an apostrophe to form the possessive case of plural words ending in -*s*.**

Students' rights are a big issue on this campus.
The *Sheldons'* stables caught fire.

4 | **Add -'*s* only to the last word to form the possessive case of compound words or word groups.**

My *brother-in-law's* arguments bore me.
The *attorney general's* dismissal was overdue.
Everyone else's paper was late.

5 | **When two or more words show individual possession, add -'*s* to them all. If they show joint possession, add -'*s* only to the last word.**

Fink and Schlenk's restaurant went bankrupt. [The restaurant was jointly owned.]
Wyatt's and *Surrey's* contributions to the sonnet form have long been acknowledged. [The two writers made separate contributions to the sonnet form.]

23b | **Don't use an apostrophe to form noun plurals or the possessive case of personal pronouns.**

Only an -*s* is needed to indicate the plurals of most nouns.

FAULTY   The three *car's* were sold yesterday.

REVISED   The three *cars* were sold yesterday.

His, hers, its, ours, yours, theirs, and *whose* are already possessive and do not need apostrophes.

FAULTY   The victory was *their's*.

REVISED   The victory was *theirs*.

23c | **Use an apostrophe to indicate the omission of one or more letters, numbers, or words in a standard contraction.**

doesn't   does not
who's   who is
it's   it is
you're   you are
'69   1969

NOTE: Don't confuse the personal pronouns *its, their, your,* and *whose* with the contractions *it's, they're, you're,* and *who's.*

FAULTY   *It's* members left *they're* votes on *you're* desk. On *who's* desk?

REVISED   *Its* members left *their* votes on *your* desk. On *whose* desk?

23d | Use an apostrophe plus *-s* to form the plurals of letters, numbers, and words named as words.

Legal prose is filled with *wherefore*'s.
Instead of drawing circles over your *i*'s, just use dots.

(See 27d on the use of italics or underlining for letters, numbers, and words named as words.)

|*Forming the possessive case*   EXERCISE **23-1**

Form the possessive case of each noun and pronoun below by adding an apostrophe, adding an apostrophe and an -*s*, or changing form as needed. Do not change singular to plural.

Example: Mike Smith   *Mike Smith's*

1. princess   _____

2. desks   _____

3. James   _____

4. everyone   _____

5. Ed Knox   _____

6. the Mileses   _____

7. vice president   _____

8. fox   _____

9. community   _____

10. Mr. and Mrs. Slocum   _____

11. they   _____

12. women   _____

13. no one   _____

14. who   _____

15. Sally Mendez   _____

16. St. Louis   _____

23

17. father-in-law   _____

18. Terre Haute   _____

19. sheep   _____

20. you   _____

21. the Bahamas   _____

22. committee member   _____

23. oxen   _____

24. *Denver Post*   _____

25. wrens   _____

,
∨

23

| *Using the apostrophe*   <small>EXERCISE</small> **23-2**

Insert an inverted caret (∨) in the following sentences where an apostrophe is required. (The caret will often have to be inserted between the letters of a word.) If the sentence is already punctuated correctly, write *OK* to the left of it.

Example: We think it˅s time for united action.

A.
1. The Hongs divorce has not been announced.

2. Thirty years on the same job will dull anyones approach to life.

3. The cows disease will kill it but wont affect the rest of the herd.

4. The mens club has voted to admit women.

5. The Smiths and Schmidts houses are as similar as their names.

6. Frances prime minister addressed the delegations.

7. The best term paper is yours.

8. IBMs technological progress has outstripped Wang's.

9. How many *if*s are in the agreement?

10. She put in a full days work.

11. The dog ran around in circles chasing its tail.

12. I can't recall whos speaking, but I do remember being excited when I heard who it is.

13. He told me that the car was yours and Teds.

14. Last Sundays sermon was better than this Sundays.

15. Everyones pay will increase because of the strike.

16. Theyre sure that the seats are theirs.

17. Its too late for an appointment.

18. The twins likeness is not surprising.

19. The class of 21 held a reunion last June.

20. The childrens habits need reforming.

’
˅

23

B.
1. Sheep and oxen grazed near the lakes edge.
2. The decision was theirs and they made it, so theres nothing we can do.
3. Bruces cats preferred meal is lettuce and tomato.
4. The flooded apartment was ours.
5. We left Sandras house at midnight.
6. The shopping malls attraction is their concentration of widely varied stores.
7. Olivers run in the marathon seemed unwise after his recent illness.
8. Larrys rooms were broken into.
9. The lecture lasts two hours each Tuesday.
10. Theirs was a difficult task.
11. Television shows seem to be getting better; at least, its possible to watch something worthwhile every night.
12. The Joneses and Whites boats are moored in the same cove.
13. The ends of both races were uneventful.
14. I did not know whose coats were left.
15. Mr. Princes son has to walk because of the bus strike.
16. The tops of the bottles had broken off.
17. The thickness of caterpillars fur indicates the severity of the coming winter.
18. She asked how many *ts* are in Cincinnati.
19. This years rainfall was greater than last years.
20. Dans kennel is always crowded because its the best in the city.

’
V
23

24 | *Quotation Marks*

Self-test

In the following sentences add single or double quotation marks wherever they are needed, being careful to place the marks correctly in relation to letters and other punctuation. If a sentence is already punctuated correctly, write *OK* to the left of it.

Example: He said, "Did you call?"

1. Were the books damaged? he asked.

2. Jeff said Okay when I asked him, Peg remarked.

3. Moon Drool is the title of her latest song.

4. Asia, Burke wrote, will remain a puzzle eternally.

5. Blake's poem The Tiger was not assigned.

6. The audience shouted Bravo! each time she came on stage, her agent reported.

7. Did the waitress say, As soon as I can?

8. He asked, Why are you home?

9. A pile of ashes, he said, is all that's left.

10. There are two reasons the poet wrote O Eager Bleat: to celebrate the sheep industry and to earn money.

Quotation marks are used primarily to enclose direct quotations from speech and writing. They always come in pairs: one before the quotation and one after.

24a | Use double quotation marks to enclose direct quotations.

> Shirer wrote that Hitler "remains, so far, the most remarkable of those who have used modern techniques to apply the classic formulas of tyranny."

Indirect quotations — reporting what a speaker said but not in his or her exact words — are not enclosed in quotation marks: *He said that he would not be late again.*

24b Use single quotation marks to enclose a quotation within a quotation.

"Graham said 'No way!' each time the coach asked him to go into the game," the reporter for the *Messenger* wrote.

24c Set off quotations of dialogue, poetry, and long prose passages according to standard practice.

Begin a new paragraph for each speaker when quoting a conversation.

"Why did you come?" the instructor asked.

"Because the course is supposed to be easy," answered the student candidly. "And besides, the subject interests me."

When you quote a single speaker for more than one paragraph, place quotation marks at the beginning of each paragraph but at the end of the last paragraph only.

Poetry quotations of one line are normally run into the text and enclosed by quotation marks. Poetry quotations of two or three lines may be run into the text and enclosed by quotation marks or set off on separate lines. If the quotation is run in, separate the lines with a slash (/).

Coleridge's beginning places the poem in an exotic land: "In Xanadu did Kubla Khan / A stately pleasure-dome decree."

Always set off poetry quotations of more than three lines. To set off a poetry quotation, separate the lines from the text and indent them ten spaces from the left margin. Double-space above and below the quotation, and double-space the quotation itself. A quotation that is set off from the text needs no quotation marks.

Emerson's poem opens with an indication of his worship of nature:

Think me not unkind and rude
That I walk alone in grove and glen;
I go to the god of the wood
To fetch his word to men.

Prose quotations of up to four lines should ordinarily be run into the text and enclosed in quotation marks. Quotations of four lines or more should be set off from the body of the paper and indented ten spaces from the left. Double-space above and below the quotation, and double-space the quotation itself. Don't enclose a set-off quotation in quotation marks.

24d Put quotation marks around titles according to standard practice.

Use quotation marks to enclose the titles of songs, short poems, articles in periodicals, short stories, essays, episodes of television and radio programs, and the subdivisions of books. For all other titles, use italics (underlining) (see 27a).

The song "Night and Day" is one of Cole Porter's best.
"Anecdote of the Jar" is a poem by Wallace Stevens.

The article entitled "The Perceptive Abilities of Rats" put me to sleep.
Mansfield wrote the short story "The Fly."
I still remember an essay we read, called "The Spider and the Wasp."
An episode called "Red Baiter" was one of the show's best.
Chapter 24, "Quotation Marks," was fascinating.

24e | Occasionally, quotation marks may be used to enclose defined words and words used in a special sense.

The "correct" version actually included fifteen errors.
Determining the meter of a line of poetry is called "scanning."

NOTE: Italics may also be used in definitions. (See 27d.)

24f | Avoid using quotation marks where they are not required.

Don't enclose the titles of your papers in quotation marks unless they contain or are themselves direct quotations.

NOT	"Rites of Passage in One Story by William Faulkner"
BUT	Rites of Passage in One Story by William Faulkner
OR	Rites of Passage in "The Bear"

Common nicknames, technical terms not being defined, slang, or trite expressions should not be enclosed in quotation marks. If slang or trite expressions are inappropriate, rewrite the sentence.

| NOT | The government should "get its act together" on national health care. |
| BUT | The government should develop a comprehensive program for national health care. |

24g | Place other marks of punctuation inside or outside quotation marks according to standard practice.

1 | Place commas and periods inside quotation marks.

They sang "America the Beautiful."
It replaced "The Star-Spangled Banner," which no one could sing.

2 | Place colons and semicolons outside quotation marks.

He said his footing was "precarious"; he was on a high wire.
The label said "for relief of itching"; so we bought a bottle.

3 | Place dashes, question marks, and exclamation points inside quotation marks only if they belong to the quotation.

The lawyer's one comment — "Immaterial" — sent a buzz through the courtroom.
Did I hear you say, "No"?

BUT

Did I hear you ask, "Why?"

Name _____ Date _____ Score _____

|*Quotation marks*   EXERCISE **24-1**

In the following sentences insert an inverted caret (∨) and single or double quotation marks as required. Be sure to place the caret or carets correctly in relation to other punctuation marks. If a sentence is already punctuated correctly, write *OK* to the left of it.

Example: How many of you, the instructor asked, have read the assigned story, Araby?

A. 1. He made the following comment: I am determined to win.

2. Did Cohan write You're a Grand Old Flag?

3. The nucleus of a cell is its center, where its vital work goes on.

4. Did I hear you say, The show is sold out?

5. The committee declared, America would be a more appropriate national anthem than the Star-Spangled Banner is.

6. When asked how he felt about guarding Jones, Geiger answered: He has to check me, too.

7. The student replied that she hadn't noticed it.

8. Never take Route 1 unless you like traffic jams, he stated.

9. African man, writes Mbiti, lives in a religious universe.

10. Dickinson's poem first sets the mood: A quietness distilled, / As twilight long begun.

11. I have been trying to shed my nickname, Bernie, ever since I acquired it.

12. Truman stated, I fired General MacArthur because he would not respect the authority of the President.

13. Do you have to be macho to love Minnesota's winters? the visitor asked.

14. Remember the Alamo! was first used as a battle cry at San Jacinto.

15. Dandruff is the code name that CB operators give to snow.

" "

24

B. 1. Coleridge was ridiculed for writing I hail thee brother in his poem To a Young Ass.

2. Her only response was Maybe! my father shouted.

3. The Congo is a poem that experiments with rhythmic effects.

4. Why did you shout Eureka! as you left? she asked.

5. The band played Auld Lang Syne from midnight until two in the morning, and no one seemed to notice.

6. The waitress asked, Did you leave me a tip?

7. We spent a whole class discussing the word moral; yet we never agreed on its meaning.

8. The characters in the story are, in the author's words, anti-heroes; however, none is realistic.

9. Huckleberry Hawkins played center for three years.

10. Her article, The Joy of Anguish, was reprinted in six languages.

11. Sotweed is a synonym for tobacco.

12. Ray owns twenty different recordings of Stardust.

13. How many of you know the To be or not to be speech from *Hamlet?* asked the drama coach.

14. He said that the test would be challenging; he should have said that it would be impossible.

15. William Blake's poem The Fly includes this stanza:

> Am not I
> a fly like thee?
> Or art not thou
> A man like me?

|*Writing quotations*   EXERCISE **24-2**

Rewrite each sentence according to the instructions that follow it. Use double or single quotation marks as necessary, observing correct placement of other punctuation marks.

1. Is this the way to the registration desk? (Begin with *Juan asked.*)

2. I will corrupt the town. (Begin with *The man who had been offended by Mark Twain's Hadleyburg announced.*)

3. It finally dawned on me what I had done. (End with *said Harold.*)

4. Edith was asked, "Did you find any new species?" (Begin with *According to the book.* Use indirect quotation.)

5. You're lost now. (Begin with *Admiral Byrd wrote.*)

6. Did you reread the last seven lines of Aesop's "The Hare and the Tortoise"? (Begin with *Mr. Delgadillo asked.*)

" "

24

7. The collie is a particularly loyal dog. (Begin with *It is said that,* using indirect quotation.)

8. Canaan was "a land flowing with milk and honey." (Begin with *God told Moses that,* using indirect quotation.)

9. I am a part of all that I have met. (End with *writes Tennyson in "Ulysses."*)

10. "Busy old fool, unruly sun, / Why dost thou thus, / Through windows and through curtains call on us?" (Begin with *Was John Donne an irritable morning riser, since he asks.*)

396

25 | *Other Punctuation Marks*

Self-test

In the following sentences add colons, dashes, parentheses, brackets, ellipsis marks, or slashes wherever they are needed or wherever they should replace other punctuation marks. When more than one mark would be correct in a sentence, choose the mark that seems most appropriate. If a sentence is already punctuated correctly, write *OK* to the left of it.

Example: The speaker dwelled on a single problem; the destructive power of ideals.

1. J. S. Mill 1806–1873 was considered the brightest man of his time.
2. A good student, he still lacks an important quality patience.
3. First editions especially rare ones can be costly.
4. The pool will be closed on the following days July 4 and September 2.
5. "The movie . . . is truly his worst effort in years," wrote one critic.
6. "The lessor and-or the agent is responsible," the attorney stated.
7. The rebate $250 prompted her to buy the car.
8. The ad read, "Buy now for tremendous saveings [*sic*]."
9. We were given a choice of 1 a term paper, 2 five book reports, or 3 a lab project.
10. Of the cities we investigated, three cities Rockville, Monroe Heights, and West Greenway had a surplus of rental housing.

:—0[]…/

25

THE COLON

25a | **Use the colon to introduce and to separate.**

1 | **Use a colon to introduce summaries, explanations, series, appositives ending sentences, long or formal quotations, and statements introduced by *the following* or *as follows.***

Note that a complete main clause precedes the colon.

The essence of his warning was this: obey the law or lose the funds.

EXPLANATION

Old Order Amish teaching requires separation from the world: members are forbidden to go to war, to hold public office, and to use modern appliances.

SERIES

The winners could choose one of three prizes: a new car, a trip to Europe, or a lifetime supply of canned crab meat.

FINAL APPOSITIVE

A good career has one essential quality: challenge.

LONG OR FORMAL QUOTATION

The senator issued this statement: "I repudiate those who question my honesty, and I call on my constituents to do the same."

STATEMENT INTRODUCED BY *THE FOLLOWING* **OR** *AS FOLLOWS*

The winners were as follows: Harriet Joyce, Bonnie Chapman, and Charleen Oliver.

`:—0[].../`

25

2 | Use a colon to separate subtitles and titles, the subdivisions of time, and the parts of biblical citations.

TITLE AND SUBTITLE   *Poetry: Sound and Image*

TIME   5:45, 9:00

BIBLICAL CITATION   Luke 5:12

3 | Avoid misusing the colon.

Use the colon only at the end of a main clause. Don't put a colon between a verb and its object or complement, between a preposition and its object, or when a formal introduction (such as *the following*) is lacking.

FAULTY   The subjects of the painting were: a cow, a bear, and a zebra. [The colon separates the verb *were* from the subject complement.]

REVISED   The subjects of the painting were a cow, a bear, and a zebra.

FAULTY   Ships sailing the Amazon River carry raw materials such as: animal skins, Brazil nuts, lumber, and rubber. [The colon separates the preposition *such as* from its objects.]

REVISED   Ships sailing the Amazon River carry raw materials such as animal skins, Brazil nuts, lumber, and rubber.

THE DASH

25b | **Use a dash or dashes to indicate sudden changes in tone or thought and to set off some sentence elements.**

1 | **Use a dash or dashes to indicate sudden shifts in tone, new or unfinished thoughts, and hesitation in dialogue.**

Jasper's sense of humor might appeal to you — if you are as witless as he is.

In response I said — well, my reply is unprintable.

"My father —" she blurted out and then stopped.

2 | **Use a dash or dashes to emphasize appositives and parenthetical expressions.**

To set off appositives and parenthetical expressions, dashes may be used in place of commas to achieve more emphasis and in place of parentheses to gain less separation.

Many animals — the elephant for one — are in danger of extinction.

The dash is particularly useful for setting off appositives that contain commas.

Some of the largest animals — elephants, rhinoceroses, and blue whales — are in danger of extinction.

3 | **Use a dash to set off introductory series and concluding series and explanations.**

Care, tenderness, a sense of humor — Gunther possessed all of these.

Reservoirs store water for several purposes — irrigation, power, water supply, and recreation.

4 | **Avoid misusing or overusing the dash.**

Don't use a dash when a comma, semicolon, or period is more appropriate. Keep in mind that too many dashes can give writing a choppy or jumpy quality.

FAULTY   The envelope — torn and scuffed — arrived on Tuesday — my birthday — and when I opened it, I found a bent birthday card — and a torn check.

REVISED   The envelope, torn and scuffed, arrived on Tuesday, my birthday. When I opened it, I found a bent birthday card and a torn check.

PARENTHESES

25c | **Use parentheses to enclose nonessential elements within sentences.**

1 | **Use parentheses to enclose parenthetical expressions.**

Parenthetical expressions include explanations, examples, and minor digressions that are not essential to meaning. Setting them off with parentheses rather than with commas or dashes separates them from the rest of the sentence and indicates their relative lack of importance to the sentence meaning.

> The zoo places animals in settings that simulate their natural environments (forest, desert, swamp, and so forth).
> William Butler Yeats (1865–1939) was not only a poet but also a playwright and an essayist.

Writers using parenthetical expressions should consider omitting them entirely. If they are so unimportant as to be included in parentheses, perhaps the piece of writing can get along without them.

When a sentence requires a comma in addition to the parentheses, the comma follows the final mark of parenthesis.

> The writer of "The Lake Isle of Innisfree," William Butler Yeats (1865–1939), was not only a poet but also a playwright and an essayist.

2 | **Use parentheses to enclose letters and figures labeling items in lists within sentences.**

> The course has three requirements: (1) an oral report, (2) a midterm examination, and (3) a final examination.

BRACKETS

25d | **Use brackets only within quotations to separate your own comments from the words of the writer you quote.**

> Brooke writes that "the essence of the religion [Islam] is legalism."

Use the word *sic* (Latin for "in this manner") in brackets to indicate that an error in a quotation appeared in the original and was not introduced by you.

> The manual pointed out that "proofreading is an important job that must be performed caerfully [*sic*]."

THE ELLIPSIS MARK

25e | **Use the ellipsis mark to indicate omissions within quotations.**

The **ellipsis mark** is three spaced periods (. . .).

> ORIGINAL   "Riley's works must be read aloud for the reader to get the fullest possible enjoyment."
>
> WITH ELLIPSIS   "Riley's works must be read aloud for . . . the fullest possible enjoyment."

When the ellipsis mark follows a sentence, it is used in addition to the period that ends the sentence: *"The plans went awry. . . . The 'perfect' crime was a failure."*

:—0[].../

25

THE SLASH

25f | Use the slash between options and to separate lines of
poetry that are run in to the text.

OPTION   We faced an either/or situation: either sell or be taken to
court.

POETRY   Wallace Stevens paints autumn differently: "The rain falls.
The sky / Falls and lies with the worms."

Using the colon, the dash, parentheses, brackets, the ellipsis mark, the slash

EXERCISE **25-1**

Circle the place in each sentence where punctuation should be added or is used incorrectly, and write the correct punctuation, along with the adjacent words, on the blank to the left. (The mark may be used to replace another mark that is used incorrectly.) When more than one mark would be correct in a sentence, choose the mark that seems most appropriate. If a sentence is already punctuated correctly, write *OK* on the blank.

Example: _**exhibit : the**_____ Adams was fascinated by one thing in the exhibit**O** the power of steam.

_____ 1. Of the nine regions surveyed, only one New England had a low suicide rate.

_____ 2. The ring was priced reasonably ($200).

_____ 3. "Iamb," "trochee," "spondee" all are terms for poetry analysis.

_____ 4. "The penalty is a $500 fine and or a year in jail," the lawyer said.

_____ 5. There are two basic defenses: 1 the zone and 2 the man to man.

_____ 6. A good worker, he lacks only one quality tact.

_____ 7. Our savings $100 are not enough for the trip.

_____ 8. The recipe my aunt's favorite calls for three eels.

_____ 9. The discount on the new car was insignificant only $50.

_____ 10. Two of the contestants (Perry and Hughy are my roommates.

:—()[]...∕

25

11. In two lines of the poem, Robinson portrays Richard Cory as "a gentleman from sole to crown, / Clean favored, and imperially slim."

12. The paper said, "People waved from the poop-site (*sic*) shore."

13. I got a high grade in only one course; Elementary Education 101.

14. The kit contained the following items, a flare, a wrench, two screwdrivers, one hammer, and a fan belt.

15. The life of Ernest Hemingway 1899–1961 was exciting by almost anyone's standards.

16. His new title [associate fireman] brought no increase in pay.

17. The hide — (alligator) — could not be imported.

18. The assignment for Friday was a long one pages 200–290.

19. The cathedral, built in 1295?, was open to tour groups.

20. "The state's largest drinking fountain" that is what Mayor Belotti called the new reservoir.

21. However, she then said, "Let's not forget how difficult it was to bring this water here and . . how much it means to us."

22. Among the recruiters were IBM, Olivetti, and TRW.

23. Tolstoy's *Works* [volumes 2 and 3] were on sale for $7.95.

24. The course depended on only one assignment . . . the term paper.

25. The teacher, actually, his assistant wrote that my paper was "flabby and pointless."

:—0[].../
25

Punctuation: Review
of Chapters 20–25

EXERCISE **25-2**

In the following paragraphs, insert a caret (∧) wherever punctuation is missing, and write the correct punctuation above the caret.

Sunlight is made up of three kinds of radiation 1 infrared rays which we cannot see 2 visible rays and 3 ultraviolet rays which also are invisible. Especially in the ultraviolet range sunlight is harmful to the eyes. Ultraviolet rays can damage the retina the area in the back of the eye and cause cataracts on the lens. Wavelengths of light rays are measured in nanometers nm or millionths of a meter. Infrared rays are the longest measuring 700 nm and longer and ultraviolet rays are the shortest measuring 400 nm and shorter. The lens absorbs much of the ultraviolet radiation thus protecting the retina however in so doing it becomes a victim growing cloudy and blocking vision.

You can protect your eyes by wearing sunglasses that screen out the ultraviolet rays. To be effective sunglasses should block out at least 95 percent of the radiation. Many lenses have been designed to do exactly this but many others are extremely ineffective. When you are buying sunglasses you can test their effectiveness by putting them on and looking in a mirror while you stand in a bright light. If you can see your eyes through the lenses the glasses will not screen out enough ultraviolet light to protect your eyes.

People who spend much time outside in the sun really owe it to themselves to buy a pair of sunglasses that will shield their eyes.

:—0[].../

25

VI | Mechanics
26 | Capitals

Self-test

In the following sentences draw a line through any letter that *should not* be capitalized, and circle any letter that *should* be capitalized. If the capitalization in a sentence is already correct, write *OK* to the left of it.

Example: Horace ~~M~~et Angela in ⓙune.

1. He has a fondness for asian art.
2. Woodworth's lyric entitled "the old oaken bucket" gives me chills.
3. My Mother sent Grandfather a box of Cuban cigars.
4. He is the president of the American Sculpture Society.
5. "The worst season here is Summer," professor Ellis said.
6. Joan, a Professor of Music, owns many Classical music tapes.
7. The East side of the woods borders Claytor lake.
8. His latest book is *The Era of the Frog: a Study in Green.*
9. She has thirty copies of "Ode to my Bunny."
10. Elmo majored in Physics at Greenburg state college.

26a | Capitalize the first word of every sentence.

The snows came early.
Why must we go?

26b | Capitalize words in the titles of works according to standard practice.

In titles, capitalize the first and last words, any word after a colon or semicolon, and all other words except articles (*a, an, the*) and prepositions and conjunctions of fewer than five letters.

Pope: A Metrical Study
Albee: His Position Among Tragedians
"How a River Got Its Name"
"Sexist Language in Television Commercials"

26c | Always capitalize the pronoun *I* and the interjection *O.* Don't capitalize *oh* unless it begins a sentence.

"But O heart! heart! heart!" wrote Whitman on the death of Lincoln.
My interview was short, but, oh, did I have to answer hard questions.

26d | Capitalize proper nouns, proper adjectives, and words used as essential parts of proper nouns.

1 | Capitalize proper nouns and proper adjectives.

Common nouns name general classes of persons, places, and things. **Proper nouns** name specific persons, places, and things. **Proper adjectives** are formed from some proper nouns. Capitalize all proper nouns and proper adjectives but not the articles (*a, an, the*) that precede them.

COMMON NOUNS	PROPER NOUNS	PROPER ADJECTIVES
country	Mexico	Mexican
man	Milton	Miltonic
building	Arizona State Prison	—

SPECIFIC PERSONS AND THINGS

Joe Smith   the Liberty Bell

SPECIFIC PLACES AND GEOGRAPHICAL REGIONS

Louisville, Kentucky   the Gulf of Mexico
the South   the Rocky Mountains

DAYS OF THE WEEK, MONTHS, HOLIDAYS

Tuesday, March 13   Labor Day

HISTORICAL EVENTS, DOCUMENTS, PERIODS, MOVEMENTS

the Civil War   the Bill of Rights
the Magna Carta   the War of 1812
the Stone Age   the Reformation

GOVERNMENT OFFICES OR DEPARTMENTS AND INSTITUTIONS

Atomic Energy Commission   Department of Defense
Centerville High School   State Department

**POLITICAL, SOCIAL, ATHLETIC, AND OTHER ORGANIZATIONS
AND ASSOCIATIONS AND THEIR MEMBERS**

Democratic Party   Houston Astros
American Kennel Club   Knights of Columbus
American Medical Association   National Council of Trade Unions

RACES, NATIONALITIES, AND THEIR LANGUAGES

Italian   Swede
Caucasian   Swedish

RELIGIONS AND THEIR FOLLOWERS

Judaism   Jews
Christianity   Christians
Islam   Moslems

cap

26

the Almighty   God
the Old Testament   Allah

2 | Capitalize common nouns used as essential parts of proper nouns.

Center *Street*   *Mount* Rushmore
Lake Mead   Canadian *Embassy*
Williams *County*   Union *Station*

3 | Capitalize trade names.

Coca-Cola   Burger King
Xerox   Ford Mustang

26e | Capitalize titles when they precede proper names but generally not when they follow proper names or are used alone.

Foreign Minister Khalil   Khalil, the foreign minister
Professor G. M. Dunning   G. M. Dunning, professor of
                                 history

26f | Avoid unnecessary capitalization.

1 | Don't capitalize common nouns used in place of proper nouns.

NOT   The Stadium was closed for repairs.

BUT   Landrum Stadium was closed for repairs.

OR   The stadium was closed for repairs.

2 | Don't capitalize compass directions unless they refer to specific geographical areas.

Travel *east* for a visit, but live in the *West*.

3 | Don't capitalize the names of seasons or the names of academic years or terms.

fall color   spring semester
winter rains   sophomore year

4 | Don't capitalize the names of relationships unless they form part of or substitute for proper names.

my uncle   Uncle John
my grandmother   Grandmother

NOTE: If you have any doubt about whether a particular word should be capitalized, consult a recent dictionary.

cap

26

| *Using capitals*

In the following sentences draw a line through any letter that should not be capitalized, and circle any letter that should be capitalized. If the capitalization in a sentence is already correct, write *OK* to the left of it.

Example: Steve and (S)helly got married last ~~S~~ummer.

1. "Helga is part American indian," her Mother said.
2. The freedom of information act has been costly to implement.
3. The Governor gave a radio talk on Christmas.
4. Edith Farrara, president of Grendel corporation, makes monsters for a living.
5. Carol titled her painting *All Alone in The Wheat.*
6. The Riley County Pumpkin-Growing contest was won by Travis and Tyler.
7. John still tells world war II stories on memorial day.
8. The waiter explained, "the soup changes every day."
9. Mike asked grandmother Collins where she was born and heard a fascinating reply.
10. Heffeltooth is a local leader of the republican party.
11. Our family attends the First Methodist Church on Main Street.
12. My Grandfather always forgets to put in his teeth, and Granny then complains.
13. The islamic group distributed literature on friday.
14. His Mother, Martha, plans to give him a new Dodge Station wagon.
15. The U.S. Postal Service becomes less efficient every year.
16. The National Geographic society was founded in 1888.
17. The American consulate would not issue Alphonse a visa.
18. My friend Joe lives on the East side of the Park.

cap

26

19. The best hunting is in the western part of the state.

20. Ed thinks Wrigley field will have lights by Spring.

21. The book was titled *How to deal with stress*.

22. My friends report that the most enjoyable way to cross the Atlantic ocean is to take a British Ship.

23. We pulled into a texaco station to fill the gas tank.

24. Both players are Seniors this year.

25. I had to memorize the dimensions of over 200 paintings for my art course last term; yet I learned almost nothing about their contents.

cap

26

27 | *Italics*

Self-test

In the following sentences underline any words that should be in italics (underlined), and circle any words now in italics that should not be. If a sentence is already correct, write *OK* to the left of it.

Example: The word <u>hoopla</u> comes from the French.

1. The selections were from the musical *Godspell*.
2. The Parkersburg Herald wrote a feature on Hull's painting "The Bernasek Porch."
3. Bardiglio is the name for a variety of marble.
4. *"Never* try that again!" she screamed.
5. Common Sense was a pamphlet urging revolution.
6. I often pronounce the t in *often*.
7. The U.S.S. Gompers set sail for the Pacific on April 3.
8. Mr. Tucker read out of *Exodus* from the Bible.
9. Omar lisped when he said isthmus.
10. Her *Newsweek* subscription has run out.

ital

27

    Type that slants to the right is known as *italic type*. It is used to distinguish or emphasize words. In handwriting or typing, underline to indicate italics.

27a | Underline titles according to standard practice.

    Underline the titles of books, long poems, plays, periodicals, pamphlets, published speeches, long musical works, movies, television and radio programs, and works of visual art. Enclose all other titles in quotation marks (see 24a).

BOOK *Ivanhoe*	MUSICAL WORK *Madame Butterfly*
LONG POEM *Lycidas*	MOVIE *On Golden Pond*
PLAY *Hamlet*	TELEVISION OR RADIO PROGRAM
PERIODICAL *The New York Times*	*Hill Street Blues*
SPEECH *Gettysburg Address*	WORK OF ART *Mona Lisa*

Don't underline the Bible or parts of it: Genesis, Matthew.

27b | **Underline the names of ships, aircraft, spacecraft, and trains.**

the U.S.S. *Turner Joy*   the U.S. *Enterprise*
the *Spirit of St. Louis*   the *Southern Crescent*

27c | **Underline foreign words and phrases that are not part of the English language.**

Deadly nightshade belongs to the genus *Atropa*.
Osborn's manners were *trés gauche*.

27d | **Underline words, letters, numbers, and phrases named as words.**

Why does *sour grapes* mean scorning something?
Even small children know there are four *s*'s in *Mississippi*.

27e | **Occasionally, underlining may be used for emphasis.**

When its trainer held out a chair, the lion *ate* it.

Be careful with this use of underlining, however. Too much underlining for emphasis makes writing sound immature or hysterical.

ital

27

414

| Using italics (underlining)   exercise **27-1**

In the following sentences underline any words that should be in italics (underlined), and circle any words now in italics that should not be. If a sentence is already correct, write *OK* to the left of it.

Example: The word <u>emotion</u> pertains to (feelings.)

1. The tankers were blockaded for a week in the *Persian Gulf.*

2. *TNT* was used to demolish the building.

3. The Washington Star usually printed conservative views.

4. The yard became overgrown with *Swedish ivy.*

5. We took a tour of a ship, the North Carolina, for only $2.50.

6. Hamlet contains more violence than does any crime drama on television.

7. The clams were so *gritty* that we could not eat them.

8. Life magazine is a show place for photography.

9. Shaw's *Man and Superman* is more often read than viewed on stage.

10. *The Great Wall of China* was completed in the third century *B.C.*

11. The strange form was the mem of the Hebrew alphabet.

12. She makes the dots on her i's so large that the page looks like an aerial view of the Charles County Balloon Festival.

13. We read the Bible's first five books and discussed them in class.

14. We had to report on the P. W. Joyce book Old Celtic Romances.

15. *Gree* is an archaic word meaning "satisfaction."

16. A new journal, Fun with Caries, reprinted an article by Brady Hull, D.D.S.

17. The documentary program 60 Minutes continues to be quite profitable for *CBS.*

ital

27

18. Miserere is the fiftieth psalm in the *Douay Bible*.

19. Eijkman won the *Nobel Prize* for medicine in 1929.

20. The expression *c'est la vie* never gave me much comfort.

21. The professor published her article in the sociology journal Studies in Poverty.

22. I was surprised to see that Wyeth's Christina's World is not a larger painting.

23. The foxglove belongs to the genus *Digitalis*.

24. My husband, for instance, repeatedly mispronounces the word asterisk.

25. My twenty-year subscription to *Boys' Life,* given to me by my uncle, has finally expired.

ital

27

28 | *Abbreviations*

Self-test

In the following sentences cross out each abbreviation that is inappropriate and write the correct form above it. If the abbreviation in a sentence is appropriate, write *OK* in the left margin.

Example: He bought ten ~~gals.~~ *gallons* of gasoline.

1. The prof. was late only once.

2. Geo. Meany headed the union for many years.

3. She finally got her B.A. in 1982.

4. Browning Corp. interviewed seniors today.

5. Dr. Schmidt recently resigned.

6. She returned to the U.S.A. in March.

7. On Mon. the team visits Ogden.

8. We arrived early on Feb. 16.

9. NATO remains an effective deterrent.

10. Agnes majored in econ. and French.

28a | Use standard abbreviations for titles immediately before and after proper names.

BEFORE THE NAME	AFTER THE NAME
Dr. Peter Green	Peter Green, M.D.
Mr., Mrs., Gen., Msgr.	Ph.D., D.D.S., S.J., Sr., Jr.

The abbreviations *Mr., Mrs., Rev., Hon., Prof., Rep., Sen., Dr.,* and *St.* (for *Saint*) are used only if they appear with a proper name. Spell them out in the absence of a proper name.

NOT	The dr. was late.
BUT	The doctor was late.
OR	Dr. Smith was late.

NOTE: The title *Ms.* takes a period even though it is not an abbreviation (*Ms.* Shumway). The title *Miss* does *not* take a period (*Miss* Olmsted).

Abbreviations such as *Jr., Sr., Esq., M.D., D.D., Ph.D.* and *S.J.*, which generally appear after proper names, are rarely spelled out. Within a sentence they should be preceded and followed by commas. Abbreviations for academic degrees may be used without a proper name.

> Arthur Garcia, Sr., sold his business.
> Hester Mainz, M.D., practices medicine in Detroit.
> He is still trying to earn an M.A.

28b Familiar abbreviations and acronyms for the names of organizations, corporations, people, and some countries are acceptable in most writing.

An **acronym** is an abbreviation that spells a pronounceable word and is written without periods: NATO, UNESCO. As long as they are well known, acronyms and abbreviations for the names of organizations, corporations, people, and some countries are acceptable in most writing. When the abbreviation consists of three or more letters, it is usually written without periods.

CIA	ABC	JFK	USA (or U.S.A.)
UAW	AFL-CIO	FDR	USSR (or U.S.S.R.)

ab

28

28c Use B.C., A.D., A.M., P.M., *no.,* and *$* only with specific dates and numbers.

44 B.C.	A.D. 54	10:15 A.M.	no. 344	$3.60

28d Generally, reserve common Latin abbreviations such as *i.e., e.g.,* and *etc.* for use in source citations and comments in parentheses.

I.e. stands for *id est,* "that is." *E.g.* stands for *exempli gratia,* "for example." *Etc.* stands for *et cetera,* "and so forth." Note that when they are used, they are not italicized.

> The council (i.e., the three voting members of the committee) decided against the rule change.
> Hardwoods (e.g., maple) make durable furniture.
> The hardwoods (maple, oak, etc.) burn well in fireplaces.

28e | Don't use *Inc., Bros., Co.,* or *&* (for *and*) except when it is part of the official name of a business firm.

NOT   The *Brown bros.* won the contract.

BUT   The *Brown brothers* won the contract.

OR   *Brown Bros.* won the contract.

28f | In most writing don't abbreviate units of measurement; geographical names; names of days, months, and holidays; names of people; courses of instruction; and labels for divisions of written works.

NOT   The book, which was a fraction of an *in.* thick and had two *chs.*, was about *Robt.* Ash's struggles every *Tues.* to master *econ.* at the school he attended in *Mo.*

BUT   The book, which was a fraction of an *inch* thick and had two *chapters,* was about *Robert* Ash's struggles every *Tuesday* to master *economics* at the school he attended in *Missouri.*

ab

28

| *Using abbreviations*

In the following sentences cross out each abbreviation that is inappropriate and write the correct form above it. If the abbreviation in a sentence is appropriate, write *OK* in the left margin.

Example: My gas guzzler has a 350-cubic-~~in~~. engine. *(inch)*

1. The prof. was usually available after class.

2. Television & radio reach a broad audience.

3. Twelve gals. of fuel cost over $15.

4. Mt. Vernon recently raised its admission fee.

5. Greg tried for years to earn a Ph.D.

6. The metric liter equals 1.057 qts.

7. My senator favors greater understanding between the U.S.A. and China.

8. No one remembered when the sgt. had been promoted.

9. The school that I attended was so small that the phys. ed. instructor also taught English.

10. The reunion was held in Hope, Kans., in July.

11. Rep. Tidwell lost in the primary.

12. My fiancé and I have known each other since we were in jr. high.

13. The FBI has lost much of its prestige since J. Edgar Hoover died.

14. The guide was from Sunset Tours, Inc.

ab

28

15. Second St. needs to be repaved.

16. Mr. and Mrs. Key worked hard all their lives.

17. Axel T. Goldfarb, Jr., raised cats for fun.

18. WTOP broadcasts news all P.M.

19. The winning ticket was no. 21-12.

20. All I got was an oz. of shrimp.

21. The juniors, led by Robt. Benz, beat the seniors in intramural basket-ball.

22. The assignment to read pp. 60 to 190 was unreasonable for a single night's work, and the students objected.

23. Some persons cannot study effectively because of learning problems; e.g., they are unable to concentrate or they read poorly.

24. The rules are meant for freshmen, sophomores, etc.

25. She demanded "compensation" (i.e., cash).

26. The YWCA offers good athletic facilities for a small fee.

27. On Christmas Eve we customarily eat dinner with the Dr. and her family.

28. We invited Dr. Wiona and Msgr. Martignetti to the opening of the Red Cross blood drive.

29. ABC televised all the Olympics until the one in 1980.

30. N.C. State went all the way to the national championship that year.

29 | Numbers

Self-test

In the following sentences cross out any figure that should be spelled out in most writing, and write the spelled-out number above it. Circle any spelled-out number that should be written in figures, and write the figures above it. If numbers are used appropriately in a sentence, write *OK* in the left margin.

Example: *~~1~~ Two* were lost, but (one hundred and two) *102* were saved.

1. Heath's batting average is .200.

2. The store closed at nine o'clock.

3. Volume three is on reserve at the library.

4. The paint cost six dollars and ten cents.

5. One hundred and ninety pounds is her weight.

6. There were 36 cousins absent from the reunion on May third.

7. The truck broke down 3 days ago.

8. At the meeting, 406 demonstrators were arrested.

9. The tank leaked 100 gallons of fuel.

10. The teacher assigned only two hundred and forty lines of poetry.

num

29

29a | Use figures for numbers that require more than two words to spell out.

Enrollment this term is *9002*.
My smallest class has *127* students in it.

Spell out most numbers of two words or less.

Last year my smallest class had *ninety-seven* students in it.
The administration expects enrollments to climb to *eleven thousand* and then level off.

When you use several numbers together, though, consistently spell them out or consistently express them in figures: *The broker bought 110 shares of mining stock at $10 each, 15 shares of oil stock at $50 each, and 4 municipal bonds at $500 each.*

29b | Use figures instead of words according to standard practice.

Even when spelling out a number would require only one or two words, writers conventionally use figures for days and years; pages, chapters, volumes, acts, scenes, and lines; decimals, percentages, and fractions; addresses; scores and statistics; exact amounts of money; and the time of day.

DAYS AND YEARS

January 10, 1975   A.D. 56   4 B.C.

NOTE: When the day of the month is not followed by a year, it may be expressed in words: *January tenth, April first; the first of April;* but *not April 1st* or *the 10th of January.*

PAGES, CHAPTERS, VOLUMES, ACTS, SCENES, AND LINES

volume 1, pages 67–68
Chapter 13
Act 3, Scene 2, lines 14–16

DECIMALS, PERCENTAGES, AND FRACTIONS

1.2 liters
3½ years
62 percent (or 62%)

ADDRESSES

327 Linden Avenue
3840 W. 148th Street *but* 315 First Street
Bloomington, Illinois 61701

SCORES AND STATISTICS

a score of 18 to 3   an ACT composite score of 21
a mean of 87   a .305 batting average

EXACT AMOUNTS OF MONEY

$6.28 $4.9 million (or $4,900,000)

NOTE: Round dollar or cent amounts may be expressed in words: *seven dollars, forty cents.*

THE TIME OF DAY

9:27   4:23 A.M.   12:00 M. (meridian)
          or 12:00 noon

NOTE: Express the time in words when using *o'clock: nine o'clock.*

num

29

424

29c | Always spell out numbers that begin sentences.

NOT   *397* people attended the lecture.

BUT   The lecture was attended by *397* people.

OR   *Three hundred and ninety-seven* people attended the lecture.

num

29

| *Using numbers* | EXERCISE **29-1** |

In the following sentences cross out any figure that should be spelled out in most writing, and write the spelled-out number above it. Circle any spelled-out number that should be written in figures and write the figures above it. If numbers are used appropriately in a sentence, write *OK* in the left margin.

Example: ~~67~~ *Sixty-seven* people attended the public meeting, although only (one hundred and fifty) *150* had been expected.

1. The fees rose by 21 percent in 1983.

2. A book of 12 tickets costs $10.

3. Seaver has won more than 300 games in his career.

4. They bought a house at Five Cove off Cork Lane.

5. There were 4070 seats in the auditorium, but the audience occupied only seventy-nine.

6. My 7-year-old sister can read and comprehend the Bible.

7. My grandmother bought the stock in 1946 at a cost of three dollars and twenty-five cents a share.

8. If you take Route 66 to the Marbury Street turnoff and follow that road east for 2½ miles, you will find the 1492 Restaurant, famous for its Spanish food.

9. One hundred and twelve yards was Jim's rushing total at the end of the game.

10. 2 volumes of poetry remained unsold.

num

29

427

11. The nine o'clock bus came an hour late.

12. After I dropped out of high school, my parents thought I would never go to college, but 6 years later here I am.

13. August twenty-seventh is her birthday.

14. The confirmation class had 30 members.

15. The Tigers won by the score 7 to 3.

16. $20 was the cost of the psychology text.

17. In high school I had to memorize over 100 lines from *Romeo and Juliet*.

18. Only eight nations attended the economic summit on June fourth.

19. The most famous eruption of Mt. Vesuvius was in A.D. seventy-nine, when the cities of Pompeii and Herculaneum were destroyed.

20. For 14 gallons of gasoline I paid $24.60 to a station owner who was later arrested for price gouging.

21. The commuter train leaves at 8:15, and the trip takes only twenty minutes.

num

29

22. Volume 5 of the encyclopedia is missing pages 12–506, as well as the last 4 pages.

23. Within 3 miles of the intersection are 12 bars.

24. The package contained 20 cookies and two jars of coffee.

25. Since he is barely 5 feet tall, Uncle Cosmo could not qualify for the police force; so he established his own detective agency and today makes 6 times what he would have made as a police officer.

Self-test

Many of the following word divisions would be inappropriate in a final paper. Some of these words should not be divided, and some should be divided differently. If a word should not be divided, write the word on one blank to the right. If a word should be divided differently, write the correct division on two blanks. Write *OK* on the blank beside any word that is divided correctly.

Example: purp-   *pur-*

ose   *pose*

1. drug-   _____

   ged   _____

2. all-   _____

   ow   _____

3. luck-   _____

   y   _____

4. pan-Ameri-   _____

   can   _____

5. mul-   _____

   tiply   _____

6. compel-   _____

   led   _____

7. self-in-   _____

   dulgent   _____

8. throu-   _____

   gh   _____

9. cosig-   _____

   ned   _____

10. obli-   _____

    que   _____

div

30

Whenever possible, avoid dividing words. If you find at times that you must break a word at the end of a line, do so only between syllables, consulting your dictionary for syllabic divisions. Indicate your break with a hyphen at the end of the line, never at the beginning of a line, and don't divide the last word on a page. Here are a few additional rules.

30a | **Don't make a division that leaves a single letter at the end of a line or fewer than three letters at the beginning of a line.**

NOT a- gree	BUT agree	NOT e- quip	BUT equip
NOT boot- y	BUT booty	NOT report- er	BUT reporter

30b | **Don't divide one-syllable words.**

NOT drop- ped	BUT dropped	NOT strai- ght	BUT straight

30c | **Divide compound words only between the words that form them or at fixed hyphens.**

Compound words are made up of two or more words. If they are joined by a hyphen, the hyphen is called **fixed.**

NOT for- ty-two	BUT forty- two	NOT mid- dle-aged	BUT middle- aged
NOT sec- ondhand	BUT second- hand	NOT pseudosci- ence	BUT pseudo- science

30d | **Avoid confusing word divisions.**

Even when a word is correctly divided into syllables, the first or second half of the word may form a different word or a wrongly pronounced syllable that will momentarily confuse the reader.

NOT poet- ical	BUT poetical	NOT the- ory	BUT theory
NOT rein- force	BUT reinforce	NOT ide- alism	BUT idealism

div

30

| *Dividing words correctly*   EXERCISE **30-1**

Many of the following word divisions would be inappropriate in a final paper. Some words should not be divided, and some should be divided differently. If a word should not be divided, write the word on one blank to the right. If a word should be divided differently, write the correct division on two blanks. Write OK on the blank beside any word that is divided correctly.

Example: good-na- *good-*

        tured *natured*

1. stew- _____

   ed _____

2. rel- _____

   igious _____

3. control- _____

   led _____

4. curr- _____

   ent _____

5. accomp- _____

   lish _____

6. Marx- _____

   ist-Leninist _____

7. ach- _____

   ieve _____

8. fin- _____

   ished _____

9. head-hunt- _____

   ing _____

10. gui- _____

    ding _____

11. poe- _____

    try _____

12. car- _____

    nival _____

13. pan-Afri- _____

    can

14. swarth- _____

    y _____

div

30

15. techniq-
ue   _____
                    _____

16. usa-
ges   _____
                    _____

17. cover-
ed   _____
                    _____

18. drag-
ged   _____
                    _____

19. self-in-
flicted   _____
                    _____

20. res-
earch   _____
                    _____

21. lit-
tle   _____
                    _____

22. sig-
ner   _____
                    _____

23. nutrit-
ion   _____
                    _____

24. leng-
th   _____
                    _____

25. divis-
ion   _____
                    _____

26. litera-
ture   _____
                    _____

27. bro-
ught   _____
                    _____

28. assig-
ned   _____
                    _____

29. rent-
ed   _____
                    _____

30. regis-
ter   _____
                    _____

div

30

VII | Effective Words
31 | *Controlling Diction*

Diction is the choice and use of words. Sometimes writers use words that don't quite express the meaning they have in mind, sometimes they use words repetitiously without intending to do so, and sometimes their words are too informal or too formal for the writing situation. The effect is that the reader gets the wrong impression of what kind of person the writer is, what idea the writer is trying to convey, or what the writer's attitude is toward the subject. It is imperative, therefore, that writers develop a sense of language, a feeling for words and their effects on readers. The following guidelines can be helpful, but ultimately you the writer must make distinctions and choices. You can develop your sense of how to use words by becoming a careful reader, reading not only to understand what writers are saying but also to discover how they use their words.

31a | Choosing the appropriate word

The words you use in any piece of writing depend on the components of the writing situation: what your subject is, who your audience is, and how you want to present yourself and your subject to that audience. Most academic, business, and professional writing is serious and straightforward, meant to convey information, explain something, interpret facts or ideas, or defend a position. But much of our everyday, conversational language may have a purpose no more serious than to pass the time, to joke around, to tease, or just to keep the channels of communication open. For such purposes we use the language that is common to our group, the words our friends and colleagues expect and understand. That language may be slang, colloquial, or nonstandard — appropriate only for that situation. For most nonfiction writing in and after college, however, the appropriate vocabulary is the standard English commonly used and understood by educated writers and readers.

d

31

1 | Avoiding slang

Slang should be avoided in formal writing because it is a special conversational vocabulary of a particular group of people. To others its meaning may not be clear: a word may have different meanings or no meaning at all for different groups of people. The slang adjective *straight*, for instance, may mean "honest," "heterosexual," "inclined to wear a vest and tie," or "not on drugs," among other things. Moreover, since slang is generally short-lived, it can quickly become dated when committed to paper.

2 | Using colloquial language with care

Another kind of conversational vocabulary is **colloquial language.** It is informal and entirely appropriate in everyday speech. We might say that we have *figured out* how to do something or that we *gave someone a hard time.* Colloquial words are generally clearly understood. In writing they give the impression of conversation. When writers want to convey a conversational tone they will deliberately use colloquial words and expressions. Generally, however, such words are avoided in academic and professional writing because of their informality. Dictionaries label them *colloquial* or *informal.*

3 | Avoiding regional words and expressions

In writing for a general audience, avoid expressions that carry their intended meaning only in certain regions or that vary in meaning from one part of the country to another. Examples of local expressions are *redd up,* meaning "tidy or prepare," and *wheel,* meaning "bicycle"; an example of expressions that vary by region is *poke,* which means "sack" in some areas and "sum of money" in others. Dictionaries label such expressions *regional* or *dialect.*

4 | Avoiding nonstandard language

Variant words and expressions that are often not acceptable even in conversation — *ain't got no, hadn't ought to, theirselves* — should be avoided in writing as well. Dictionaries use *nonstandard* or *substandard* to label such usages.

5 | Avoiding obsolete or archaic words and neologisms

You should also avoid words the dictionary labels *obsolete* or *archaic* because they are no longer part of the current American vocabulary. (An example is *dispensatory,* meaning dispensary.) *Neologisms* are recently invented words that are not yet (and may never be) part of the common vocabulary; they are inappropriate unless you are sure your readers will understand them and appreciate them. (An example is *prioritize.*)

6 | Using technical words with care

In every academic or technical field, practitioners use certain terms to convey special, highly specific meanings. Sometimes, these words are newly invented or adapted from words in the general vocabulary. Botanists speak of an *etiolated* leaf, sociologists of the *ethos* of a culture, baseball players of a *fly* ball, psychologists of *reinforcing* a behavior, literary critics of an *intentional fallacy.* Such terms are useful for expressing common ideas precisely and economically. However, in writing for a general audience you should avoid such terms if possible because not all readers will understand them. When you must use specialized terms, explain them when you introduce them.

d

31

7 | Avoiding euphemisms and pretentious writing

A **euphemism** is an inoffensive substitute for a word that is potentially offensive or blunt. Examples are *the dread disease* as a substitute for *cancer, passing away* for *dying*. Since euphemisms may be vague or misleading, use them only when direct, truthful words would needlessly offend members of your audience. Don't use them to hide your real meaning, like calling a nuclear warhead a *re-entry vehicle*.

Pretentious writing contains more words or longer words than are needed. For example, *She obtruded her presence into my realm of awareness* can be restated simply and unpretentiously as *I noticed her*.

d

31

|*Choosing the appropriate word*   EXERCISE **31-1**

Complete the following sentences by circling the word or expression in parentheses that is most appropriate to standard written English. Avoid slang, colloquial language, regional words and expressions, nonstandard language, obsolete or archaic words, neologisms, unnecessarily technical words, euphemisms, and pretentious words. Consult a dictionary as needed to verify your choice.

Example: Though the acting was competent, the play itself was (*lousy, no good,* ⟨*bad*⟩).

1. The committee met to review the (*pres's, president's*) report.

2. Yelling at a referee is not (*wise, cool, kosher*).

3. Sarah, once the best tennis player in town, (*died, passed away*) recently.

4. The book sale will (*surely, sure*) make enough money to repay the club's debts.

5. I was very (*angry, teed off, mad*) when I heard my grade.

6. A (*used, preowned*) Mercedes is expensive.

7. Lowe's humor is always (*whacko, unconventional*).

8. My paper contained twenty-seven (*errors, typos, goofs*).

9. The dean's expression was (*real, really*) tense.

10. When his sister came to him for help with her chemistry, he felt (*dumb, dopey, inadequate*) at not being able to help her.

11. (*Dough, Money, Bread*) is all the doctor cared about.

12. We studied how New York is doing (*economywise, economically*).

13. I hoped my (*dad, old man, father*) would help me through school, but I was wrong.

14. Though the projector was (*broken, busted, bust*) the audience could still see the slides.

d

31

437

15. The (*cops, bears, police*) knocked on the door.

16. He claims he can (*learn, teach*) anyone to use a pesonal computer in less than an hour.

17. Even elementary schoolchildren are (*becoming interested in, getting into, digging*) rock music these days.

18. How can I do well in the course when the teacher will not try to (*deal straight, level, communicate*) with me?

19. The office computer is (*down, busted, not working*).

20. He felt (*beat, bushed, fatigued*).

21. He was (*indisposed, sick*).

22. I had to learn to (*take it easy, relax, be cool*) before I did well in examinations.

23. When children misbehave, parents should (*get tough with them, discipline them, crack down on them*).

24. The janitor finally realized he was not going (*anywheres, anywhere*) in his company.

25. The snow (*began, commenced*) on Friday afternoon and continued until Monday morning.

d

31

31b | Choosing the exact word

Because two words in English rarely mean exactly the same thing, a writer's choice of words is crucial to the effectiveness of his or her communication with readers.

1 | Using the right word for your meaning

A precise expression of meaning depends on the writer's awareness of the denotation and connotation of words. A word's **denotation** is its dictionary meaning. Confusion about denotation can cause a writer to make such mistakes as writing *depreciate* (to lower or underestimate the value of something) in place of *deprecate* (to show mild disapproval). Often a reader's problem with denotation (understanding what a writer means) results from the writer's problem with spelling, as when someone writes *desert* when he means *dessert*. Always check a dictionary when you are uncertain about the meaning or spelling of the words you are using.

A word's **connotation** is what the word implies, the emotional associations it calls up in the reader. Reactions to words vary from one individual to another, depending on one's experiences; for example, the person who has had a family member die of cancer will have a different emotional reaction when hearing the word *cancer* from someone who has not been touched by the disease personally. However, people have many emotional associations in common. We react more positively to the words *love* and *home* and *mother* than to *affection* and *house* and *female parent*. Most of us react more favorably to being described as *thin* or *slender* than to being called *skinny*. We would rather call our new shirt *inexpensive* than *cheap*. Be sure that the connotations of the words you choose contribute to rather than clash with the impression you want to create. There is a great difference, for instance, between *Her skin was as smooth as silk* and *Her skin was as smooth as marble*. To help you choose the right word, examine the different nuances of synonyms in your dictionary.

2 | Balancing the abstract and concrete, the general and specific

Words are your medium for getting ideas and images transferred from your head into the mind of your reader. If you describe a dog as small, your reader can imagine any kind of dog and can picture it as being any size relative to his or her experience with dogs. By using a general term (*dog*) and an abstract one (*small*), you have probably failed to create in the mind of your reader the same image you have in your head.

Abstract words name qualities or ideas: *small, beauty, anger, reality*. **Concrete words** name things we can touch or otherwise know by our senses: *typewriter, flower, cake, sweet*.

General words name classes or groups of things: *dog, tree, building, rain*. **Specific words** name particular members or varieties of a class: *dachshund, oak, Curtin Hall, drizzle*. In trying to make your writing more specific, you need to be aware that general and specific words are relative to the situation. *Dog*, for example, is more specific than *animal*, but *young* *brown and black dachshund with a tail that never stops moving* is more specific than *dachshund; pin oak* is more specific than *oak.*

Compare the following vague sentences made up of abstract and general words with the more exact revisions, which use words that are more concrete and specific.

VAGUE	Mites are small creatures that annoy people and animals.
EXACT	Mites are microscopic, spiderlike creatures that can burrow into the skin of people and animals, sucking the blood and causing itching.
VAGUE	A physician of ancient Rome made important contributions to medicine.
EXACT	The Greek physician Galen, who practiced medicine in Rome in the second century A.D., formulated the first medical theories based on scientific experimentation.

In writing, abstract and general words often introduce and sum up concepts: *Apartheid is a policy of racial segregation.* Specific and concrete words then present supporting details: what the policy is and how it works, what races are segregated, what the segregation consists of, and so forth.

3 | Using idioms

Idioms are expressions in our everyday language that often cannot be analyzed grammatically and whose meaning cannot necessarily be determined from the usual meanings of the words that make them up (for example, *out of his mind,* or *to make believe*). They make learning the language difficult for nonnative speakers; even people who have grown up with English have trouble with some idiomatic expressions. For this reason most dictionaries include many idiomatic usages. For example, look at the listings in your dictionary under the word *get.*

Many idioms include prepositions whose correct use is not always logical. For instance, we say that we *search for* something or are *in search of* it. But we do not say *in search for;* this expression is unidiomatic. A list of some common idioms with appropriate prepositions follows. If you are unsure of which preposition to use with an idiom, check your dictionary (32b-2).

acquitted *of* a crime

angry *with* someone

charged *for* service
charged *with* a crime

comply *with* an order

correspond *to* the architect's plans
correspond *with* a friend

differ *from* someone of contrasting appearance
differ *with* someone of contrasting views

identical *with* (or *to*) the original

impatient *with* someone
impatient *for* a result

independent *of* each other

occupied *by* an invading army
occupied *with* a customer

reward *by* giving a present
reward *with* a present

stay *at* my grandmother's
stay *in* town

vary *from* his usual habits
vary *in* length

wait *for* Godot
wait *on* tables

4 | Using figurative language

Figures of speech add richness to writing by comparing the action or thing being described with some other action or thing, using vivid, specific qualities. A **simile** makes the comparison explicitly, using *like* or *as: She's like a rainbow. He's built like a panda.* A **metaphor** implies the comparison, omitting *like* or *as: Life is a carnival. When my soul was in the lost and found, you came along to claim it.* When using a metaphor, be sure to stick with it. A **mixed metaphor** combines incongruous figurative language, destroying the image the writer is trying to create.

MIXED	The Chinese and American ships of state march to different drummers.
REVISED	The Chinese and American ships of state are sailing in different directions.

Personification treats an idea or object as if it were human: *Despair seized her in its merciless grip.* **Hyperbole** is an exaggeration for the sake of emphasis: *She was paralyzed by his stare.*

5 | Avoiding trite expressions

Avoid **clichés,** expressions that have been used so often they have lost their freshness and impact.

TRITE	I had to *work like a dog.*
REVISED	I had to *work with all the concentration of a demolition expert.*
TRITE	He *ate like a pig.*
REVISED	He *ate four large anchovy pizzas.*

d

31

Understanding denotation EXERCISE **31-2**

Circle the word in parentheses whose established denotation fits the meaning of the sentence. Consult a dictionary as needed.

Example: Our personalities are (*complimentary,* (*complementary*)).

1. By 9 P.M. we were all hungry and (*eager, anxious*) for the dinner to begin.

2. The old house was the first in Cornwall to have (*dormant, dormer*) windows.

3. Josey became (*historical, hysterical*) when told of her dog's death.

4. The charge is (*presently, currently*) too high.

5. My sister told a (*barefaced, bearfaced*) lie.

6. They lost (*conscience, consciousness*) when the gas leaked from the stove but were fortunate to be saved by a neighbor.

7. Even a weak opponent should not be taken for (*granite, granted*).

8. The (*enormity, vastness*) of the ranch was impressive.

9. The advice is (*patiently, patently*) ridiculous.

10. The lecturer's comments seemed (*irreverent, irrelevant*) to the topic, but I wrote them down anyway.

11. My being late (*irritates, aggravates*) her.

12. By Tuesday the campus decorations reflected that Homecoming was (*immanent, imminent*).

13. The judge listened intently but remained (*disinterested, uninterested*) in the libel case.

14. Most people's casual conversation is too full of (*anecdotes, antidotes*).

15. The (*statute, stature*) that prohibits kissing under water is still on the books.

d

31

16. There were (*fewer, less*) pages assigned today than yesterday.

17. We asked him (*respectively, respectfully*) to give us an extra week, but still he said no.

18. Though the governor had (*formally, formerly*) invited them to his dinners, he omitted them from his guest list after they were rude to him.

19. The seniors are divided into (*clichés, cliques*) and will not talk to new students.

20. Our grandfather (*immigrated, emigrated*) to the United States from Italy when he was a boy.

21. He (*flouted, flaunted*) my authority once too often.

22. Her angry outburst had not been (*expected, suspected*).

23. When he kept harping on the same mistakes days after I had made them, I could see I had a (*hypocritical, hypercritical*) boss.

24. Our supervisor was so (*credulous, credible*) that she believed our story.

25. The lawyer provided sound (*advise, advice*).

Using general and specific words, abstract and concrete words EXERCISE **31-3**

Each sentence below contains an italicized word that is general or abstract. Write above each italicized word a word or words that are more specific or concrete.

clear and crisp

Example: The weather was *beautiful.*

1. Mortgage interest rates have been *high.*

2. My roommate is *unsanitary.*

3. Being a *liberal,* she was in favor of the proposed law.

4. The cat's *light* fur reflected sunlight.

5. Children who live in the inner city are *different from* children who live

   in the suburbs.

6. We won *a lot of* games last fall.

7. A *powerful* wind blew the tower over.

8. The new student union is *more nearly complete* than the old one.

9. All of us have been inspired by her *success* to work harder.

10. The *situation* called for quick action.

11. Though it was hearty, Chuck's *meal* was strange.

12. The fire department needs a new *vehicle.*

13. The commanding officer was *short.*

14. Foreign cars are *better* (or *worse*) than anything made by American

    manufacturers.

d

31

15. The *animal* started toward us and then changed its mind.

16. All the students clustered around the *car*.

17. On the *chair* sat a tiny man with delicate features.

18. A *tree* fell into the power line.

19. We thought the movie was *awful*.

20. Hoping not to attract anyone's attention, I *walked* across the room.

21. Mary Lin is from *Asia*.

22. *Something* in the air of the room reminded me of my grandmother's house.

23. I am majoring in *science*.

24. A *bug* rested on the sill.

25. The *look* on the lecturer's face told us as effectively as words to stop giggling.

d

31

| *Using idioms*

Drawing on the list on pages 440–41 or consulting a dictionary as needed, circle the appropriate preposition in parentheses to complete the idioms in the following sentences.

Example: After much debate, we finally agreed (*with,* (*on*) a new policy.

1. You will never keep up (*to, with*) me.

2. I was impatient (*for, with*) the class to end.

3. Differing (*from, with*) each other only over money, the couple nonetheless decided to divorce.

4. When I returned to class after the break, my seat was occupied (*by, with*) a large, unkempt boy.

5. The room measured six feet (*to, by*) four feet.

6. The request seemed unreasonable, but she complied (*with, to*) it anyway.

7. Though we were angry (*at, with*) each other, we continued to study together.

8. They corresponded (*to, with*) the same woman for seven years before they learned the truth.

9. The dangers (*in, for*) someone learning to ski are slight.

10. The officer locked the suspect up and charged him (*for, with*) robbery.

11. College is different (*from, than*) high school in unexpected ways.

12. When the jury acquitted O'Reilly (*for, of*) murder, the townspeople were delighted.

13. During his visit the pope stayed (*in, at*) New York only briefly, but he electrified the city.

d

31

14. Although rewarded (*by, with*) increasingly flavorful foods, the pigeon would not learn any new tricks.
15. I waited (*on, for*) his arrival with friends.
16. At the age of fourteen, Lucy was independent (*of, from*) her parents.
17. My courses vary (*in, from*) difficulty, so I have no trouble setting my priorities when I study.
18. Some researchers are impatient (*at, with*) the arguments of the theorists.
19. I was preoccupied (*with, by*) my work.
20. The shop charged me (*with, for*) a purchase that I had forgotten.

d

31

| *Using figurative language*

If any figures of speech in the following sentences are inappropriate, re-write the sentences to introduce appropriate figures. If the figures are appropriate, write *OK* to the left of the sentence.

Example: The distinguished-looking man had hair the color of a cement block.

> *The distinguished-looking man had hair the color of gray flannel.*

1. His serve hit the tennis court with all the power of a hand grenade.

2. The test was so difficult it would have made a sailor blush.

3. The opposing team's center charged at me as quickly as a frightened deer.

4. From atop the telephone pole, the kitten eyed my rescue efforts like a trapped rat.

d

31

5. The academic rat race comes to a head at exam time.

6. His steel-gray eyes enhance his cold stare.

7. Taking his position as the basketball team's center, Wilt was as proud as Napoleon.

8. I was deserted by the others, locked high and dry in the basement.

9. The oil slick spread over the blue water like cream poured over peaches.

10. Each passing year stamps our new college with a nail of respectability.

d
31

| *Avoiding trite expressions* | EXERCISE **31-6** |

Identify the trite expression or expressions in each sentence below, and revise the sentence to eliminate the expressions.

Example: She was meek as a lamb, though she was a superb public speaker.

> *She was exceedingly shy, though she was a superb public speaker.*

1. He writes well, but he is no Shakespeare.

2. The food at Six Chefs restaurant is like Mom's home cooking.

3. A budding genius, my little brother won a mathematics award and two science awards.

4. The student wanted out of the rat race.

d

31

5. The job of moving my grandfather to a nursing home was easier said than done.

6. I did not know for sure, but I had a sneaking suspicion that my friends were planning a surprise party.

7. Our not getting the lease was a crying shame.

8. The sight of my old rival scared me out of my wits.

9. The pregnant woman was as big as a house.

10. I nearly died when I saw the utility bill.

31c | Avoiding wordiness

Make sure that all your words contribute meaning to your sentences, and avoid those that simply fill up space or repeat what you have already said. However, be careful not to confuse conciseness with brevity. For concise writing you need to cut out all unnecessary words; but excessive brevity eliminates specific details and words that otherwise help explain what you mean.

1 | Cutting empty words and phrases

Writers sometimes resort to empty words and phrases because they don't have much to say. Sometimes they use them because they think such phrases will make their writing sound authoritative. Whatever the reason, the writing is *padded;* it is stuffy and boring. Avoid adding length to your writing without adding substance. Here are some filler phrases that take several words to say what one word can usually say just as well.

FOR	SUBSTITUTE
at all times	always
at the present time	now
at this point in time	now
in the nature of	like
for the purpose of	for
in order to	to
until such time as	until
for the reason that	because
due to the fact that	because
because of the fact that	because
by virtue of the fact that	because
in the event that	if
by means of	by
in the final analysis	finally

Some padding can simply be cut without any loss in meaning.

PADDED	Gray is of the opinion that at this point in time it is no longer acceptable to the American people that their government should lend its support to an agency specializing in activities that are by their very nature covert.
REVISED	Gray believes that Americans no longer want their government to support an agency specializing in covert activities.

2 | Avoiding unnecessary repetition

Another form of padding is saying the same thing in two different ways. While writers use repetition effectively to emphasize main points and link important ideas (see 17b and 18b), thoughtless repetition can weaken writing.

WEAK	REVISED
my theory that I have come up with	my theory

WEAK	REVISED
the program's purposes and goals	the program's purposes
at the corner where Main Street meets High Avenue	at the corner of Main Street and High Avenue

3 | Simplifying word groups and sentences

Use the grammatical construction that states your meaning in the simplest and most direct way. Don't use a clause if a phrase will do; don't use a phrase if a word will do. Whenever you can, use direct, active verbs. Avoid passive verbs (see 18d) and noun constructions substituting for verbs. Also be wary of indirect sentence beginnings such as *there is* and *it is* (see 18e).

WORDY   The largest member of the deer family, *commonly known as the moose*, sometimes weighs as much as 1800 pounds.

REVISED   The largest member of the deer family, *the moose*, sometimes weighs as much as 1800 pounds. [Phrase reduced to two words.]

WORDY   Moose prefer to spend their summers in forest land *that contains willow swamps and lakes.*

REVISED   Moose prefer spending their summers in forest land *containing willow swamps and lakes.* [Clause reduced to phrase.]

WORDY   In the winter, protection from cold winds is found by the moose by gathering together in the woods and swamps.

REVISED   In the winter, moose find protection from cold winds by gathering together in the woods and swamps. [Passive voice revised to active. The subject now is the performer of the action.]

WORDY   There are moose living in northern regions throughout the world.

REVISED   Moose live in northern regions throughout the world. [*There are* construction eliminated to make the sentence begin with its subject.]

4 | Avoiding jargon

Jargon is the special vocabulary of a professional, academic, or technical group. (See 31a-6.) But the term also refers to any language that tries to sound professional, academic, or technical by stating simple ideas in complicated ways.

JARGON   To be interdependent means to recognize that wholeness in human relationships depends on a giving and receiving dynamic.

REVISED   To be interdependent means that we help one another.

d

31

Cutting empty words and phrases

Revise the following sentences to eliminate empty words and phrases.

Example: The aspects of poetry that I like best are its imagery and its rhythm.

I like the imagery and the rhythm of poetry.

1. Due to the fact that they were no longer able to care for him, my parents decided in the final analysis to place my grandfather in a nursing home.

2. There was a call put in by someone for a plumber to come and fix the dishwasher, which was broken and would not work.

3. The problem that arose when the committee could not reach an agreement prolonged the meeting an additional hour of time.

d

31

4. The burglar gained access to a crawl space by means of a ladder and then punched a hole in the ceiling in order to enter the apartment.

5. The nature of the changes in the rules makes it difficult to follow them.

6. I was eager to go on the backpacking trip, but two of the others were concerned with the element of risk involved.

7. We asked for laboratory tests, which were for the purpose of giving us a diagnosis of the illness that the pup had.

8. It is important to realize the value of patience, which is always worthwhile.

9. She was excited about having the opportunity for a chance at getting an interview.

d

31

10. The reason that the weather was so severe last night was that there was a blizzard.

| *Avoiding unnecessary repetition* exercise **31-8**

Revise the following sentences to eliminate needless or confusing repetition.

Example: The electoral college is involved in the presidential elections in this country because in the U.S. Constitution it says that the President is to be elected by the electoral college.

The U.S. Constitution specifies that the President be elected by the electoral college.

1. He decided to retire and not work at his job beyond the age of sixty.

2. In conclusion, the final point I want to make clear and plain is that many students need to be free of diverting distractions while studying.

d

31

3. The blue ribbon, which signified first place in the 100-yard dash, was awarded to Susan for winning the race.

4. Engaged in agriculture, the farmer is governed by a wide variety of government regulations put out by the Department of Agriculture.

5. The subway system is an important form of urban mass transit to move large numbers of people throughout the city.

6. We were assigned a Hardy novel as required reading for our homework outside class.

7. The commercial I find most interesting is the new one I just finished watching, which is the one that is on television these days for an abrasive soap.

8. Picking up trash yourself is a way that you should contribute to helping to keep the city park in a state of cleanliness.

d

31

9. The editorial claimed in its argument that capital punishment should not be used to put murderers to death.

10. Just after sunset in the evening is the time when other people's houses look most inviting.

Simplifying word groups and sentences

Revise the following sentences to simplify word groups and to introduce strong, active verbs.

Example: A red sky and thin, horizontal clouds at sunset are signals that the winds to come will be blustery.

A red sky and thin, horizontal clouds at sunset signal blustery winds to come.

1. He was feeling angry because the game was delayed.

2. Owners who applied for tax relief were given it, and all of them applied.

3. She has the ability to be able to fall asleep anywhere she chooses to do so.

d

31

4. Federal laws prohibit the buying and selling of handbags made out of alligator skin.

5. The essays and writing assignments were required to be turned in on Monday.

6. He had the idea that the pay raise would make his check bigger in the month of November.

7. Both the two of us had a fear of going on the mountain road.

8. The drink, made from ice, water, sugar, and lemon juice, really made us cooler, and the heat did not bother us as much as it had before we had the drink.

9. We have a suspicion that the administration has a plan to cut the faculty by a third.

d

31

10. The Museum of Modern Art in New York had on exhibit a sports car that is red and low-slung and that was built in the 1930s.

32 | *Using the Dictionary*

A dictionary can tell you how to spell and pronounce a word, give you the forms of irregular nouns and verbs, tell you the meaning of an unfamiliar word, and introduce you to new words. Besides containing an alphabetical list of words with their meanings, many dictionaries include synonyms, word origins, biographical and geographical listings, material on the history and grammar of English, and other useful supplements. In addition, most dictionaries indicate whether the words are slang, colloquial, regional, or otherwise restricted in their use.

32a | Choosing a dictionary

There are many different types of dictionaries, including abridged, unabridged, and special dictionaries.

1 | Abridged dictionaries

Abridged dictionaries, while not exhaustive, contain most commonly used words and brief descriptions of their meaning and usage. The following abridged dictionaries (listed alphabetically) are recommended.

> *The American Heritage Dictionary*. 2nd coll. ed. Boston: Houghton, 1982.
> *Oxford American Dictionary*. New York: Oxford UP, 1980.
> *The Random House College Dictionary*. Rev. ed. New York: Random, 1980.
> *Webster's Ninth New Collegiate Dictionary*. Springfield: Merriam, 1983.
> *Webster's New World Dictionary of the American Language*. 2nd coll. ed. New York: Simon, 1982.

2 | Unabridged dictionaries

The most scholarly and comprehensive dictionaries, unabridged dictionaries emphasize the history of words and the range of their uses. When you need detailed information about a word or want to find an obscure word, consult one of the following.

> *The Oxford English Dictionary*. 13 volumes plus 4 supplements (in progress). New York: Oxford UP, 1933, 1972, 1976. Also available in a photographically reduced, two-volume edition, 1971.
> *The Random House Dictionary of the English Language*. New York: Random, 1980.
> *Webster's Third New International Dictionary of the English Language*. Springfield: Merriam, 1981.

32

3 | Special dictionaries

Special dictionaries limit attention to a particular type of word, problem, or field. Especially helpful for writing are dictionaries of usage, which discuss common problematic words and constructions, and dictionaries of synonyms, which list together words that are similar in meaning. The following are recommended.

Bernstein, Theodore M. *The Careful Writer.* New York: Atheneum, 1965.
Webster's New Dictionary of Synonyms. Springfield: Merriam, 1973.

32b | Working with a dictionary's contents
1 | Finding general information

Dictionaries contain a wide range of information — for instance, famous people's birth and death dates and major achievements; facts about plants, animals, chemicals, and events; pictures of architectural elements and musical instruments; interpretations of concepts; names and locations of colleges and universities. Every dictionary's table of contents lists the special sections that supplement the word listings.

2 | Answering specific questions

A dictionary's function is to provide information about words. The main entry first shows spelling and word division — where to break the word if you have to divide it at the end of a line. Next comes the pronunciation, usually including all major variations. (Most dictionaries explain their pronunciation symbols in their opening pages and at the foot of every page or every other page.) The word is then identified by part of speech, and its principal parts are given. Its **etymology** — its origin — may follow; in some dictionaries, etymology is given last. Meanings are given next, grouped by part of speech if the word can function as more than one. Sometimes major differences in meaning and usage are listed under separate entries. Various definitions may be labeled as obsolete, slang, foreign, and the like. Often a word's main **synonyms** (words with similar meaning) and **antonyms** (words with opposite meaning) are also given.

32

I *Using the dictionary* exercise **32-1**

Use a college-level desk dictionary to answer the following questions.

Name of dictionary _____

Publisher _____

Date of publication _____

A. Abbreviations and symbols

1. On what pages does your dictionary explain the abbreviations and symbols used in its entries? (The guide to abbreviations and symbols may be listed separately in the table of contents, or it may be included in an overall guide to the dictionary.)

_____

_____

2. Write out the meaning of the following abbreviations or symbols. If any of them are not used in your dictionary, leave the spaces blank.

Example: n. pl. *or* pl. n. ___*plural noun*___

a. syn._____

b. dial._____

c. LL._____

d. lit._____

e. var._____

f. [ ] (bracketed matter)_____

g. Icel._____

h. obs._____

i. mil._____

j. intr. v._____

32

B. Spelling

On the following blanks, reproduce the way your dictionary lists the words given. Provide capitalization, syllable breaks, word spaces, and hyphens as well as spelling. Note that the form provided here is not necessarily the only correct option.

Example: dessertspoon *des·sert·spoon*

1. riverbed _____
2. speakeasy _____
3. backwater _____
4. living room _____
5. catlike _____

6. hayloft _____
7. freeze-dry _____
8. Italy _____
9. self-government _____
10. suckerfish _____

C. Pronunciation

1. On what pages does your dictionary explain the symbols used in its guides to the pronunciations of words? (The symbols are probably listed in a separate pronunciation key. They may also be included in full or abridged form at the bottom of the dictionary's pages.)

_____

_____

2. Copy out exactly the pronunciation given by your dictionary for the following words. If the dictionary gives more than one pronunciation for a word, provide both. Consulting the pronunciation key, sound out the word until you can pronounce it accurately and smoothly.

Example: beguile *bĭ-gīl'*

a. pastoral _____
b. err _____
c. invalid _____
d. schism _____
e. often _____

f. statistics _____
g. Caribbean _____
h. kiln _____
i. irrelevant _____
j. puberty _____

3. In what order does your dictionary list two or more pronunciations of

32

Name _____

the same word? (The principle is described in the guide to the dictionary.)

_____

_____

D. Grammatical functions and forms

1. List and label the past-tense and past-participle forms of the following verbs exactly as provided in your dictionary. Note that most dictionaries provide both forms only if they are different. Check the guide to your dictionary to determine its practice. If it provides only one form, list only one.

   Example: have *had (past tense and past participle)*

   a. prefer _____

   b. work _____

   c. break _____

   d. echo _____

   e. wring _____

2. List and label the comparative and superlative forms of the following adjectives and adverbs exactly as given in your dictionary. Note that some dictionaries provide the comparative and superlative forms only when they are formed by a means other than the simple addition of *-er* and *-est*; and most dictionaries do not provide comparative and superlative forms when they can be made only by adding *more* and *most*. Check the guide to your dictionary to determine its practice. Write below only what the dictionary actually includes in the entry.

   Examples: small *smaller (comparative), smallest (superlative)*

   beautiful *(no forms given)*

   a. inner _____

   b. lovely _____

32

465

c. cross (*adj.*)_____

d. ill_____

e. median_____

E. Etymology

1. Trace the origins of the words listed below as they are given in your dictionary. List (1) the initial language and word from which our word is derived; (2) the meaning of the initial word (sometimes not listed separately if it is the same as the given word); and (3) the other languages through which the word has passed on its way to us. Use the full names of languages, not abbreviations (consult the key to the dictionary's abbreviations if necessary). The guide to the dictionary will tell you how to read the etymology of a word if you need help.

Example: logic (1)___*Greek logos*_____

(2)___*Speech, reason*_____

(3)___*Late Latin, Old French, Middle English*___

a. induce (1)_____

(2)_____

(3)_____

b. lieutenant (1)_____

(2)_____

(3)_____

c. quake (1)_____

(2)_____

(3)_____

d. shirt (1)_____

(2)_____

(3)_____

32

e. rhythm (1) _____

(2) _____

(3) _____ _____

2. Provide the origins of the following words as they are given in your dictionary.

Example: ohm *After Georg Simon Ohm (1787-1854), German physicist*

a. zipper _____

b. jargon _____

c. astronaut _____

d. jerk _____

e. quisling _____

F. Meanings

1. How does your dictionary arrange the different meanings of the same words: chronologically, as they developed, or in order of current common use? Consult the guide to the dictionary.

_____

_____

2. List two different meanings for each of the following words as they appear in your dictionary.

a. specie (n.) (1) _____

(2) _____

b. gall (n.) (1) _____

(2) _____

32

c. hound (v.) (1)_____

(2)_____

d. go (v.) (1)_____

(2)_____

e. card (v.) (1)_____

(2)_____

G. **Synonyms**

The synonyms listed below for the noun *pay* differ slightly from each other in meaning. Consult your dictionary for the precise meaning of each word, and use the word in a sentence. (Your dictionary may provide under one of the words a paragraph that explains the distinctions among them.)

1. *pay:* meaning_____

sentence_____

_____

2. *wage:* meaning_____

sentence_____

_____

3. *salary:* meaning_____

sentence_____

_____

4. *stipend:* meaning_____

sentence_____

_____

32

H. Labels

1. Consult the guide to your dictionary for the labels it uses to designate words or meanings of words with restricted usage. (The description of labels is usually under a heading like "Usage" or "Labels.") List below the specific labels mentioned in the guide.

   _____

   _____

2. Provide the label applied by your dictionary to each of the following words or meanings of words. If your dictionary does not apply a label to a given word, write *No label* in the space. From the description of labels in the guide to the dictionary, what does each label indicate about the word's usage?

   Example: ain't *nonstandard (not appropriate for standard written English)*

   a. critter (noun meaning "animal") _____

   _____

   b. enthuse (verb meaning "to show enthusiasm") _____

   _____

   c. knock (verb meaning "to criticize") _____

   _____

   d. rod (noun meaning "revolver") _____

   _____

   e. humdinger (noun meaning "something remarkable") _____

   _____

32

I. Other information

1. Where does your dictionary provide biographical information on important persons: in the main alphabetical listing or in a separate section (give the page numbers if a separate section)? _____

_____

2. Where does your dictionary provide geographical information on countries, cities, rivers, mountains, and so on: in the main alphabetical listing or in a separate section (give the page numbers if a separate section)? _____

_____

3. Does your dictionary contain a history of the English language?

_____

4. Does your dictionary contain a guide to punctuation and mechanics?

_____

5. Does your dictionary contain a list of colleges and universities?

_____

6. List below the other special features of your dictionary.

_____

_____

_____

32

33 | *Improving Your Vocabulary*

Students are often frustrated at the size of their vocabulary when they are trying to express an idea. The thought is clear in their own heads, but when they try to write it on paper they cannot think of the right words. They correctly surmise that they need to increase the stock of words they can draw on. But they incorrectly think that this can be accomplished by doing some sort of relatively painless exercise. The truth is that vocabulary improvement takes time — a lifetime, in fact. Vocabulary can be improved not only by increasing the store of words the writer can draw on but by using words more precisely as well.

Both types of improvement are accomplished by *input* and *output:* hearing and reading words, speaking and writing them. If you want to increase your vocabulary, you first sharpen your perception. Listen to people whose vocabulary you admire to see how they use words. And *read.* How much do you read beyond what is assigned? When you read, do you pay attention to how writers use words? Do you try to grasp the meaning of new words within their context? Do you look up words that are not clear to you in context? Increasing your perception of words you hear and read improves your knowledge and understanding of them. As you speak and write, make a conscious effort to use words you have added to your vocabulary through your sharpened perceptions. Check the meanings in your dictionary if you need to make sure you're using words correctly. By increasing your sensitivity to words, especially through frequent reading and writing, you'll see your vocabulary improve.

This chapter offers no guaranteed vocabulary improvement. It does, however, show you ways to look at words and understand how they are used. It presents the background of English words and suggests ways for you to add new words to those you already know.

33

33a | Understanding the sources of English

English is part of the Indo-European language family, whose origins go back perhaps seven thousand years. The earliest known language in England was Celtic. But the English we speak is descended from the language of Germanic tribes that conquered the Celts in the fifth and sixth centuries, leaving us with such common words as *heaven, earth, our, three,* and *day.* The vocabulary of Old English, as this early form of English is called, was later enriched by Danish invaders in the ninth and tenth centuries and by the French-speaking Normans who conquered England in 1066 and reigned for nearly two hundred years. The resulting Middle English included large numbers of words derived from French, such as *catch, cattle,* and *cavalry.* In the fifteenth and sixteenth centuries, the Renaissance and the introduction of the printing press caused further changes in our language and vocabulary, introducing many Latin and Greek words and leading to Modern English. English continues to change today as we drop old words, coin new ones, and adopt others from languages throughout the world.

33b | Learning the composition of words

Breaking up a word into its component parts is often a good way to see where it came from and to figure out what it means.

1 | Learning roots

At least half the words in English have Latin or Greek roots. Some Greek words that commonly serve as roots in English words are *theos,* "god" (*theology, atheist*); *philia,* "loving" (*Philadelphia, bibliophile*); *demos,* "people" (*democracy, epidemic*); and *sophia,* "skill" or "wisdom" (*sophisticated, philosophy*). Some common Latin roots are *pater,* "father" (*paternal*); *mater,* "mother" (*matron*); *bellum,* "war" (*bellicose, antebellum*); and *dictum,* "something said" (*dictate, indict*).

2 | Learning prefixes

A **prefix** is one or more syllables that can be added to the front of a word or root to change its meaning. Many standard prefixes come from Latin or Greek. A list of common prefixes follows.

a-, an-	without, not, away from (*atheist*)
ad-	toward, next to (*adjacent*)
ante-	before (*antecedent*)
anti-	opposite, against (*antipathy*)
arch-	chief (*archduke*)
auto-	self (*automobile*)
col-, com-, con-	with (*concur*)
demi-	half (*demitasse*)
dis-	not (*dissatisfied*)
ex-	from, out of (*exhaust*)
extra-	beyond (*extrasensory*)
hyper-	excessive (*hypertension*)
il-, im-, in-, ir-	not (*immobile*)
inter-	between, among (*international*)
intra-	within (*intramural*)
mal-	wrong, bad (*malcontent*)
pan-	all (*pan-American*)
poly-	many (*polyglot*)
post-	after (*postwar*)
pre-	before (*premeditate*)
pro-	before, forward, in favor of (*propose*)

semi-	half (*semisweet*)
sub-	under (*submarine*)
super-	above (*supervisor*)
sym-, syn-	together (*sympathy*)
trans-	across (*transport*)
un-	not (*unhealthy*)

3 | Learning suffixes

A **suffix** is one or more syllables that can be added to the end of a word or root to change its meaning or function. Common noun suffixes include the following:

-ity	*-er* or *-or*	*-ship*
-ence or *-ance*	*-ist*	*-hood*
-sion or *-tion*	*-ism*	

Common verb suffixes include the following:

-en	*-ify*
-ize	*-ate*

Common adjective suffixes include the following:

-ful	*-able* or *-ible*	*-ous*
-ish	*-al* or *-ial*	*-ive*
-ble	*-ic*	*-ant* or *-ent*

33c | Learning to use new words

Examining a word's components is one way to understand its meaning. Other ways are examining its context and looking it up in the dictionary.

1 | Examining context

The way a word is used in a sentence or paragraph often gives clues to its meaning. Take the sentence *Most aficionados of musical comedy admire Lerner and Loewe's <u>My Fair Lady</u>.* If you did not know the word *aficionado,* you could guess from its relation to *musical comedy, admire,* and <u>*My Fair Lady*</u> that it means something like "fan" or "enthusiast."

Sometimes you can infer the meaning of an unfamiliar word if it is used in parallel structure with a more familiar word: *Casual theatergoers think of <u>My Fair Lady</u> as a pleasant musical comedy; but the true aficionado of musical comedy knows that it is based on George Bernard Shaw's biting play <u>Pygmalion</u>.* Since the sentence contrasts the *true aficionado* and the *casual theatergoer,* you know that the aficionado is not casual but the opposite, perhaps enthusiastic.

Expressions like *also known as, sometimes called,* and even *is* point to a definition of an unfamiliar word. Or a definition may be set off by dashes, parentheses, or commas: *To the aficionado — the devoted follower of musical comedy — <u>My Fair Lady</u> is a gem.* Examples also can help you figure out what a word means: *Such aficionados as Walter Kerr of <u>The</u>*

33

New York Times and Brendan Gill of *The New Yorker* — both long-time the-ater critics — have applauded this new production of *My Fair Lady.*

2 | Using the dictionary

The dictionary can give you the precise meaning of a word whose general sense you have guessed from its context. The dictionary may also help you fix the word in your memory by showing its spelling, pronunci-ation, grammatical functions and forms, etymology, and synonyms and antonyms.

33

Using roots, prefixes, suffixes EXERCISE 33-1

By referring to the lists of roots, prefixes, and suffixes given on pages 472–73, identify each word below as a noun (*n.*), verb (*v.*), or adjective (*adj.*) and guess at its meaning. If you are unable to guess, look the word up in your dictionary.

Example: antebellum __*before a war (adj.)*__

1. belligerent _____

2. demigod _____

3. anterior _____

4. quadrennial _____

5. prorate _____

6. retroactive _____

7. advocate _____

8. Francophile _____

9. interdict _____

10. theosophy _____

11. polymer _____

12. synchronize _____

13. subvert _____

14. preposterous _____

15. transceiver _____

16. atheism _____

33

17. kilocycle _____

18. intersperse _____

19. demimonde _____

20. maladjusted _____

21. demagogue _____

22. archdeacon _____

23. amoral _____

24. illaudable _____

25. transcend _____

33

Learning new words through context

Use contextual clues to guess at the meanings of the italicized words in the passages below. Write out the meanings. Then check your definitions in your dictionary.

Example: From a lance among the lead band of warriors fluttered a *pennon* bearing the symbol of Armingild.

pennon *narrow banner or streamer; flag*

1. The *impresario* who developed the oil field considered the private jet as one of his *perquisites.*

   impresario _____

   perquisite _____

2. His sole aim in *augmenting* his income was to buy a swimming pool, a luxury car, and other trappings of *hedonism.*

   augment _____

   hedonism _____

3. The newspaper's *spurious* argument was based on forged statistics and a *paucity* of real evidence.

   spurious _____

   paucity _____

4. A *genealogist* may spend hours looking through birth records, baptismal certificates, marriage licenses, death warrants, and ship passenger lists and still not find any *substantive* information on your family.

   genealogist _____

   substantive _____

33

5. The *diminutive* woman peered up at the cans of soup on the grocery shelf and then stood on tiptoe to grasp one.

   diminutive _____

6. His *caustic* reply to my request for help stung me.

   caustic _____

7. The *philanthropist* set up a trust fund for homeless cats, and that act left his heirs *bemused* but not angry.

   philanthropist _____

   bemused _____

8. His *gaffe* of calling the teacher by the wrong name went unnoticed, for the teacher was *immersed* in a calculus problem.

   gaffe _____

   immersed _____

9. She took *umbrage* at the boss's comments, but he had not meant to criticize her.

   umbrage _____

10. Sue seemed to be *ubiquitous*. When I went to the post office, she was there. When I went to the bank, she was there. When I came home, she was in front of the house, walking her dog.

    ubiquitous _____

33

34 | *Spelling*

As you probably know, English spelling is not always easy to understand. You may at times even harbor the thought that some sadist has made a conscious effort to convert spelling into a sort of code that only the most clever can crack. However, our difficult spellings have come to us through a variety of natural causes, the major ones being our liberal borrowing of words from other languages (see 33a) and the fact that pronunciation is constantly changing while spelling remains relatively constant.

If spelling is troublesome for you, you might have noticed the seemingly inequitable way that correct spelling comes almost effortlessly to some people but requires nearly constant surveillance by others. You may be convinced that no matter how much time you take with your spelling, you always end up with some misspelled words. And you can be sure that your readers will notice at least a few of them. While we all know that good writing does not depend solely on correct spelling, readers do seem to have more respect for ideas expressed in correctly spelled words. This chapter will help you understand spelling problems and will explain a few fairly dependable rules.

34a | Avoiding typical spelling problems

Most spelling difficulties relate to differences between how a word sounds and how it is spelled. The same spelling may be pronounced more than one way, and the same pronunciation may have different spellings.

1 | Avoiding excessive reliance on pronunciation

George Bernard Shaw is said to have observed that the word *fish* could be spelled *ghoti: gh* as in *tough, o* as in *women,* and *ti* as in *action.* Shaw's point was that the pronunciations of English words can often lead us to misspell them. When in doubt about how to spell a word, look it up in your dictionary; and if you don't find it, try to think of other ways the word's sound might be spelled.

Frequent sources of confusion are *homonyms,* words that are pronounced the same but spelled differently, and near homonyms, which are pronounced similarly but not identically. Here are some examples of both types:

sp

34

479

accept, except	hole, whole
affect, effect	its, it's
allusion, illusion	no, know
board, bored	peace, piece
brake, break	right, rite, write
capital, capitol	their, there, they're
desert, dessert	to, too, two
fair, fare	which, witch
formally, formerly	who's, whose
hear, here	your, you're

2 | Distinguishing between different forms of the same word

Often the root of a word changes slightly in spelling when the word's form and function change.

VERB	NOUN	ADJECTIVE	NOUN
breathe	breath	brief	brevity
choose	choice	curious	curiosity
devise	device	deep	depth
envelop	envelope	long	length
proceed	procedure	wide	width
succeed	success	wise	wisdom

Many verbs form their principal parts irregularly: *drive, drove, driven; throw, threw, thrown; swim, swam, swum.* Some nouns also change their root spelling from singular to plural: *foot, feet; leaf, leaves; mouse, mice.*

3 | Using preferred spellings

Some words can be spelled more than one way. Often variants of the preferred spelling are British: *our* instead of *or* (*colour, color*); *ae* instead of *e* (*anaemic, anemic*); *ise* instead of *ize* (*realise, realize*); *ll* instead of *l* (*travelled, traveled*). Use the form in your writing that the dictionary designates as preferred, usually the first form listed.

34b | Following spelling rules

Even though spelling rules always have exceptions, they're worth the trouble to learn because by practicing them you can avoid misspelling those words to which the rules apply.

1 | Distinguishing between *ie* and *ei*

The rule for *ie* and *ei* is "*I* before *e* except after *c*, or when pronounced 'ay' as in *neighbor* and *weigh*": thus, *believe* (*i* before *e*) but *receive* (except after *c*). There are some exceptions: common ones are *either, foreign, forfeit, height, leisure, neither, seize, seizure,* and *weird.*

2 | Keeping or dropping a final *e*

When adding an ending such as *-ing* or *-ly* to a word that ends in a silent *e*, drop the *e* if the ending begins with a vowel (*change* + *ing* =

changing), but keep the *e* if the ending begins with a consonant (*brave + ly = bravely*). There are a few exceptions to this rule. Words that could be confusing if the *e* were dropped keep the *e* (*dye + ing* does *not* become *dying*). Words ending in a soft *c* or *g* keep the *e* when an ending is added that begins with *a, o,* or *u* (*notice + able = noticeable*). Sometimes when the *e* is preceded by another vowel, it is dropped before an ending that begins with a consonant (*due + ly = duly*).

3 | Keeping or dropping a final *y*

When a final *y* is preceded by a consonant, the *y* changes to *i* when an ending is added (*baby + s = babies*), except if the ending is *-ing* (*babying*). When a final *y* is preceded by a vowel, or when it ends a proper name, the *y* stays as is (*say + s = says; Kelly + s = Kellys*).

4 | Doubling consonants

Consonants at the ends of words are sometimes doubled when suffixes are added. Whether to double them depends on the sound of the vowels in the word: a doubled consonant gives a short sound to the vowel that precedes it: the vowel in *hopping* is short, the one in *hoping* long. When adding a suffix, double a final consonant if all of the following factors are present:

1. The word is one syllable or has stress on the final syllable.
2. The final consonant is preceded by a single vowel.
3. The suffix begins with a vowel.

In the following words, the final consonant is doubled.

admit, admitted	prefer, preferred
begin, beginning	ship, shipped
flat, flattened	sit, sitting
occur, occurred	stop, stopping

In the following words, the consonant is *not* doubled because the word does not have one of the factors listed above.

benefit, benefited (stress is not on final syllable)
differ, different (stress is not on final syllable)
equip, equipment (suffix does not begin with a vowel)
repair, repaired (final consonant is not preceded by a single vowel)

5 | Attaching prefixes

The addition of a prefix does not change the spelling of the word it is attached to: *un + necessary = unnecessary; un + able = unable; mis + spell = misspell; mis + adventure = misadventure.*

6 | Forming plurals

For most nouns, form the plural by adding *-s* to the singular form (*horse + s = horses; pea + s = peas*). For some nouns ending in *f* or *fe*, change the ending to *ve* before adding *-s* (*life + s = lives*). For singular nouns ending in *-s, -sh, -ch,* or *-x,* add *-es* (*mess* + *es* = *messes; bash* + *es* = *bashes; itch* + *es* = *itches; box* + *es* = *boxes*). For nouns ending in *o* preceded by a vowel, add *-s* (*scenario* + *s* = *scenarios*); but if the *o* is preceded by a consonant, add *es* (*potato* + *es* = *potatoes*). A few nouns that were originally Italian, Greek, Latin, or French form the plural as in their original language (*solo* becomes *solos,* not *soloes; datum* becomes *data,* not *datums*).

　　　　Compound nouns form plurals in two ways. When two or more main words (usually nouns, verbs, or adjectives) form the compound, make only the last word plural (*streetwalker* = *streetwalkers; superman* = *supermen; strongbox* = *strongboxes*). When the parts of the compound are not equal — when a noun is followed by one or more other parts of speech — make only the noun plural (*sister-in-law* = *sisters-in-law*).

| *Spelling and pronunciation* EXERCISE **34-1**

Choose the correct spelling from the pairs given in parentheses. On the blank to the left, divide the correct word into syllables, with the help of your dictionary if necessary, and indicate which syllable has the primary accent.

Example: _ath·let'·ics_ Our school has spent nearly $50,000 making the girls' (*atheletics*, *athletics*) program equal to the boys' program.

_____ 1. The community (*accepted*, *excepted*) the company's (*preference*, *prefrence*) for (*nucular*, *nuclear*)
_____ power.

_____

_____ 2. Barry Maison cross-examined the witness for
more than an (*hour*, *our*) in an attempt to (*illicit*,
_____ *elicit*) evidence of Miss Fallana's allegedly (*illicit*, *elicit*) activities.

_____

_____ 3. The (*government*, *goverment*) provided a good
(*enviorment*, *environment*) for the (*immagrants*,
_____ *immigrants*).

_____

_____ 4. Later Miss Fallana herself refused to (*brake*,
break) under his (*ineffective*, *inaffective*) ques-
_____ tioning. She remained (*discretely*, *discreetly*)
(*bored*, *board*).

_____

_____

sp

34

483

_____

_____

_____

_____

_____

_____

5. Finally, Judge Krater's (*patience, patients*) failed, and with a (*mischievous, mischievious*) (*allusion, illusion*) to Miss Fallana's (*guerrilla, gorilla*) (*past, passed*), he ruled Maison's line of questioning (*irrevelant, irrelevant*).

| Distinguishing between
different forms of the same word;
using preferred spellings   EXERCISE **34-2**

A. Write on the blanks to the left the appropriate forms of the words in parentheses. If necessary, check your spellings in a dictionary.

Example: _discussion_ The candidate declined to enter into a (*discuss*)
omissions about (*omit*) from his disclosure of campaign fund sources.

_____ 1. We (*swim*) at the pool last week for the (*nine*) time.

_____

_____ 2. The drama was termed a great (*tragic*), and it (*whole*) met our expectations.

_____

_____ 3. Her (*Britain*) (*pronounce*) drew smiles.

_____

_____ 4. He (*ordinary*) (*omit*) the roll call during all of last term.

_____

_____ 5. Last night she (*mean*) to frighten both (*thief*) by screaming.

_____

_____ 6. He thought it (*desire*) to be in charge of building (*maintain*).

_____

_____ 7. All the (*woman*) thought (*persevere*) would pay off.

_____

_____ 8. His act was the (*high*) of (*hypocrite*).

_____

sp

34

_____ 9. Do not seek to (*deception*) her with a false
_____   (*argue*).

_____ 10. After the (*occur*) of the accident, both drivers
_____   lost their (*license*).

B. The following paragraph was written by an English exchange student. Underline the British spellings and write the American spellings below. The first one is done for you.

There are differences between the American sense of <u>humour</u> and the British. One British comedian told an American audience of a kidnapper who sought a licence for his criminal activity so that he would not have to go to gaol. It was a real labour for the audience to laugh, especially since many had travelled several miles to get to the theatre in which the comic performed. The comedian took the next aeroplane out of the country, having done little to honour his profession in America.

_____*humor*_____   _____

_____   _____

_____   _____

_____   _____

Distinguishing between ie *and* ei

Insert *ie* or *ei* in the following blanks. Remember: *"I* before *e* except after *c* or when sounded 'ay' as in *neighbor* or *weigh."* Also keep the exceptions in mind, and check the dictionary as needed.

Example: for _*ei*_ gners

1. ach____ve

2. w____ght

3. fr____nd

4. ch____f

5. sl____gh

6. h____ght

7. rec____ve

8. gr____ve

9. n____ther

10. conc____ve

11. f____nd

12. b____ge

13. c____ling

14. bel____ve

15. hyg____ne

16. p____rce

17. ____ghth

18. forf____t

19. conc____t

20. perc____ve

21. l____sure

22. fr____ght

23. s____ze

24. w____rd

25. dec____t

sp

34

Keeping or dropping a final e or y

Keep or drop the final vowels as necessary when adding endings to the following words. Consult your dictionary as necessary.

Example: supply + -er _*supplier*_ _____

1. suspense + -ful _____

   suspense + -ion _____

2. desire + -able _____

   desire + -ous _____

3. gay + -ly _____

   gay + -ity _____

4. beauty + -ful _____

   beauty + -ous _____

5. apply + -ed _____

   apply + -s _____

6. die + -ing _____

   die + -d _____

7. defy + -ing _____

   defy + -ance _____

8. service + -er _____

   service + -able _____

sp

34

9. true + -est _____

   true + -ly _____

10. gratify + -ed _____

   gratify + -ing _____

11. practice + -ing _____

   practice + -able _____

12. lone + -ly _____

   lone + -some _____

13. duty + -ful _____

   duty + -s _____

14. love + -ly _____

   love + -able _____

15. solve + -ing _____

   solve + -able _____

16. notice + -ing _____

   notice + -able _____

17. glory + -ous _____

   glorify + -ed _____

18. hate + -ing _____

   hate + -ful _____

19. sure + -ly _____

   sure + -est _____

20. agree + -ing _____

   agree + -able _____

*Doubling consonants;
attaching prefixes;
forming plurals*   EXERCISE **34-5**

A. Write on the blanks to the left the appropriate forms of the words in parentheses. Check your dictionary as needed.

Example: ___*hopping*___ There is a kangaroo (hop) across the plain.

_____ 1. There is no (*differ*) in the approaches.

_____ 2. Have you (*ride*) a horse before?

_____ 3. Has he (*travel*) far?

_____ 4. She was my (*advise*).

_____ 5. He (*submit*) his resignation yesterday.

_____ 6. Have you been (*refer*) to a doctor?

_____ 7. When will an eclipse (*re + occur*)?

_____ 8. The reservation was (*cancel*).

_____ 9. Your concern is (*un + necessary*).

_____ 10. We were not (*permit*) to enter.

_____ 11. The car needed (*anti + freeze*).

_____ 12. Ten words were (*mis + spell*).

_____ 13. The shuttle (*re + enter*) the atmosphere.

_____ 14. They were (*co + conspirators*).

_____ 15. He (*dis + approved*) of the movie.

_____ 16. Your (*remit*) was due last week.

_____ 17. Her position is (*pre + eminent*).

sp

34

491

_____ 18. She (*transfer*) last fall.

_____ 19. He was heard (*admit*) guilt.

_____ 20. They were innocent of (*mis* + *spending*) the funds.

B. Write the plurals of the following words and compounds, checking your dictionary as needed.

Example: chief____*chiefs*____

1. buffalo_____

2. tomato_____

3. mother-in-law_____

4. sheep_____

5. amoeba_____

6. fox_____

7. series_____

8. shelf_____

9. index_____

10. bureau_____

11. handful_____

12. passerby_____

13. analysis_____

14. economy_____

15. ox_____

34c | Developing spelling skills

You can improve your spelling by pronouncing words carefully, using memory tricks, and studying words you are likely to misspell.

1 | Pronouncing carefully

Many common misspellings come from inaccurate pronunciation. Be careful with words like *library, February, recognize, nuclear, mischievous,* and *athlete;* don't add or omit letters when either pronouncing or spelling them. For words that are particularly troublesome, you might try correcting the faulty syllable by stressing it; write on a piece of paper or note card: *FebRUary, reCOGnize, govERNment.*

2 | Using mnemonics

Mnemonics are tricks for memorizing. Some are standard: *stalactites* grow down from the ceiling, but *stalagmites* grow up from the ground; *stationery* has an *er* like *letter paper.* But you can also make up your own. For instance, remember that *embarrass* has two *r*'s and two *s*'s to match the double letters in *stutter* and *stammer,* an embarrassed person's actions. *Inoculate* has no double letters — one shot is enough.

3 | Studying spelling lists

Below is a list of some of the most commonly misspelled words in the English language. You probably know how to spell most of them. To find out which ones you *don't* know how to spell, have someone read the entire list to you while you write the words. Checking your words with the list will tell you which ones you need to work on. On a card or piece of paper write each word you don't know; on the reverse side write a sentence using the word. Then study the words a few at a time, testing yourself occasionally.

absence	athlete	dictionary	harass
abundance	attendance	dining	height
academic	audience	embarrass	illiterate
accommodate	basically	emphasize	indefinite
achieve	believe	entirely	independent
acknowledge	benefited	entrance	infinite
acquaintance	Britain	environment	license
across	calendar	etc.	luxury
address	category	exaggerate	marriage
aggravate	cemetery	existence	mathematics
aggressive	certain	fascinate	medicine
all right	column	February	necessary
all together	conceit	foreign	neither
a lot	condemn	forty	occasion
already	definite	fourth	occur
altogether	descendant	friend	occurrence
appearance	describe	government	omission
argument	develop	grammar	parallel

perform	quizzes	seize	than
perhaps	receive	separate	then
possess	recommend	sergeant	tragedy
precede	reference	several	truly
prejudice	referring	similar	until
prevalent	reminisce	sincerely	usually
primitive	renown	sophomore	vacuum
privilege	rhythm	sponsor	villain
procedure	roommate	succeed	weird
proceed	safety	supersede	writing

34d | Using the hyphen to form compound words

1 | Forming compound adjectives

When two or more words function as a single adjective before a noun, hyphenate the words: *well-heeled benefactor*, a *decision-making problem*. When the same word group stands alone or follows the noun, hyphens are not needed: *We need a benefactor who is well heeled. Decision making is her main problem.*

2 | Writing fractions and compound numbers

Fractions and compound numbers from twenty-one to ninety-nine are always hyphenated: *one-half; thirty-six.*

3 | Forming coined compounds

Hyphenate a group of words you are linking to serve as a temporary (coined) adjective if they precede the word they modify: *The dog let out her there's-a-squirrel-in-that-tree bark.*

4 | Attaching some prefixes and suffixes

Most prefixes do not take a hyphen: *prewar, semiannual.* When a prefix consists of or precedes a capital letter, however, use a hyphen: *anti-British.* Prefixes that are complete words by themselves usually take hyphens: *self-indulgent, all-around.* Also hyphenate *ex-* meaning "former": *ex-president.*

Suffixes usually do not take hyphens, except *-elect: senator-elect.*

5 | Avoiding confusion

Use a hyphen after any prefix or in any compound when the resulting word might be misread without the hyphen (*re-echo, anti-intellectual*) or confused with another word (*re-create, un-ionized*). Also hyphenate adjective groups that could be misread: *new-gas prices* (meaning the prices for newly discovered gas).

Name _____ Date _____ Score _____

Using the hyphen in compound words, fractions, compound numbers

EXERCISE **34-6**

A. Write out the following numbers, using hyphens when appropriate.

Example: 4500 _*forty-five hundred*_

1. 10¼ _____

2. ²¹/₂₂ _____

3. 39 _____

4. 102 _____

5. 3,000,152 _____

6. 92 _____

7. 25 _____

8. 25,095 _____

9. ³/₁₀ _____

10. 260 _____

B. As appropriate for correct spelling, leave each of the following pairs of words as two words or make each pair one word by inserting a hyphen or closing up the space. Check your dictionary as needed.

Example: anti Soviet _*anti-Soviet*_

1. ante bellum _____

2. pro American _____

3. self serving _____

4. car port _____

5. porch light _____

6. news stand _____

7. hot dog _____

8. non partisan _____

9. ninth century (adj.) _____

10. co author _____

11. post Victorian _____

12. red eyed _____

13. re shuffle _____

14. long handled _____

15. red handed _____

16. soft hearted _____

17. pre fabricated _____

18. life boat _____

19. life like _____

20. anti imperialist _____

sp

34

496

Answers to Self-tests

Numbers in parentheses refer to sections applying to the answers.

Chapter 6 | Case of Nouns and Pronouns

1. I (6a) 2. them; us (6b) 3. us (6c)
4. me (6b) 5. we (6a) 6. whom (6g-2)
7. he; I (6a) 8. me (6b) 9. she; I (6a)
10. he; she (6a)

Chapter 7 | Verb Forms, Tense, Mood, and Voice

1. swam (7a) 2. broken (7a) 3. were
(7g-1) 4. showed (7f-2) 5. sat (7b, 7e-2)
6. were (7g-1) 7. lying (7b) 8. rung
(7a, 7e-2) 9. lasted (7e-2) 10. mistaken
(7a)

Chapter 8 | Agreement

1. is (8a-4) 2. his (8b-3) 3. its (8b-4)
4. his (8b-3) 5. are (8a-3) 6. his (8b-3)
7. is (8a-4) 8. were (8a-2) 9. asks (8a-1)
10. was (8a-10)

Chapter 9 | Adjectives and Adverbs

1. most (9e-4) 2. really (9a) 3. bad (9b)
4. good (9b) 5. worse (9e-2, 9e-4) 6. nicer
(9e-4) 7. slowly (9a) 8. naturally (9a)
9. worst (9e-2) 10. carefully (9a)

Chapter 10 | Sentence Fragments

Incomplete sentences: 2 (10e) 4 (10b)
6 (10c) 8 (10d) 10 (10c)

Chapter 11 | Comma Splices and Fused Sentences

1. c (11a) 2. b (11b) 3. c (11a) 4. a
5. b (11a) 6. b (11a) 7. b (11a) 8. b (11b)
9. c (11c) 10. c (11b)

Chapter 12 | Pronoun Reference

1. When I saw my teachers greeting my friends, I said hello to them. (12a)
2. The man's shadow loomed against the wall, which alarmed John. (12c-1)
3. After Hilda's snake escaped, Martha would not go into her room. (12a)
4. As long as the council members refused to meet the developers, there would be no end to their frustration. (12a)
5. When he saw how much the parts cost for the repairs, he decided to obtain them elsewhere. (12a)
6. OK
7. It says on the bottle not to drink its contents. (12d, 12c-2, 12e)
8. In Agnes's glove compartment, she kept a revolver. (12c-2)
9. After my roommate insulted my father, he refused to speak to him. (12a)
10. Alice told Karen that Esther found her purse. (12a)

Chapter 13 | Shifts

1. We entered the museum not knowing you were supposed to pay. (13a)
2. She wanted to know whether to take the job and did it pay well. (13d)
3. We planned to commute by car, but bus was found to be cheaper. (13c)
4. Oliver had no way of knowing we were there until he walks through the door. (13b)
5. The intensity of a person's feelings can cause you to act foolishly. (13a)
6. OK
7. A person should always have professional playing experience before they coach. (13a)
8. To revise a paper, read it through for

497

errors, and then you should examine its structure. (13b)

9. OK

10. I had to decide whether to go on the trip and could I afford it? (13d)

Chapter 14 | Misplaced and Dangling Modifiers

1. Art only walked to the campus once last month. (14c)

2. Looking in the mirror, the new suit was very becoming. (14g)

3. She kept the dog in the closet that was housebroken. (14b)

4. After calling the repairman, the furnace started working. (14g)

5. He kept the marble cups that he bought in Taiwan during his tour last spring in the closet. (14a)

6. Having hired an attorney, the lawsuit was under way. (14g)

7. OK

8. Two teams were in the play-offs that were undefeated. (14b)

9. To gain entry, a special pass is necessary. (14g)

10. Six of us ordered drinks at the bar that tasted like after-shave lotion. (14b)

Chapter 15 | Mixed and Incomplete Sentences

1. M(15a) 2. M(15b) 3. I(15d-1) 4. OK
5. I (15d-3) 6. I (15d-4) 7. M (15a) 8. I (15c) 9. M (15b) 10. M (15a)

Chapter 16 | Using Coordination and Subordination

1. a (16b) 2. b (16b) 3. a (16b) 4. b (16b) 5. b (16b) 6. b (16c-1) 7. a (16b) 8. b (16b) 9. a (16b) 10. b (16b-2)

Chapter 17 | Using Parallelism

1. Going to a professional football game is better than to watch one on TV. (17a- 3)

2. The Episcopalians and those who are Catholics have more ritual in their services than Methodism has. (17a-1, 17a-3)

3. OK

4. Men's clothing styles and the clothes that women wear have grown similar in recent years (17a-1)

5. In both the campus and in the town, sentiment for drug control was strong. (17a-2)

6. OK

7. The seniors, juniors, and the sophomores all helped raise money. (17a-4)

8. To coach professional baseball and coaching professional football were both career possibilities for him. (17a-1)

9. Listening to records and attendance at live concerts are both enjoyable. (17a-1)

10. In many aspects of technology, the Japanese excel over England. (17a- 3)

Chapter 18 | Emphasizing Main Ideas

1. a (18a-2) 2. b (18a-1, 18a-2) 3. a (18d)
4. b (18e) 5. a (18a-1) 6. b (18e) 7. b (18a-2) 8. a (18a-1, 18a-2) 9. a (18a-1)
10. b (18a-1)

Chapter 19 | Achieving Variety

1. a 2. b

Chapter 20 | End Punctuation

1. The sign on the mailbox read, "William Morris, Esq." (20b)

2. He asked whether I had played varsity. (20a)

3. OK (20a, 20b)

4. "Did you return the package?" she asked. (20c)

5. OK (20a)

6. Hiram P. Luce, B.A., edited the anthology. (20b)

7. Her former home is Washington, D.C. (20b)

8. "Ready!" he shouted. (20f)

9. The talk was titled "When Will We Have Rights?" (20c)

10. The report will be available at noon. (20a)

Chapter 21 | The Comma

1. Some walls in the old house were painted yellow, and others were covered with dark paneling. (21a)

2. Before the mail arrived this morning, we were waiting impatiently for word. (21b)

3. Tuition, of course, is high this year. (21c-3)

4. OK

5. The vandalized, dilapidated building was the gym. (21f-2)
6. At sixty, workers are eligible for retirement. (21i)
7. "I can't," she said, looking apologetic. (21h-1)
8. OK
9 The time to act is now. (21j-1)
10. The rally ended with the familiar song "We Shall Overcome." (21c-2)

Chapter 22 | The Semicolon

1. A foreign coin jammed the vending machine; however, the coin was soon dislodged. (22b)
2. OK (22e-1)
3. She called to say she would arrive at noon; therefore, we ran out for groceries. (22b)
4. His face tightened with tension; he clenched his fists. (22a)
5. OK (22e-1)
6. They had met twice before; nevertheless, he did not remember her. (22b)
7. OK (22c)
8. OK (22b)
9. The following gave generously: E. E. Edwards, a broker; R. Zikowicz, a contractor; and L. Peters, a banker. (22d)
10. OK (22e-1)

Chapter 23 | The Apostrophe

1. The princes' reputations have been impugned. (23a-3)
2. At today's prices, we can't afford to eat out. (23a-1; 23c)
3. The women's coats were left in the pew. (23a-1)
4. The child asked how many s's are in *Mississippi*. (23d)
5. Karen will graduate in the spring of '86. (23c)
6. OK (23b)
7. OK (23b)
8. Students' privileges are limited. (23a-3)
9. Children's art will be featured. (23a-1)
10. "It's a big job," she said. (23c)

Chapter 24 | Quotation Marks

1. "Were the books damaged?" he asked. (24a; 24g-3)
2. "Jeff said 'Okay' when I asked him," Peg remarked. (24a; 24b; 24g-1)

3. "Moon Drool" is the title of her latest song. (24d)
4. "Asia," Burke wrote, "will remain a puzzle eternally." (24a; 24g-1)
5. Blake's poem "The Tiger" was not assigned. (24d)
6. "The audience shouted 'Bravo!' each time she came on stage," her agent reported. (24a; 24b; 24g-1, 24g-3)
7. Did the waitress say, "As soon as I can"? (24a; 24g-3)
8. He asked, "Why are you home?" (24a; 24g-3)
9. "A pile of ashes," he said, "is all that's left." (24a; 24g-1)
10. There are two reasons the poet wrote "O Eager Bleat": to celebrate the sheep industry and to earn money. (24d; 24g-2)

Chapter 25 | Other Punctuation Marks

1. J. S. Mill (1806–1873) was considered the brightest man of his time. (25c-1)
2. A good student, he still lacks an important quality: patience. (25a-1)
3. First editions — especially rare ones — can be costly. (25b-2)
4. The pool will be closed on the following days: July 4 and September 2. (25a-1)
5. OK (25e)
6. "The lessor and/or the agent is responsible," the attorney stated. (25f)
7. The rebate ($250) prompted her to buy the car. (25c-1) (Or "... rebate — $250 — prompted"; 25b-2)
8. OK (25d)
9. We were given a choice of (1) a term paper, (2) five book reports, or (3) a lab project. (25c-2)
10. Of the cities we investigated, three cities — Rockville, Monroe Heights, and West Greenway — had a surplus of rental housing. (25b-2)

Chapter 26 | Capitals

1. He has a fondness for Asian art. (26d-1)
2. Woodworth's lyric entitled "The Old Oaken Bucket" gives me chills. (26b)
3. My mother sent Grandfather a box of Cuban cigars. (26f-4)
4. OK (26e, 26d-1)
5. "The worst season here is summer," Doctor Ellis said. (26f-3; 26e)

6. Joan, a professor of music, owns many classical music tapes. (26e; 26d-1)
7. The east side of the woods borders Claytor Lake. (26f-2; 26d-2)
8. His latest book is *The Era of the Frog: A Study in Green.* (26b)
9. She has thirty copies of "Ode to My Bunny." (26b)
10. Elmo majored in physics at Greenburg State College. (26d- 1)

Chapter 27 | Italics

1. OK (27a)
2. *The Parkersburg Herald* wrote a feature on Hull's painting *The Bernasek Porch.* (27a)
3. *Bardiglio* is the name for a variety of marble. (27c)
4. OK (27e)
5. *Common Sense* was a pamphlet urging revolution. (27a)
6. I often pronounce the *t* in *often.* (27d)
7. The U.S.S. *Gompers* set sail for the Pacific on April 3. (27b)
8. Mr. Tucker read out of Exodus from the Bible. (27a)
9. Omar lisped when he said *isthmus.* (27d)
10. OK (27a)

Chapter 28 | Abbreviations

1. The professor was late only once. (28a)
2. George Meany headed the union for many years. (28f)
3. OK (28a)
4. Browning Corporation interviewed seniors today. (28e)
5. OK (28a)
6. OK (*or* USA) (28b)
7. On Monday the team visits Ogden. (28f)
8. We arrived early on February 16. (28f)
9. OK (28b)
10. Agnes majored in economics and French. (28f)

Chapter 29 | Numbers

1. OK (29b)
2. OK (29b)
3. Volume 3 is on reserve at the library. (29b)
4. The paint cost $6.10. (29b)
5. OK (29c)
6. There were thirty-six cousins absent from the reunion on May third (or 3). (29a; 29b)
7. The truck broke down three days ago. (29a)
8. OK (29a)
9. The tank leaked one hundred gallons of fuel. (29a)
10. The teacher assigned only 240 lines of poetry. (29a)

Chapter 30 | Word Division

1. drugged (30b)
2. al-
low (30a)
3. lucky (30a)
4. pan-
American (30c)
5. OK
6. com-
pelled
7. self-
indulgent (30c)
8. through (30b)
9. co-
signed (30d)
10. oblique (30d)

Index

Boldface page numbers indicate exercises.

Plan of the book and guide to correction code and symbols